Aeschylus' *Oresteia*

A LITERARY COMMENTARY

Traditionally, books on Greek tragedy tend to fall into two classes: scholarly editions with commentaries on textual, linguistic, and detailed interpretative points, and literary-critical studies which sometimes include summary treatments of questions involving a detailed study of the text. Classics specialists tend, for obvious reasons, to concentrate on the former. Readers of translations have, of necessity, been limited to the latter kind of aid in their reading of the works of the Greek tragedians, works that are often unfamiliar particularly in their cultural context. D.J. Conacher has brought these two approaches together in this comprehensive study of the three plays of Aeschylus' *Oresteia*.

The major part of Conacher's work is a detailed running commentary on, and dramatic analysis of, the three plays. It is supplemented in notes and appendixes by discussions of the philological problems relevant to the interpretation, and by a sampling of other scholarly views on a number of controversial points.

Designed to meet the needs of readers with varying degrees of specialization, the book contains generous selections from, and discussions of, scholarly opinions in various commentaries and journal articles which students may not be able to consult for themselves. Here, as in the text of his commentary, Conacher has attempted to keep the detailed discussions understandable by students at various levels, and has provided translations or paraphrases for words and passages quoted in the original Greek.

This supporting material adds considerable value to Conacher's detailed analysis and appreciation of the form and meaning of Aeschylus' trilogy, and makes the plays much more accessible to a wider audience.

D.J. CONACHER is Professor Emeritus of Classics at University of Toronto. He is the author of *Euripidean Drama: Myth, Theme, and Structure* and *Aeschylus' Prometheus Bound: A Literary Commentary*.

UNIVERSITY OF TORONTO PRESS

Toronto   Buffalo   London

D.J. CONACHER

Aeschylus' *Oresteia*

A LITERARY COMMENTARY

© University of Toronto Press 1987
Toronto   Buffalo   London
First paperback edition 1989

ISBN 0-8020-5716-0 (case)
ISBN 0-8020-6747-6 (paper)

∞

Printed on acid-free paper

Canadian Cataloguing in Publication Data

Conacher, D.J., 1918–
Aeschylus' Oresteia

Bibliography: p.
ISBN 0-8020-5716-0
1. Aeschylus. Oresteia. I. Title.
PA3825.C66 1987   882'.01   C87-093085-0

Contents

PREFACE   vii

ONE / *AGAMEMNON*

1 Introductory comment: the play and the trilogy   3
2 Prologue and parodos (vv 1–257)   7
3 First episode and first stasimon (vv 258–487)   16
4 Second episode (the 'Herald scene') and second stasimon (vv 489–781)   24
5 Third episode (Agamemnon and Clytemnestra) and third stasimon (vv 782–1034)   29
6 Fourth episode, including first kommos (the 'Cassandra scene') (vv 1035–1330)   40
7 Fifth episode and second kommos (the off-stage murder and its aftermath) (vv 1343–1576)   48
8 Exodos (the 'Aegisthus scene') (vv 1577–1673)   55
   Appendix 1 to chapter 1: Problems in the parodos of *Agamemnon*
   i The anger of Artemis   76
   ii 'Knowledge through suffering' in the 'Hymn to Zeus'   83
   iii The guilt of Agamemnon   85
   Appendix 2 to chapter 1: The entry of Clytemnestra, with particular reference to vv 489–502   97

TWO / *CHOEPHORI (THE LIBATION BEARERS)*

1 Preliminary comment   102
2 Prologue, parodos, and first episode (vv 1–305)   103

3 The 'great kommos' (vv 306–478)   108
4 Second episode and first stasimon (vv 479–651)   113
5 Third episode (vv 652–782)   118
6 Second stasimon (vv 783–837)   121
7 Fourth episode (vv 838–934) and third stasimon (vv 935–72)   122
8 Exodos (vv 973–1076)   124

THREE / *EUMENIDES*

1 Prologue, parodos, and first episode (vv 1–234)   139
2 Second episode, part 1 (vv 235–53); second parodos (vv 254–75); second episode, part 2 (vv 276–306)   147
3 First stasimon (vv 307–96)   150
4 Third episode (vv 397–488)   152
5 Second stasimon (vv 490–565)   156
6 Fourth episode (vv 566–777): the 'trial scene'   159
7 The 'conversion' of the Erinyes (vv 778–1020); the escorting of the Erinyes to their new home (vv 1021–47)   169
  Appendix to chapter 3: Some views on the political and social aspects of the *Eumenides*
   i Preliminary comment   195
   ii Political aspects of the *Eumenides*   197
   iii The 'male-female conflict' in the *Eumenides* and in the trilogy   206

BIBLIOGRAPHY   223

Preface

In the present circumstances of classical studies, there seems to be a need, in the field of Greek tragedy as in other fields, to cater for a wider variety of students and other readers than ever before. This variety includes classics specialists, particularly graduate students with considerable familiarity with the original texts; students with some Greek, who may be reading works such as the *Oresteia*, or parts of it, for the first time; and a large number of readers, many of them highly sophisticated in literary matters, who now read Greek literature, and particularly Greek drama, in translation. Traditionally, the books available on Greek tragedy tend to fall into two classes: editions with commentaries (ranging from voluminous works of scholarship to what used to be called 'school editions', also learned but less detailed) and literary-critical studies which sometimes include more summary (and often more subjective) treatments of questions involving a detailed study of the text. Readers 'in translation' have, of necessity, been limited to the latter kind of aid in their reading of the strange and often unfamiliar (particularly in their cultural context) works of the Greek tragedians; classics students tend, for obvious reasons, to concentrate on the former, with perhaps a brief scamper through the chapters of the 'lit-crit' books which are relevant to special assignments or to essay questions on final examinations.

I have found, however, in my own teaching of Greek drama to the several kinds of students described above that the good 'translation' students often ask questions concerning precise meanings and interpretative details not 'covered' in the more general literary studies, while the more literary among the classics students look in vain in the learned commentaries (and often in the literary studies) for detailed discussion of the structure and technique of the works which they are linguistically digesting.

The present study attempts, however inadequately, to meet at least some of these complex requirements within a single book. The classics student will, of course, always require the commentaries of the learned editions (in the case of the *Oresteia* one hopes that more of these will be forthcoming for the last two plays of the trilogy) and both classicists and those reading in translation will rightly wish to extend their critical awareness by original interpretations more in tune with contemporary 'lit-crit' fashions than the present work can claim to be. My own intention is to supply a detailed running commentary on, and dramatic analysis of, the three plays of the trilogy, supplemented (in the notes and appendixes) by discussion of philological problems relevant to the interpretation, and by at least a sampling of other scholarly views on particularly crucial points of that interpretation. The format of the book, the fairly rigid relegation of controversial points of interpretation and of other scholars' views to the notes and appendixes, is dictated partly by the different levels of 'readership' envisaged, partly by the concern that readers should not lose the thread of the dramatic analysis by such intrusions into the text of the commentary.

It is, of course, impossible to gauge accurately which parts (if any) of this 'three-tiered' study may be useful to one or another of the kinds of readers of the *Oresteia* mentioned above. Generally speaking, the notes and appendixes are aimed at the more specialized students, or at least at those reading the plays in Greek; however, many of our 'Greekless' students do ask questions of the kind which I have indicated and it is hoped that for these at least some of the notes and appendixes will be of interest as well. Thus, with both types of reader in mind, I have, in the notes, made generous selections from the best-known editions-with-commentaries, which the student may not be able, in all cases, to consult in detail for himself. On other, more discursive matters, of interpretation, dramatic technique, use of imagery and so on, I have attempted (again in the notes and appendixes) to provide a fair sampling of scholarly opinion to be found in other books and, particularly, in journal articles, to which students interested in a particular point or topic are referred for further study. Here, as in the text of my commentary, I have attempted as much as possible to keep the detailed discussions understandable to students at various levels of scholarly attainment and have provided translations or, occasionally, paraphrases for words and passages quoted in the original Greek.

My discussion of the *Oresteia* is based, in the first instance, on Gilbert Murray's Oxford Classical Text of *Aeschylus* (first edition 1938, second edition 1955) augmented by constant consultation of (and reference to) various other texts, most notably Denys Page's Oxford Classical Text of *Aeschylus* (1972).

Several important Aeschylean studies have appeared since the completion of this book in manuscript in 1983 or too late in its preparation for more than limited use or (in some cases) mere bibliographical reference. These include two major editions, *L'Agamemnon d'Eschyle* (Lille 1981–2) by Jean Bollack and Pierre Judet de la Combe and A.F. Garvie's edition of Aeschylus' *Choephori* (Oxford 1986); A.J.N.W. Prag, *The Oresteia. Iconographic and Narrative Tradition* (Warminster 1985); and Philip Velacott, *The Logic of Tragedy, Morals and Integrity in Aeschylus' Oresteia* (Durham, NC 1984). John Herington's recent introductory work, *Aeschylus* (New Haven and London 1985), in the Hermes Books series, contains, as well as its interesting discussions of Aeschylus' plays, an excellent account, for the general reader, of the background, mythological and historical, to Aeschylean thought. Also useful for the Greekless reader (though more for scholarly information than for literary criticism) is James Hogan's line-by-line commentary, *A Commentary on the Complete Greek Tragedies–Aeschylus* (Chicago and London 1984), the first of a series of companion volumes to the University of Chicago Press' distinguished series of translations of Greek tragedy, edited by Grene and Lattimore. Among recent more specialized articles appearing too late for discussion here are A.L. Brown, 'The Erinyes in the *Oresteia*, Real Life, the Supernatural and the Stage' *JHS* 103 (1983) 13–34, and David Sansone, 'Notes on the *Oresteia*' *Hermes* 112 (1984) 1–9.

I should like to express my thanks to the anonymous readers for the Canadian Federation of the Humanities and the University of Toronto Press (as well as to the copy editor, Ms Judy Williams, for the latter) for various helpful suggestions and criticisms, and to Ms Carol Ashton and Ms Ruth Anne MacLennan for their patience and efficiency in typing this book.

This book has been published with the help of grants from the Canadian Federation for the Humanities, using funds provided by the Social Sciences and Humanities Research Council of Canada, and from the University of Toronto Women's Association. I should also like to express my grateful acknowledgment of a Research Grant from the Social Science and Research Council of Canada in 1980 which I made use of for research at Oxford University and which consequently assisted me greatly in the preparation of this book.

Aeschylus' *Oresteia*
A LITERARY COMMENTARY

CHAPTER ONE

Agamemnon

1 Introductory comment: the play and the trilogy

In *Agamemnon*, the seeds of the action on which the tragic meaning depends are all certain violent deeds of the past: the crime of King Agamemnon's father, Atreus, against his brother, Thyestes, when Atreus served Thyestes a banquet of his own children's flesh; the abduction of Helen, wife of Menelaus (Agamemnon's brother) by the Trojan prince Paris, adulterous guest at Menelaus' table; the sacrifice by Agamemnon of his daughter Iphigenia to Artemis, to win favourable winds for the expedition bringing 'Zeus' justice' against Troy. Each of these deeds, it will be noted, involves a crime against the house or the home, either by an outrage of hospitality ('Zeus-of-the-guests' is invoked early in the play)[1] or by the 'avenging eagles' destroying one of their own young in the course of their vengeance. One of these dread events belongs to the remote familial past of King Agamemnon; one involves 'fatal Helen,' sister of Queen Clytemnestra who will herself prove fatal in another way to Agamemnon; one belongs to the more immediate past of Agamemnon himself. Yet another ingredient from the past must still be mentioned: Aegisthus, Thyestes' sole surviving son, sworn to fulfil his father's curse against the house of Atreus, has become the paramour of Clytemnestra while Agamemnon is away at Troy. Thus in the 'given material' from which *Agamemnon* begins, there already appears something of the complex causality with whose interrelations the tragic meaning of this play and ultimately of the whole trilogy will be concerned. All these events are known to the audience before the play begins; so, too, are the future deeds of violence (hence the reader, too, should be aware of them).[2] For what has happened in the remote and in the more recent past, Agamemnon will die by Clytemnestra's hand aided by Aegisthus, Thyestes' son; later in the trilogy, Agamemnon's son Orestes will slay the slayer and will, in turn, flee from the remorseless Furies of his mother's blood.

The audience's foreknowledge, far from spoiling the tragic effect, will be exploited to the full in the poet's achievement of it. Relying on this awareness, Aeschylus translates this succession of known events, and the latent ironies involved, into a sequence of tragic inevitability by the particular treatment which he gives them. Nor are we to be concerned solely with a chain of violence and retributive violence. By the end of the trilogy we are to find a solution of – even an advance beyond – the apparently unending requital of blood by blood and the ever recurrent pollution which such vengeance involved.

The theme, as has often been said, of both *Agamemnon* and the trilogy as a whole is 'justice' (*Dikē*), yet it undergoes significant, even extreme, modulations as the trilogy progresses. The most significant of these (the change in attitude even on the part of the Olympians as to how Justice should be administered) we shall consider later when we have discussed each of the three plays. Certain preliminary observations should be made, however, about the changing thematic material of the individual plays. In the first play, we are concerned chiefly with watching the awful spectacle of Agamemnon's past (both familial and personal) catching up with him. Here the dramatist concentrates on individual decisions, deeds, and destinies, though this need not imply, as it might in later (even in Euripidean) tragedy, an analytic interest in character and motivation of the tragic sufferer.[3] Even in *Agamemnon*, however, the larger theme of the House of Atreus and its destiny is also present, as various passages in the choral odes and in the 'Cassandra scene' make clear. As the trilogy proceeds, the emphasis on individual decisions, and individual fates, decreases – not all at once but in a gradual diminuendo. In the second play, *The Libation Bearers* (*Choephori*), for example, there is *some* concern for Orestes' own motives in slaying the usurpers but more for the powerful movement of vengeance arising from both chthonic (Underworld) and Olympian powers. In the third play, the *Eumenides*, we are made aware from the beginning that the chief issue will be between the old order of Justice, represented by the Furies pursuing Orestes, and a new order of Justice, represented by Apollo and later implemented by Athena. Orestes' fate is still of some concern to us but by the time the play is only two-thirds finished this has been decided and our attention is freed to concentrate entirely on the 'solution,' the new dispensation of Justice introduced by Athena, and on the conversion of the Furies to support that new dispensation. Whereas in the second play Aeschylus moves from individual concerns (such as the dispossessed poverty of Orestes and Electra, on which Euripides will dwell much longer) to the reestablishment of the House[4] and the vindication of outraged Justice from the nether world, by the end of the third play even the House of Atreus is replaced by the larger social unit, the *Polis* (the State, viewed as a body of citizens), as the recipient of the ultimate blessings produced from the long sequence of suffering individuals and dynasties.[5] (That the *polis* concerned turns out to be the Athenian, not the Argive *polis* of the House of Atreus, is another matter which will be considered later.)

In thus summarizing the trilogy development, however inadequately, as a shift of concentration from the individual to the House, and from the House to the *Polis*, we must not forget that at each stage of the development the other stages are always kept in mind by the poet, either in anticipation or in retrospect. As to why Aeschylus has chosen this particular kind of enlargement of his theme, a proper answer must await our discussion of the finale of the trilogy. Some preliminary indication may, however, be suggested here. In the first place, the shift from the old to the new order of justice will be seen inevitably to involve the community as a whole in its operation and, in the treatment of this particular myth, the House, as avenged and restored by Orestes, provides the necessary transition between the individual and the community. Secondly, the form of justice to emerge at the end of the trilogy will, particularly in the new institution to be established, be endowed with a political as well as a judicial authority. It will, of necessity, be one to which the poet's fifth-century audience (the Athenian *polis*) can relate, for the order which it seeks to preserve will (as that audience would expect) be of a political as well as a judicial nature. Further than this, in our anticipation of the *telos* to which Aeschylus has shaped his trilogy, we should not venture before following the path which the poet himself has laid down for its achievement.

The theme, the moral statement, of a tragedy may be a very simple, 'well-known,' though always important, truth. What makes a tragedy great is the on-stage expression of that theme in such a way that the audience *feels* it as an immediate experience, inescapable once the essential connections are made. The past of Agamemnon and his house, and the increasing sense of the inevitability of his violent death, must be injected into the very blood-stream of the action.

In this process, the role of the Chorus is immense. First of all, it can light up crucial moments in the past in a lyrical and emotional, as opposed to a historical, manner. Freed from the need to be logical, to spell out the connections which it makes, choral lyric can be evocative in technique and immediate in effect. Faster even than the beacon signals which announce Troy's fall, it can travel over the years and over the seas, selecting and juxtaposing a series of apparently disparate events. A word or phrase here, an image cluster there, can suggest, especially to a tutored audience, a multiplicity of meanings and associations all at once, and leave in darkness and in silence the intervening (and irrelevant) gaps of time and sense.[6]

Furthermore, the Chorus, in limning these fatal present-past relations, has a certain universalizing power. It can make us aware (in a way that particular speeches and particular actions cannot) of certain recurrent patterns in human destiny and in the Justice of Zeus. Such warning may take the form of some great mythical paradigm such as the operation of dread Temptation (*Peithô*), child of scheming *Atê*, in the career of Paris (as in the first stasimon), or (as in the third stasimon) it may take the form of some generalizing ethical 'coda,' following the description of a particular, fatal sequence of events from the past.

Finally (and this, the subtlest of the Chorus' functions, one has already observed in Aeschylus' *The Persians*), the Chorus in *Agamemnon* sets up a sort of rhythm of disaster by the very sequence of themes within each ode. This sequence – a confident, even triumphant overture, an intermezzo full of doubting questions, a finale trailing off in dark despair – occurs again and again in the choral odes of this play and is repeated, in more obvious form, in certain dramatic episodes.

Lyric evocations of the past, repeated patterns of Zeus' power and justice and the insistent tragic rhythms of disaster: an analysis of the choral odes of *Agamemnon* in their dramatic context will enable us to see these effects in operation.[7] But fundamental as these odes are to our understanding of the play, we must remember that, even in Aeschylus, the Chorus is subsidiary to the dramatic action which it elucidates. Moreover, in the dramatic passages, the speeches of Clytemnestra and the Herald, the confrontation between Agamemnon and Clytemnestra and the all-too-prescient ravings of Cassandra all play their parts, along with the Chorus, in the ever-increasing expectations of catastrophe so fundamental to the tragic effects of the play.

2 Prologue and parodos (vv 1–257)

Prologue

> I pray the gods relief from the woes of this year-long watch in which,
> lying dog-like on the Atreidae's roof, I've come to know the company of
> stars, bright dynasts conspicuous in the sky, ushering in winter's
> storms and summer's heat by when they set and rise ... (1–7)

So Clytemnestra's Watchman, stationed on the palace roof to watch for the beacons signalling Agamemnon's victory at Troy. In some forty lines, this prologue sets up the tragic rhythm – hope and fear, weariness and refreshment, triumph with ruin lurking in the wings – which is to be repeated, in numerous lyric and dramatic variations, throughout the play. In each particular, the Watchman (now conning the movements of the stars, those 'bright dynasts ... as they wax and wane' [6–7]; now, as the Chorus soon will do, curing his anxieties with song) reflects in his own experience the larger weal and woe. The foreboding gloom of this initial mood (framed, in vv 1 and 20, by the repeated prayer for 'relief from woes!') suddenly vanishes in the cry of joy and the happy little dance with which he greets the long-awaited beacon flare.

> Only grant [the Watchman concludes] that with this hand I grasp the
> dear hand of my master home again! [Suddenly his joy is quenched.] For
> the rest, I'm silent. A great ox sits upon my tongue. The house itself,
> if it had speech, might speak most clearly ... (34–8)

Parodos

> This is the tenth year since Priam's great adversary, strong yoke of the
> Atreidae, even Menelaus and lord Agamemnon, twin-throned, twin-
> sceptred in their power from Zeus, first put to sea a thousand Argive
> ships. ... (40–7)

The long anapaestic sentence with which the Chorus begins its opening chant celebrates in consistently triumphant tones (till its close with the paroemiac at v 59) the glorious departure of the Kings, Agamemnon and Menelaus, leading vast hosts and screaming their warlike fury, like vultures wheeling above nests robbed of their young

(48 ff). And so the soaring confidence continues: Zeus *xenios* (guardian of hosts and guests) himself has sent the Atreidae against Alexander (Paris), because of that 'many-manned woman,' Helen (60–2). ... Then, suddenly, we are in the press of battle, of twisted limbs, shattered spears, and woes innumerable upon the Trojans and the Greeks alike. The Chorus wavers. 'Everything will, surely, be brought to its appointed end. Neither by burnt offerings nor by libations will one appease the stubborn wraths [of the gods] for unlawful sacrifices' (67–71). Trojan sacrifices, of course, are to be understood in the immediate context. Yet already in ἀπύρων ἱερῶν ὀργὰς (70–1) we hear an echo of a Greek sacrifice, far more terrible, to come.[8]

Suddenly, all is sadness, old age, the sere and yellow leaf:

> We, the old ones, weary in our ancient flesh, the army's left-behind, we can but wait, resting our feeble strength upon our staffs ... Thus man, in his last old age, his foliage shed, wanders his three-footed way, a waking-dream, in strength no better than a child. (72–82, in part)

This swift descent from triumph to gloom in the opening anapaests anticipates the movement of the ensuing ode.

Like the melancholy Watchman of the prologue, the Chorus is suddenly revived by the flash of flame – this time, the flame of sacrificial fires which Clytemnestra is mysteriously lighting (or supervising) at the nearby altars of the gods.[9]

> What news? What have you heard? What message persuades you [τίνος ἀγγελίας πειθοῖ] to command these sacrificial fires? ... One after another, on all quarters, the heavens-seeking flames leap up, bewitched by the soft, guileless persuasions of holy oil from deep within the royal store. (85–96, in part)

Such persuasions – and from such a source – are to recur in circumstances more sinister when Clytemnestra welcomes Agamemnon home.[10] Unanswered, yet with confidence somehow restored, the Chorus swings into the 'triumphant' opening strophe of the parodos:

κύριός εἰμι θροεῖν ὅδιον κράτος αἴσιον ἀνδρῶν
ἐκτελέων· ...

Full power is mine to sing of the heroes' fated victory, proclaimed by the portent as they journeyed forth. For persuasion [πειθώ] from

the gods breathes down upon me; for songs of others' valorous deeds
now suit my years. (104–6)[11]

An omen of victory at Troy is, then, to be the first subject of the
Chorus' song. This sudden portent of two eagles – one black, one
white – appearing to the right (or 'spearhand side') of the royal camp
(108 ff) recalls the triumphant and righteous image of the avenging
vultures, evoked by the Chorus in their opening lines (49 ff). There
is, however, a significant difference. The vultures of the metaphor,
bereft of their young, scream their fury to the gods, who hear them;
the eagles of the portent swoop down upon a pregnant hare and
destroy her with her young. Just avengers and cruel predators: the
two aspects of the royal leaders shine clearly through these two passages and the savage swoop of the eagles upon the mother helpless
to protect its young must, from the first, suggest to the audience the
awful sacrifice which it knows the Kings will make.

Both aspects of the 'eagle omen' appear in Calchas' comments on
it. First, the clear interpretation: the eagles are, of course, Agamemnon
and Menelaus, and their feast portends the successful sack of Troy
and all the 'plentiful possessions' of its people.[12] The second part of
Calchas' utterance, a prophetic warning (followed by prayer) based
on that interpretation, is more complex and obscure:

'Only may no ill-will from the gods cast a shadow over this great curb
of Troy forged from military might. For, through pity, holy Artemis
holds a grudge against the winged hounds of the father feasting on the
labouring hare, young and all, before the birth of the young was
accomplished. She hates the feast of the eagles.' Cry pity, pity, but may
the good prevail! 'O Lovely one [the prophet continues] *kindly though you
are to helpless young of savage lions and sweet to the unweaned whelps of
all creatures who roam the wild, grant the things portended by these signs. [I
distinguish] the favourable and the blameable aspects of the portent ...* ' (131–45)

In this passage, then, Calchas introduces the 'second aspect' of the
omen of the eagles feasting on the pregnant hare, features involving
divine disapproval (κατάμομφα δέ, 145), in addition to the favourable
features (δεξιὰ μέν, 145), previously described in his prophecy (126
ff) of Troy's destruction.

The anger of Artemis has, of course, been the subject of unending
discussion and rationalization by the commentators on this play. Let
us, for once, take it at its face value; let us understand it as poetically

– and as illogically – as the poet himself expressed it. Artemis (Calchas fears, and rightly) may be angry at the eagles' feast on the pregnant hare because she is the protectress of the young of all wild things.

The poet is concerned first of all to provide a portent in which we can see, in a flash of the mind's eye, without rational analysis, the sack of Troy, the sacrifice of Iphigenia, and the awful feasting on Thyestes' young – three horribly related events which we, the audience, already know have happened. He is also concerned, in keeping with the tragic rhythm already established, to provide a portent suggestive first of triumphant, then of catastrophic, meanings. Thirdly, the poet requires an *occasion* for the anger of Artemis, not of course for its own sake (Artemis is not important here) but for the sake of the all-important dilemma which its appeasement is to cause the King. Fraenkel has judged well Aeschylus' reason for avoiding mention of the traditional explanation of Artemis' anger:[13] it would involve Agamemnon in an offence against the gods *prior* to the ethical situation (the dilemma at Aulis) on which the poet, for his play's sake, must concentrate. Hence, by 'spreading' the guilt of Agamemnon, it would distract attention from the essential moral issue with which the play is, at this point, to be concerned.

Whatever the *cause* of Artemis' anger, there can be no doubt, from Calchas' despairing prayer to Apollo the Healer (Artemis' brother), as to what the prophet fears as its result:

> I pray ... that she may not contrive ship-delaying, adverse winds thus
> hastening on another sacrifice, a particularly outrageous one [ἄνομον,
> 'lawless'], not to be stomached [ἄδαιτον: lit, 'inedible'], an architect
> of strife, clinging to the race, which fears not the husband-king himself
> [οὐ δεισήνορα]. For the fearful, treacherous house-keeper of the race
> abides, late to be aroused, the ever-remembering, child-avenging wrath.'
> (147–55)

Thus from one originally triumphant portent, the feast of the swooping eagles, the poet has let loose a flood of sinister reminders and anticipations. The language of this passage, pregnant with those multiple meanings which only lyric expression can simultaneously convey, suggests the whole sweep of horror: Atreus' savage banquet of Thyestes' children, the sacrifice of Iphigenia (ἄδαιτον 151, like Thyestes' banquet) which Artemis' anger, boldly 'occasioned' by the portent itself, will require for its appeasement, and finally even the vengeance on Agamemnon by Clytemnestra ('fearing not her husband') which that sacrifice must bring. The ambiguities persist to the last line of Calchas' prophetic speech, for the rich and terrible image of the last sentence quoted above applies both to Clytemnestra (certainly a 'treacherous house-keeper') avenging Iphigenia's death *and* to the 'wrath' from the slaughter of Thyestes' children, which is to be Aegisthus' goad to vengeance.

As in the anapaestic introduction, so now in the ode proper, the vigorous description of the great expedition against Troy stalls on a new note of anxiety and fear. Pondering the grim destinies (τοιάδε ... μόρσιμα) such as Calchas has just prophesied along with 'great goods,' from the portent of the eagles' feast, the Chorus repeat their ambiguous refrain ('Cry pity, pity, but may the good prevail!'),[14] then abruptly abandon these particular speculations about the future in favour of a larger, more consoling theme. Others have, to be sure, viewed the passage somewhat differently, but surely the so-called 'Hymn to Zeus' which follows in the next three stanzas (160–83) can be seen as the Chorus' ultimately hopeful response to the forebodings (including the hints of Iphigenia's sacrifice and its bloody aftermath) which Calchas' final prophecies have engendered.[15] For Zeus, the Chorus declare, is the only one on whom they can think of calling, if they are to cast the vain burden of care from their minds.

The basis of this confidence is twofold and is expressed in the next two stanzas, each encapsulating, in very different ways, a hope for the future (despite the suffering to be entailed) which the poet is ultimately to fulfil in the action of the trilogy. First the *power* of Zeus, the 'triple thrower,' and the manner of its establishment, is celebrated in a brief, elliptical description of his total victory over Kronos, himself the absolute conqueror of Ouranos. Second, the moral policy of Zeus' rule of human destiny is celebrated:

... Zeus who has put men on the way to wisdom by establishing as valid law, 'By suffering they shall win understanding.'[16]

This 'mixed blessing' from Zeus understandably does not (as yet, at any rate) quite bring the Chorus that relief from care which they are seeking:

The painful memory of woe drips, replacing sleep, over the heart. Even to those who are unwilling, discretion [σωφρονεῖν] comes. There is, somehow, a grace-that-comes-by violence [χάρις βίαιος, after Turnebus][17] from the gods seated on their dread bench of the helmsmen. (179–83)

The blend of suffering, of which the Chorus are aware both from their knowledge of what has happened thus far and from Calchas' prophetic warnings, and of learning-through-suffering expresses precisely the sequence of pain and victory anticipated in the prayerful refrain. It is important to note, too, the generalizing power of this passage: the knowledge (μάθος), discretion (σωφρονεῖν), the 'grace so hardly won' (χάρις βίαιος) need not be limited to any particular 'sufferer,' be it an Agamemnon, a Clytemnestra, a Paris, or an Orestes. (Indeed, in the case of the murdered Agamemnon, such terms would be singularly inappropriate, for what time will he have in which to 'learn,' to experience the violent *grace*?) Thus these 'lessons' mentioned by the Chorus should not be equated (as some have equated them) with its later saying that 'the doer will suffer' (παθεῖν τὸν ἔρξαντα, 1564), though the process may well *include* this particular fact. Bearing this long-term process of 'learning-through-suffering' in mind, we may, perhaps, postulate a reason for the particular terms in which the power of Zeus, expressed as the victory of the triple thrower, was described in the preceding stanza (167 ff). The victory of Zeus as the third and final ruler of the universe (after the violent overthrow of Ouranos and Kronos, respectively) anticipates, perhaps, the advance in understanding and, in particular, in σωφρονεῖν, which, under Zeus' new dispensation, society will learn at the end of the sufferings experienced in the present trilogy.[18]

Suddenly (for 'lyric action' can effect these leaps) we are transported, once the 'Hymn to Zeus' is over, back to Agamemnon's expedition, now in the midst of the ominous delay at Aulis ('Winds from Strymon ... wearing out ships and cables, crush, by their long delayings, the flower of Argive valour,' 192 ff, in part). We hear of Calchas' awful remedy (too awful for clear expression) for Artemis' anger and are plunged, without further warning, into the dread dilemma of the King. Agamemnon, seen earlier (187) as 'breathing with the sudden blasts of mischance,' and now as 'breathing his mind's own changing-wind' (219) reaches his unspeakable decision (the poet does not let him utter it) to sacrifice his daughter. (These wind-images expressing the King's dilemma and his choice fit grimly with the situation of his wind-stayed fleet.)[19] That Agamemnon *has* a choice (the point has been much debated),[20] albeit of one of two evils, is surely clear both from his own statement of the dread alternatives and from the absence, from both of them, of any indication of supernatural compulsion.[21] Indeed, the King expresses the extreme grievousness of *each* alternative with surprising clarity: the horror of staining his paternal hands at the altar with the streams of his maiden daughter's blood ($\pi\alpha\rho\theta\epsilon\nu o\sigma\phi\acute{a}\gamma o\iota\sigma\iota\nu\ \acute{\rho}\epsilon\acute{\iota}\theta\rho o\iota\varsigma$, 209–10: an image showing acute awareness of the ghastly nature of the deed) as opposed to the unthinkable possibility (for Agamemnon, the commander-in-chief) of being a betrayer of the expedition ('how can I become a ship-deserter [$\lambda\iota\pi\acute{o}\nu\alpha\upsilon\varsigma$], betraying the alliance?' 212–13). A choice of evils, to be sure ($\tau\acute{\iota}\ \tau\hat{\omega}\nu\delta'\ \check{\alpha}\nu\epsilon\upsilon\ \kappa\alpha\kappa\hat{\omega}\nu$; 211), but one which Agamemnon resolves, by putting public duty, 'responsibility' as leader of the alliance, before private outrage and the worst form of familial pollution. That this is so is clear from the King's final utterances in which he declares 'it is *right* [$\theta\acute{\epsilon}\mu\iota\varsigma$] that they [?] [the allies?][22] should vehemently desire the sacrifice which will put an end to the adverse winds' and even prays that, once this is done, all may be well ($\epsilon\hat{\upsilon}\ \gamma\grave{\alpha}\rho\ \epsilon\check{\iota}\eta$, 216).

So Agamemnon makes his decision. Whether to the motive of public duty, military responsibility, we are to add the overtone of personal ambition, the text, at this point, gives no indication. Elsewhere, it is true, the Chorus indicates public disapproval of the expedition (citizens' deaths 'for the sake of another man's wife,' 448) and the Chorus itself echoes this disapproval (799–804) on the same grounds. But elsewhere, also, the Chorus claims Zeus' own authorization of the expedition against Paris and Troy (60 ff and, by implication, 355–80), though this, to be sure, need not affect our view of Agamemnon's own motivation. It seems better, then, to leave both these circumstantial considerations, the one deepening, the other mitigating, the responsibility of the King, out of consideration at this particular point in the drama, and to decide on the responsibility and the 'guilt' of Agamemnon strictly in the terms in which he himself has expressed the issue, and in which the poet, through the words of the Chorus, reiterates it, in the passage immediately following. Clearly Agamemnon has *chosen* to stain his hands with his daughter's blood rather than betray his position as leader of the expedition and of this terrible and personal guilt and pollution no rationalization by the critics can clear him. (That Agamemnon was ever placed in this awful dilemma – through no fault of his own, as the treatment of Artemis' anger has indicated – may well, on the other hand, be the work of the family curse from Atreus' crime: the point has already been hinted at obscurely, vv 151–5, and will surface more clearly in the utterances of the prophet Cassandra and even of Clytemnestra herself, later in the play.)[23]

Agamemnon's decision to sacrifice Iphigenia, or at least the 'rationale' of that decision, is clearly implicit in the speech from which we have just quoted. A marked distinction in tone and language occurs in the next strophe, as the Chorus describe the quasi-physical effects observable as Agamemnon crosses the terrible line between deliberation and action, and actually undertakes the unspeakable deed.

> When he put on the yoke-strap of necessity [ἀνάγκας ἔδυ λέπαδνον], breathing an impious, impure, unholy 'changing wind' [τροπαίαν] of his mind, then from that point [τόθεν] he changed his thinking to utter recklessness. (218–21)

Critics have been seduced by the powerful image, the 'yoke-strap of necessity,' into concluding that Agamemnon has no choice in his decision, despite the clear indications of choice given in the preceding speech. Rather Agamemnon at this point accepts his hard lot as military commander and all that must follow from it: ἀνάγκη, as we shall see, is not always the absolute force which some would make it,[24] though once it has been accepted (ἔδυ, 'he puts on,' perfectly describes that moment), it becomes so. It is from this point that a kind of madness (παρακοπά : 'a knocking aside of the wits') descends on him, an external force without which he could not go through with the deed. It is *then* that 'he dares to become the sacrificer of his daughter' and the insensate quality of the deed is underlined by the sardonic descriptions, 'as a help in this war for avenging a woman, as a preliminary sacrifice on behalf of his ships.' This distinction between the ability or even (in a limited sense) the freedom to make a decision about a dreadful undertaking and the need of some kind of divine invasion (παρακοπά, like ἄτη, implies this)[25] of the *psyche* for that decision to be carried out may strike the modern reader of this passage of the *Agamemnon* as an overrefinement, but it is to occur again (though in very different form) in the case of Orestes' matricide later in the trilogy.[26] In both cases it is, perhaps, the poet's way of dramatizing something almost inconceivable: the very idea of a man who is not a monster bringing himself to commit a monstrous deed, whatever the 'justifications.'

The following two stanzas of the parodos (vv 228–47) provide ample evidence both that Agamemnon must indeed be possessed by a kind

of madness and that his deed must involve him in such guilt and
pollution as to make retribution inevitable. (It is the latter aspect, of
course, which makes the Chorus' treatment of the whole 'sacrifice of
Iphigenia theme' so necessary a part of the tragic sequence of this
play.) No words are spared, in one of the most moving passages in
extant Greek tragedy, in describing the pathos and the horror of the
sacrifice itself (' ... her prayers, her vain cries of "Father", her maiden
years, the warlike chieftains set at nought,' 227–30) and the cruel
insensibility of Agamemnon himself. Indeed, the emphasis on the
father's impious insensitivity (' ... after a prayer, he bids the attendants take heart and lift her ... " 231 ff), on the unnatural substitution
involved in this sacrifice ('face down, over the altar, like some sacrificial animal, with her robes trailing around her'), and on the cor-
ruption of what was once a loving father-daughter bond ('looking ...
as if she would give voice, as often, indeed, she had sung at other
male gatherings about her father's banquet table') seems almost perverse (editors have even sought to mitigate the horror of what the
Greek seems to say in the interest of credibility)[27] until we realize that
the deed we are witnessing is simply the realization of the madness,
of the impious, impure, unholy 'changing wind' of Agamemnon's
mind, of which we have been warned in the preceding strophe.
Nevertheless, before the madness of the deed came the sober pondering leading to the fatal decision. One wonders why, if we are
meant, as so many commentators have insisted, to regard Agamemnon merely as the unwilling victim of Necessity, the poet here chooses
to arouse the 'natural feelings' of the audience so violently against
him.[28]

The Chorus ends this mighty ode with an echo of earlier consolation
(somewhat cryptic in the circumstances), 'Justice brings down [or
'weighs out,' with its scales] knowledge to those who have suffered,'
(250–1)[29] and a prayer, equally cryptic but more ominous, for the
future:

> as to what follows on this deed [the sacrifice of Iphigenia], may the
> accomplishment turn out well – as this close-clinging, sole guardian
> [ἕρκος] of the Apian land declares. (255–7)

This introduction of Clytemnestra, as she steps forward at the end
of the parodos, provides a chilling reminder of the blood-strife 'clinging to the race' (152) which Iphigenia's sacrifice was doomed to
reawaken. (Some editors, it is true, reject this ironic interpretation of

the hidden doom of Agamemnon, the 'triumphant' 'beacons speech' anticipates the Chorus' ambiguous treatment, in the coming ode, of Agamemnon's victory. 'First and last runner share the victory': Clytemnestra's closing irony (314) will be remembered when the Chorus sings (462-7) of the Erinyes closing in on Agamemnon.

In the Queen's second speech (320-50), the same blend of triumph and danger appears. Amid the scenes imagined in the captured city, the vision of 'children falling about their fathers' corpses' (327-8) provides a chill anticipation of Iphigenia's embrace, in Hades, of her slaughtered father.[32] Of the Queen's ironic expressions of fear for the conquering Argives, the last one in particular ('the suffering of the dead [at Troy? at Aulis?] may be aroused ... ' 346-7)[33] will soon be affirmed by the Chorus (456-7) in its own 'triumphant' song.

Such, then, are the various hints, themes, and anticipations which the first stasimon of the *Agamemnon* will develop. Convinced, at first, by the joyful news, the clear evidence and the vivid imaginings of Clytemnestra's speeches, the Chorus set out to celebrate the just destruction of Paris and the Trojans. But soon, as in the parodos, the note of triumph fades and the ode delineates, by a series of subtle transitions, the inevitable shift from triumph to disaster, the prelude to Agamemnon's own entanglement in the net of Justice.

The ode's prelude (in anapaests) presents two striking images of retribution: the image of *Atê*'s net cast over the walls of Troy and of the unerring marksman, Zeus-of-the-guests, bending his bow against Paris. Those who cast the net are 'King Zeus' and 'friendly Night.' The latter has already been named by Clytemnestra (265, 279) as coadjutor in the good news from Troy; here the epithets φιλία, μεγάλων κόσμων κτεάτειρα reinforce the full sense behind the Queen's conventional euphemism (εὐφρόνη) and the ambiguity of the second epithet ('possessor of star-spangled robes'/'bestower of glorious victories') allows us to see, in a single phrase, both the literal and the symbolic splendour of the image.[34]

The 'net of destruction' (στεγανὸν δίκτυον ... μέγα δουλείας γάγγαμον, ἄτης παναλώτου, 358-61) is to be a recurrent image in the play and in the trilogy. The fact that it occurs first in connection with Zeus' just destruction of Troy shows clearly the paradeigmatic relation of that event, as treated in the present play, to the deeds of violence more intimately affecting Agamemnon and his family, for it is in this connection that each subsequent occurrence of the 'net image' is used both in this play and in the trilogy. Thus, at *Agamemnon* 868, Clytemnestra's rhetorical use of this image to describe her 'wounded' husband at Troy anticipates, with hidden irony, the grim reality of the much-punctured robe in which she soon will slay him – and this is that same 'net of Hades' (δίκτυόν ... Ἅιδου, 1115), with the wife herself the snare (ἄρκυς, 1116), which prophetic Cassandra 'sees' descending on the King. Clytemnestra again, in her speech over the body of the King, refers to the boundless net, like a fishing-net (ἄπειρον ἀμφίβληστρον, ὥσπερ ἰχθύων, Ag 1382) in which she slew him; in the next play, the same word (ἀμφίβληστρον, Cho 492) is used by Electra as, with Orestes, she seeks to goad the spirit of Agamemnon to aid in their vengeance. At *Choephori* 505–7, Electra uses the net image in describing the role of the children in preserving the fame of a slain hero: 'as corks a fish-net [δίκτυον], they buoy up the line that stretches to the deep below.'[35] After the matricide, Orestes, with nice irony, recalls the earlier application of the net image, as he holds up the robe in which Agamemnon was slaughtered and calls it 'a net [δίκτυον], a hunting-snare [ἄρκυν], garments to entrap the feet' (Cho 1000). Finally, in the *Eumenides*, as the long succession of slaughters nears its resolution, the sequence of 'net images' ends appropriately with the cry of the Furies, frustrated, for the moment, in their pursuit of Orestes: 'The beast has fallen from the net [ἐξ ἀρκύων]!' (147).

'Confining net ... net of slavery, net of all-destructive *Atê*.' Of the three dread descriptions of the net (358–61), the Chorus leaves the most terrible till the last. *Atê*, a concept usually endowed with 'personality' in Aeschylus, is to recur in a particularly striking passage later in this ode.

As the image of the confining net is suited to the collective victim, Troy, so the second image (the 'archer image') of this choral prelude fits the individual victim, Paris.

> ... Zeus ξένιος [Zeus-of-the-guests] stretching his bow, these many years, against Alexander so that the arrow sped neither short of its mark nor beyond the stars. (362–6)

The image is both precise and cosmic: the arrow reaches its particular target at a particular point of time and space (μήτε πρὸ καιροῦ is, in the context, both a temporal and a spatial expression) and we are made aware of the immensity of the range by the reminder of where the arrow might have gone if Zeus had shot too far.

So much for the anapaestic overture. The ode proper now settles down (in a brisker, more relentless rhythm, predominantly iambic,[36] which is to last till the epode) to develop in its first phase the significance of this assault of Zeus and to describe, with vivid imagery, the aberration of Paris which occasioned it. The language remains metaphorical and the transition from the 'over-all' view of the introductory passage is softened by the initial 'tracking metaphor' which follows the hunting metaphor of Zeus' arrow:

> They have the blow of Zeus to tell of, this, at any rate, one can track down. (367-8)

'He has fulfilled it as he decreed' ($ἔπραξεν ὡς ἔκρανεν$, 369). Here (in the case of Paris and the Trojans) it is Zeus who is described as both decreeing and fulfilling, but the line anticipates (as so much of Paris' tale will anticipate) Agamemnon's fate, when a decree of another sort [$δημοκράντου ... ἀρᾶς ...$ 457] is soon to be fulfilled). So, too, the Chorus' initial description of Paris' situation is generalized in such a way, and in such language, as to be applicable to that other situation as well:

> A man said that the gods paid no heed to those men by whom the grace-of-things-not-to-be-touched [$ἀθίκτων χάρις$][37] was trampled on. But that man was not pious. (369-72)

The overt reference of $ἀθίκτων χάρις$ is, of course, to Helen, the wife of Paris' host, and to the crime of Paris in profaning the sacred and reciprocal rights of hospitality ($ξενία$). Both in word and idea, the expression anticipates several passages in which Helen is to appear in one form or another: $χάρις$ is to be used of statues (417), and of dream-visions (described as $χάριν ματαίαν$), of Helen (422), both of which frustrate Menelaus' desire. In the second of these passages, moreover, something of the 'untouchable quality' of Helen is ironically repeated in the elusive nature of the vision: 'slipping through his hands, the vision is gone' (424-5). But $ἀθίκτων χάρις$, 'the delicacy of things inviolable,' as Lattimore translates v 371), looks back also to the parodos, to Iphigenia, whose virgin grace was so poignantly described at vv 239-47, and to Agamemnon, to whom she was, above all others, $ἄθικτος$, and who shed her blood in sacrifice.[38]

> Destruction ($ἀρή$) manifestly exacts punishment for criminal deeds of men breathing more pride than is right, of houses filled to overflowing beyond what is best. (374-8)[39]

This second description of Paris' situation has, like the preceding one (369-72), a wider application than the one supplied by the immediate context. First of all, the idea of ἀρή ('destruction': if we accept the reading [compare *Suppl* 84] and the meaning here given to it), exacting retribution from Paris for violent deeds, anticipates, in highly ironic fashion, a similar expression used near the end of the ode (457) where ἀρά, in the sense of a curse *which brings destruction*, is used in connection with Agamemnon's coming doom. Secondly, the full treatment of the association between wealth and criminal deeds is also to appear later, at 750-81, where it is strategically placed between the Chorus' final treatment of the 'Trojan theme' (in the third stasimon) and the entry of the doomed Agamemnon. The text of the present passage is obscure, but we may discern at least the association of deeds of violence and their punishment with 'too much wealth.' The later passage (750-81, supported still later by 1007-13) repeats this association but insists emphatically that wealth alone (in, presumably, Agamemnon's and Paris' cases, as in all others) need not lead to destruction. Finally, the coda at vv 381-4, with its warning that there is no defence for the man who 'in pride of wealth spurns justice,' anticipates, though again only in partial manner, the warning in the third stasimon that, though dangerous wealth may be jettisoned, the deed of violence admits of no solution (1007-21). Thus the later and fuller development of each aspect of this sequence of disaster, here first observed in the case of Paris, emphasizes the essentially paradeigmatic nature of the whole treatment of Paris' career. Brilliant though that treatment is in itself, the destruction of Paris and Troy is but the anticipatory analogue of the destruction of Agamemnon.

The antistrophe (385-402) depicts the operation of Persuasion or Temptation (*Peithô*) on the flawed young hero, Paris: again it is a theme which, as we have seen, also affects the principal figures in the *present* tragic action. Here the process is personified in the poet's most vivid manner:

For dread Persuasion forces her way through, Persuasion [*Peithô*], the irresistible child of fore-counselling *Atê*.

In what sense *Peithô* can come to be regarded as 'the child of *Atê*,' a passage in the *Persae* has already hinted.[40] There (*Persae* 93-100) we have seen divine deception (ἀπάτην θεοῦ) luring man to his doom, while *Atê*, with smiling flattery, leads him into toils whence no man escapes. Here the personification is worked out a shade further: Persuasion (*Peithô*) replaces deception (*apatê*) of the passage in the *Persae* and now figures as the child or agent of *Atê* who is represented as both planner and executioner of the wretch's destruction.

It is significant that, as in the passage in the *Persae*, it is the divine element which is first pictured as suggesting the crime for which the doer is later to suffer at the hands of the gods. First we hear of the divine instigators, *Atê* and *Peithô*, then of the deed itself ('the baneful act [σίνος] gleams forth, an evil light,' 389), and, only at the end, of the doer of the deed:

> Like base bronze, when rubbed and battered, so he becomes indelibly black, when brought to justice (390–3)[41]

The striking simile leaves no doubt of the Chorus' (and the poet's) intention to include Paris in the chain of responsibility for Troy's downfall – a point which is made explicit a few verses later (397–402), at the end of this antistrophe. We are reminded again of the *Persae*; there, though the image of divine temptation is given first, as in the passage cited, Darius later supplies the significant qualification: 'Whenever a man himself [Xerxes, in this case] is eager [ie for deeds of outrage], then the god battens on him' [ἀλλ', ὅταν σπεύδῃ τις αὐτός, χὠ θεὸς συνάπτεται, 742). So, too, in the case of Paris (and of Agamemnon?): he may be 'divinely tempted' but he must yield to the temptation before *Atê* can seize him. The Chorus, be it noted, judge Paris to be ἄδικον (unjust) in the gods' eyes (397–8).

The heavy image of flawed bronze (Paris as the offender) suddenly gives place to a volatile image (' ... a boy chases a winged bird ...' 393–4) of Paris as the one led astray by temptation.[42] The language is consonant with all the marvellously 'elusive' images which appear whenever the presence of Helen, now an enticement, now a dream disappearing, now herself a guilty fugitive, is felt, rather than clearly perceived, in these choral songs. Thus the image for Paris' temptation is an apt preparation for the new themes of Helen the deserter ('slipping lightly through the gates, daring the undareable, she is gone ...' 407–8) and of the abandoned Menelaus, grappling with the 'mournful apparitions of dreams ... which bring a vain delight' but soon 'slip, insubstantial, through his arms, never to return thereafter along the winged paths of sleep' (420–6). Just as Paris' crime afflicts his own city (395) and shames the hospitality of the Atreidae (400 ff) so Helen 'leaves shield-and-spear-clashings for her fellow-citizens and brings to Troy like destruction, for her dowry' (403–6).[43] Once again, the images wear a Janus-like aspect, looking backward to the parodos, to the afflictions forecast for Greeks and Trojans alike (63-7) and looking forward to the next stasimon, to the grim dénouement of the 'lion-cub image':

> ... and the house was defiled with blood, an irresistible affliction for the householder, a great bane, full of slaughter. (732-6)

From Helen we pass (412-26) to the deserted Menelaus, sadly pacing the deserted halls of his palace, seeking the departed Helen in statues ('in whose blank gaze all passion perishes') and in the frustrated embraces of his dreams. It is a passage of striking and mournful beauty, but in the thematic sequence of the ode its chief function is to shift the focus of interest from the Trojans and from Helen, the cause of their destruction, back to the 'bereaved' ones at home: first to Menelaus but eventually to other mourning Greeks as well. Thus does the poet prepare for the surprise climax to which this whole ironic 'song of victory' is leading.

> These are the woes at the hearth at home, these – and others more grievous still than these. (427-8)

This is the essential transition, for now the Chorus will celebrate neither the triumphs nor even the griefs of the Atreidae but the griefs of homes throughout Greece who receive back 'dust instead of men' after the Atreidae's war.

In the parodos, Zeus ξένιος has been described as one who sent the Atreidae to war (60-2); now Ares suddenly appears as the sender (Ἄρης ... πέμπει, 438-41) in the shocking image 'Ares, trafficker in men's bodies' (ὁ χρυσαμοιβὸς δ' Ἄρης σωμάτων). Thus the poignant contrast 'dust in place of men' is sustained throughout the sordid commercial image of Ares as 'money-changer, scale-holder in battle' to emerge again, on the other side of the metaphor, as the bereaved families are pictured receiving at home 'the well-ordered urns.' The faintly 'Homeric' echo here (though the epithet itself is not Homeric) leads to another 'heroic' note: the briefly dramatized exchange between the mourners ...

> ... praising one man, that he was skilled in battle, another, that he had died nobly amid the carnage – *for the sake of another man's wife.* (445-8)

With the last phrase begins the ground-swell of Argive discontent with the Atreidae themselves:

> Thus mutters low some citizen. And over them steals grief full of resentment against the avenging Atreidae. (449-51)

From the urns at home the Chorus flashes a quick glance across the seas to those whom Troy hides buried in the land they conquered. Then, in the antistrophe, the people's curse sounds forth for the first time explicitly:

> Grievous is the talk of the citizens when they are angry;
> The curse the people has pronounced ordains that a penalty must be paid (456-7).[44]

δημοκράντου δ' ἀρᾶς τίνει χρέος : at the beginning of this ode, it was Zeus who fulfilled justice as he had decreed it (ὡς ἔκρανεν, 369) on Paris and the Trojans; now it is the decree of the people's own curse which is to exact its fulfilment on Agamemnon. The ode has travelled full cycle. Starting with the celebration of Zeus' justice over the Trojans through Agamemnon's victory, we now count Argive dead among the battle's victims and hear the people's curse for these deaths 'for another man's wife.' To the popular anger, the Chorus now adds the watchful eye of the gods against the slayers of many, the vengeance of the Erinyes (who 'set at naught': the unjust man, 463-6) and finally the awful thunderbolt of Zeus himself (469-70).

In the coda (471-4) to this last antistrophe, the Chorus shuns the lot of the city-sacker and of the conquered victim alike.

> Prosperity which is free from envy, I judge best [κρίνω δ' ἄφθονον ὄλβον] (471).

Schooled by its own observations in the preceding two stanzas, the Chorus thus makes its final comment on Agamemnon's mighty victory over Troy, a conclusion very different from the triumphant vaunt over Paris with which the ode began. So, too, in the epode, (475-87), the Chorus, governed by mood rather than logic, now question even the news of Agamemnon's victory, which has been accepted as an established fact throughout the ode.

From the good news of the beacon fires, a swift report has reached the city. Yet who knows if it be true – or some deception from the gods? (475–8)

The last expression (if this reading be sound)[45] leads our minds back to that divine deception which (as we have also seen in *the Persae*)[46] lies at the beginning of so many catastrophic sequences in Aeschylus. In the present instance, of course, the fear is not justified – the 'good news' is true: Troy *has* fallen; yet the ironic validity in the Chorus' fear may be that Agamemnon's actual victory may prove to be a snare and a delusion. How much – or, more probably, how little – of this may be in the Chorus' mind we do not know: they still speak of the beacon-fire as 'good-news-bearing' (εὐαγγέλου), but their actual receptions of the Herald's news and of the King's victorious return are, as we shall see, fraught with ambiguities, hope and congratulation constantly giving way to premonitions and even despair. As far as *mood* is concerned, what seems important to remember is that it is how the Chorus affects the mood of the audience, not the 'psychological' reasons for the Chorus' own moods, that matters. To this we should add the important dramatic point (regarded by some, though by no means all, of the commentators as the *only* explanation of this puzzling passage) that some element of uncertainty about Agamemnon's victory is necessary in order to give the Herald's imminent confirmation of the news an appropriate impact.[47] And to this dramatic point the Chorus adds a further ironic fillip by its recurrent doubts (see vv 483–7) about the too credulous nature of a mere woman's (Clytemnestra's!) mind.

> Too persuasive [or too credulous?] a woman's ordinance feeds beyond its boundaries[48] travelling on too fast; But woman-chattered rumour dies a speedy death. (485–7)

The ambiguous lines with which the ode closes reawaken a sinister motif. The Chorus (as Paris was before them and as Agamemnon soon will be) have been subjected to the power of *Peithô* vested in a woman. Here, for a moment, they reject it, but will soon find their repudiation vain.

4 Second episode (the 'Herald scene') and second stasimon (vv 489–781)

Clytemnestra now announces,[49] at the beginning of the second episode, the approach of the Herald from Troy whose news will decide 'whether the message of the beacon is true or whether, like dreams, this light which came so sweetly has beguiled our wits' (491-2). It is a brilliant device to blend in this scene the Queen's ironic message of welcome to Agamemnon (600-14) with the naïve and gradually corroded optimism of the Herald's declamations. In these three speeches of the Herald (503-37, 551-82, 636-80), his mood, like that of the Chorus in each of the preceding odes, moves from joy and confidence through doubt to gloomy admissions of catastrophe.[50]

At first, all is triumph and happy home-coming:

Hail native soil ... at last I've reached you after many broken hopes. I never thought I'd die at home in Argos and share, in burial, in this beloved land. (503-7)

Halls of my King, beloved hearth, sacred royal seat and statues of the gods who look toward the sun, now if ever before, receive with these glad-gleaming eyes our King at last returned. (518-21)

Now welcome him, for it is fitting, him who has overthrown Troy with the mattock of Zeus, bringer of justice ... And all the altars and temples are swept away and the seed of all the land is quite destroyed. (524-8)

Even here, however, in the midst of joy, we catch sinister overtones, all the more so for being unconscious from the Herald's point of view. 'To share, in burial, in this beloved land' is an ironic anticipation of the King's own death; ' ... with these glad-gleaming eyes' ($\phi\alpha\iota\delta\rhoοῖσι$ $\tauοιοῖδ'$ $\check{ο}\mu\mu\alpha\sigma\iota\nu$, 520) anticipates Clytemnestra's fawning welcome to her husband: $\lambdaοντροῖσι$ $\phi\alpha\iota\delta\rho\acute{ν}\nu\alpha\sigma\alpha$, 1109; $\phi\alpha\iota\delta\rho\acute{ο}\nuους$ 1229, in Cassandra's descriptions of the Queen. Finally, 'altars and temples swept away [$\check{α}\iotaστοι$]' fulfils the warning implied in Clytemnestra's speech (338-40) on the captured city.

It is the Chorus who gradually infect the cheerful Herald with their own mood of gloom. Talk of the Herald's longing for Argos leads to dark hints (542 ff) of woes at home:

CHORUS Long have I held silence to be my cure of ills.
HERALD But how was this? Were there some here you feared, when the Kings were far away?
CHORUS Yes, so much so that death itself were grace, as you were saying just now. (548-50)

The Herald in his second speech (551–82) allows the first hint of gloom to affect his own report.

> Well, the end has been good. In the long haul, one might say that
> things have gone well, but one might urge complaints as well ... (551–3)

The complaints (ἐπίμομφα) follow: the wearing discomforts of a long, bitter campaign, the cramped quarters on shipboard, the damp billets on shore, the lice in the hair ... 'But why grieve over these matters? The woe has passed [παροίχεται, 567].' Yet even in his brave attempts to forget, the Herald's language trips him up: 'Aye, it has passed right enough [παροίχεται, again]; so 'passed' for the dead, indeed, that they've no concern ever to rise again!' (568–70). Again the Herald seeks to reestablish confidence. 'For the survivors, for those that sped o'er land and sea to safety, the gain outweighs the woe ... For, by Zeus' favour, it is a glorious victory!' (573–82, in part).

'For the survivors ... ' Clytemnestra's message of welcome to Agamemnon[51] interrupts the Chorus' questioning of the Herald, but after it the Chorus return to this new avenue of gloom. Is Menalaus among these survivors? (See 618–19.) It is now the Herald's turn to be evasive with talk of 'lies which remain no longer fair when friends find out the truth' (620–1) ... and soon the truth, the disappearance of Menelaus and all the fleet, is out. The third and last of the Herald's speeches is a tale of unrelieved woe, a 'paean of the Erinyes' as he himself calls it. A storm 'caused not but by the wrath of gods' (649) caused the whole Aegean 'to blossom with corpses of Achaeans and wreckage of their ships'' (659–60). Only Agamemnon's ship, with some god (θεός τις, 663) steering it, escaped. 'Chance ... as saving guardian' (Τύχη ... σωτήρ, 664) is the Herald's guess as to why this happened, but the audience, and perhaps the Chorus, may think otherwise.

The 'Helen ode' (which now ensues at vv 681 ff) complements the preceding 'Paris ode.' In the latter, we saw Paris racing to his ruin and Troy's ruin, 'even as a boy chases a winged bird,' and there, too, we caught our first glimpse of Helen as Temptation (Peithô, irresistible child of Atê, 385–6). But now the song is all of Helen, ἑλένας, ἕλανδρος, ἑλέπτολις ('destroyer of ships, destroyer of men, destroyer of cities,' 689–90), a theme developed in a terrifying sequence of images which begins with beguiling sweetness but ends with the victim's blood.

... battle-wooed Helen, bride of strife ... from her softly curtained
bower she sailed on the breath of the mighty west-wind. (686 ff)

And the wrath which works its will forces the fulfilment of the marriage-bond-of-woe[52] for Troy ... (699 ff)

Too late the ancient town of Priam learns in place of the marriage-song
a song of much lamenting and cries out on Paris of the fatal marriage ...
(709 ff)

So a man nourished a lion-cub in the first encounters of life [ἐν βιότου
προτελείοις], gentle and sweet, the darling of old and young alike ...
gleaming-eyed and fawning ... (717 ff)

The lion-cub grows; in time it shows its parents' nature. Unbidden, it
fashions a banquet [δαῖτ' ἀκέλευστος ἔτευξεν] of herds foully destroyed;
a grim requital of favours received. (727-31)

By god's hand, a sort of priest of *Atê* has been nourished for the house
(735-6)

The language is as allusive as ever: ἐν βιότου προτελείοις (720)
recalls διακναιομένης τ' ἐν προτελείοις κάμακος (though the construction is different) at vv 65-6, and προτέλεια ναῶν, 'the sacrificial
expiations for the ships,' at v 227;[53] φαιδρωπός, 725, here said of the
lion-cub, echoes Clytemnestra's own description of herself at v 520,
as she prepares to receive her lord, φαιδροῖσι τοισίδ' ὄμμασιν, just
as Helen's role here prefigures that of Clytemnestra with Agememnon
in the coming carpet scene; finally, the sinister juxtaposition of words,
δαῖτ' ἀκέλευστος ἔτευξεν, 731, used here of the lion and his banquet,
reminds us of Atreus' awful banquet for Thyestes.

The seductive image of the 'bride-of-strife' who brings a marriage-bond of woe is complemented by the 'lion-cub image' and its
dénouement. It is a richly elaborated sequence. The first strophic pair
(681-716) describes the bride (both as ravished [δορίγαμβρον] and as
ravishing [ἕλανδρος]) and the disastrous results of her marriage-song
upon the Trojans celebrating it. The second strophic pair (717-36)
describes the parallel career of the lion-cub, who grows from a
seductive plaything to be the destroyer of the home which nourished

it. The point of the comparison appears most clearly in the climax of the latter description, for here the language applied to the lion-cub applies more clearly still to Helen:

> And the house was defiled with blood, an unbearable woe to the householders, a dread blight productive of much bloodshed. By the will of god it had been reared as a sort of priest of *Atê* for the house. (732–6)

In the next strophe (737–49), which concludes the sequence, the Chorus returns to Helen, describing her first, in language still more disarming and seductive, as a 'spirit of unruffled calm' (739–40), as 'a heart-piercing bloom of love' (743), and then (at the sending of Zeus *xenios*) as a bitter settler for the sons of Priam, a Curse (*Erinys*) to make brides weep (746–9).

(So bold is this image in which Helen appears both as, in one sense, the occasion, through her marriage with Paris, of Zeus' wrath, *and* as the instrument for its accomplishment, that some critics have refused to accept the identification here of Helen and the Erinys. But in the language of Aeschylean poetry there is surely nothing improbable about such a daring switch. Zeus' wrath, moreover, is directed primarily at Paris' crime against Menelaus' hospitality. Helen, who is herself outside the moral sequence concerned, acts first as a catalyst for Paris' crime; once this role is completed, she becomes, like the lion-cub, the force by which her new 'protectors' are destroyed.)[54]

The second stasimon ends with a philosophic passage (750–81), expanding this theme of retribution, which looks forward to the doom of Agamemnon as surely as it comments on the fall of Troy. Here the Chorus clearly distinguish their view from the traditional view (the παλαίφατος λόγος, 750) that great prosperity of itself begets insatiate misery. Rather,

> The impious deed (τὸ δυσσεβὲς ... ἔργον) begets more of the same stock after it ... (758–60)

> Old ὕβρις is wont sooner or later to beget new ὕβρις growing afresh [νεάζουσαν] amid men's evils, when the fated hour of birth comes 'round, and the irresistible unholy spirit of Boldness [θράσος], both of them black disasters [ἄτας] on the house, like to their parents.[55] (763–71)

It is clear that, in this part of its ethical 'coda,' the Chorus is at pains to mark the originality of its view (δίχα δ' ἄλλων μονόφρων εἰμί ... 757) that unholy deeds rather than great wealth are the source of disaster for a family. Some scholars have argued that, in fact, there was nothing novel in this view and that the distinction concerned 'had been clearly enough expressed by Solon a very long time ago (frr. 1.9 ff., 5.9–10).'[56] But, in fact, comparison of the above passage (*Ag* 750–71) with *all* the relevant fragments of Solon suggests a far greater insistence here on the impious deed (*apart* from wealth) as the cause of catastrophe than is always present in the extant Solonian fragments.[57] This is in keeping, too, with the dramatic context and the dramatic purpose of the present passage, for it occurs just after the lyric celebration of the retribution which came upon Paris from Zeus *xenios*, through Helen as Erinys, and just before the return of Agamemnon, who will face similar retribution from Clytemnestra, both for his own deed against Iphigenia and for the deeds of his father Atreus.[58]

The emphasis of the present passage is to be repeated also in the following stasimon, after the return of Agamemnon, where the Chorus' worry very clearly concerns the King. There (1008–21) we will be reminded that 'a well-measured throw' can relieve a ship foundering from excess cargo but that 'blood once shed' can never be recalled. Nevertheless, wealth is not absent from either Paris' or Agamemnon's situation. Helen as Paris' bride has been called 'gentle adornment of wealth' (ἀκασκαῖον ... ἄγαλμα πλούτου, 741) and Agamemnon is to be tempted to a wasteful display of wealth in the carpet scene. It is perhaps for this reason that the final antistrophe of the present ode, just before the entry of the King, dwells on the dangers of excessive wealth with the reminder that:

> Justice shines in smoky hovels and honours the righteous man. Abandoning with averted eyes gold-encrusted houses where unclean hands are found, she goes to holy dwellings, giving no honour to the power of wealth, which is falsely stamped with praise. (772–81)

So despite the initial emphasis on τὸ δυσσεβὲς ἔργον, the impious deed, rather than great wealth, as the cause of a family's recurrent woes, the 'dangerous wealth' theme is still present. It was a theme congenial to the fifth-century Greeks[59] as well as to the sixth. Perhaps the Aeschylean Chorus has not advanced so far beyond Solon after all.

5 Third episode (Agamemnon and Clytemnestra) and third stasimon (vv 782–1034)

As the Chorus ends its song with these ominous verses, Agamemnon makes his triumphant entry, with Cassandra, the captive Trojan princess, behind him. The main effect of this scene, of course, is to be the confrontation between the King and Clytemnestra. However, the first one to address the King, and so to be answered by him, is the Chorus-Leader, not the Queen. This is important, for the first words of the King may then more easily take the form of a general address to the city, and it is equally important that the citizens, by getting in first, should distinguish their welcome from that of the plotting Clytemnestra. Here the poet faces a real difficulty. It has been part of the 'thematic' function of the Chorus to express the darker aspects, with hints of divine retribution, of Agamemnon's past, and in this, as we have seen, the muttered curses of the citizens for the Argive dead have played their part. On the other hand, it is essential that these civic representatives be ultimately loyal: otherwise, the treasonous Clytemnestra and Aegisthus might seem to represent not merely their own and the *alastor*'s vengeance but the Argive people's will as well. Aeschylus resolves this difficulty with the simplicity of genius. After a cryptic warning against the flattery of specious welcomers (788–98), the Chorus (through their leader) make a clean breast of their own past misgivings and a ringing declaration of their present loyalty:

> When first you led the army forth for Helen's sake, your image (I'll not hide it from you) in my heart was not a pretty one, such poor judgment was it (to my mind) to spend men's lives in fetching home that willing wanton.[60] But now, from the bottom of my heart, I profess my love
> for those who have accomplished well the undertaking. (799–806)

Agamemnon, like Xerxes before him, is a tragic sufferer whose presentation on stage is almost devoid of personal characterization. He is, of course, regal and triumphant as the conventional persona of a victorious king requires. Apart from this impression, or, rather, nicely complementing it, the chief effect of his richly textured opening speech (810–54) is that of tragic irony, in its simplest and, in the tense circumstances, its most effective form. In his first sentence, Agamemnon addresses as coadjutors ($\mu\varepsilon\tau\alpha\iota\tau\acute{\iota}o\upsilon\varsigma$, 811) in his sack of Troy the native Argive gods ($\theta\varepsilon o\grave{\upsilon}\varsigma$ $\dot{\varepsilon}\gamma\chi\omega\rho\acute{\iota}o\upsilon\varsigma$) who will soon join in his own destruction. $\check{\alpha}\tau\eta\varsigma$ $\theta\acute{\upsilon}\varepsilon\lambda\lambda\alpha\iota$ $\zeta\hat{\omega}\sigma\iota$ ('The storm of *Atê* still lives on'), he reminds us grimly in his vivid picture of the smoking ruins of Troy; then, as if to underline his unconscious irony, he likens the Argive beast which destroyed Troy to a savage lion leaping on its towers to lick its fill of royal blood (827–8): the image recalls the lion-cub image (717 ff) which introduced Helen as scourge of Troy and anticipates Cassandra's image of the 'cowardly lion,' Aegisthus (1224), now plotting with Helen's sister to overthrow her lord. In the second part of his speech, the King's unconscious ironies come still closer to the immediate situation, as he reminds the Chorus of his skill in detecting the false appearance of good will; they reach their climax with his bland assurance that 'by cautery or surgery,' as needed, he'll take the sting from any civic ill.

Attempts have been made to find culpable or at least personal (and fatal) characteristics in this speech of Agamemnon as in the ensuing argument with Clytemnestra about treading on the tapestries. It has been suggested, for example, that the King shows arrogance in treating the gods as his associates ($\mu\varepsilon\tau\alpha\iota\tau\iota\circ\upsilon\varsigma$, 811) in the sack of Troy,[61] but this interpretation surely founders on the King's claim (813 ff) that the gods have answered just pleas in determining the fate of Troy. Perhaps the one individual feature observable in Agamemnon's speeches before the dialogue with Clytemnestra is his apparent coldness to his eager Queen: he addresses first 'Argos and the native gods' (810–11), then the Chorus (830 ff), and when finally he turns to Clytemnestra (914 ff) it is to rebuke, without any initial endearments, her own excessive welcome. But with Cassandra in the immediate, and Iphigenia in the remote, background, even this feature of Agamemnon's conduct is hardly indicative of a highly personal reaction.

In general, attempts to find subtle characterization of Agamemnon in this scene are misguided. The dramatist has already provided in abundant measure the kind of dramatic expectations (derived from the King's past and that of his family) necessary for the coming catastrophe. A certain nobility or stature is, of course, required of this single appearance of the tragic figure. This is indeed supplied in his first two speeches, in which a proper awareness of divine $\phi\theta\acute{o}\nu\circ\varsigma$ ('ill will' 'begrudging') and even of the requirements of human 'right-thinking' ($\tau\grave{o}\ \mu\grave{\eta}\ \kappa\alpha\kappa\tilde{\omega}\varsigma\ \phi\rho\circ\nu\varepsilon\tilde{\iota}\nu$, 927) are also (perhaps with some irony) manifested, and this effect is not entirely lost even in his ultimate submission 'against his better judgment' to the Queen's wishes. For the rest, it is the on-stage *deed* which he is led to perform, rather than questions of personality or motive, on which dramatic attention is rightly concentrated.

The confrontation between Clytemnestra and Agamemnon which now ensues is the theatrical climax of the play: 'theatrical' in that here Agamemnon is made to give, before the eyes of the spectators, a symbolic demonstration of the hybristic deed of outrage to the gods and to his royal house which he has performed at Aulis; 'theatrical' again, in that here Clytemnestra enacts in symbolic fashion (again before the eyes of the audience) that defeat and mastery of Agamemnon which she will soon consummate behind the closed doors of the palace. Since the whole presentation of Clytemnestra thus far in the play is one of the most powerful of various dramatic preparations for the catastrophe, it might be well, at this point, to review some of the preceding effects of that presentation.

We have already seen how the prologue, the first three great odes, and the three speeches of the Herald have all, in their very different ways, contributed to the dramatic expectation of the coming catastrophe. A large number of these anticipations have taken ironic form: the gradual revelation of the reality of the coming disaster beneath the appearance of triumph and prosperity. The form of Clytemnestra's contribution here is also heavily ironic but in a very different way, for unlike the Watchman, the Chorus, and the Herald she is fully aware of the sinister hidden meanings which form the most significant part of all her utterances. In her covert expression, in innocent-seeming words, of guilty passions and murderous intentions, lies an essential part of her dramatic personality. While it is acceptable, I would insist, to speak of that personality as a continuous dramatic reality through the play,[62] it is important to recognize from the outset its function in the total structure. Clytemnestra, like every other element in this tragedy, exists for the sake of the action and its meaning. Both by what she is (how she affects all who come in contact with her) and by what she says, she must make the audience more and more conscious of the inevitability of the coming catastrophe.

Our first impression of Clytemnestra – an impression, be it noted, directly related to the action of the play – has come from the Watchman's striking phrase, as he describes the heart, 'man-like in its counsels, ever expectant of news' (γυναικὸς ἀνδρόβουλον ἐλπίζον κέαρ, 11), of the woman who gives him his orders. These same qualities of man-like resolve and readiness to seize the right opportunities reappear in her scornful refutations of the Chorus (who fear that, like a credulous woman, she may be too quick to believe rumours of Agamemnon's victory) and in her enthusiastic welcome of the beacons' message (281–316). Clytemnestra is to be a mistress of persuasion in this play, but the only persuasion to which she herself succumbs (τίνος ἀγγελίας κειθοῖ ... ; 86–7, the Chorus has asked) is one in which she has every reason to be confident.

In the vivid, almost mantic speech on the captured city (320 ff) the Queen's hopes masquerade as fears as she hints with covert irony at the various dangers (all to be fulfilled) which still await the conquerors. But it is in the two speeches of welcome to Agamemnon, the first addressed as a message through the Herald (600-14), the second addressed to the citizens, in the presence of the King himself (855 ff), that we savour the full quality and significance of Clytemnestra's irony. In both speeches, the patently innocent 'Penelope-tone' of the faithful grass-widow is exquisitely blended with the sinister private irony which expresses for the Queen herself (and for the audience) her secret, delicious embracings of the deed to come. In this, the purpose of the playwright is twofold: first, the more vividly we are permitted to envisage, in the mind's eye, the murder of the King, the more powerful our anticipation of the catastrophe becomes; secondly, the more we see of the Queen's own *delight* in her secret imaginings, the more inevitable the tragic sequence, *dramatically* presented as dependent on her will, is felt to be. For there is more than mere deception in Clytemnestra's ironies: time and again, she purposely sails close to the wind, reverting with dangerous insistence to such (in the circumstances) sensitive topics as motherhood, love (conjugal and adulterous), edged weapons, nets, and wounds. Vying with the intention to deceive, to play the faithful wife, is Clytemnestra's own enjoyment of her duplicity, partly for the piquancy afforded by innocent expressions of guilty thoughts, partly for the anticipatory thrill of the deed to come. Thus Clytemnestra's language is very much a part of the woman herself just as the sinister meanings hidden in her metaphors are a part of the deed of vengeance which they anticipate.

All this, I would maintain, is essential to the plot and to the play, for, as we have seen in the discussions of choral odes and dramatic episodes so far, it is the ever-increasing sense of tragic inevitability, coming as it were from many different directions, which provides the essential tension in the pre-catastrophic portions of the play. That so much dramatic energy is expended on the agent of the catastrophe is right and proper. And if in consistent exercise of her all-consuming activity Clytemnestra reveals herself – and achieves an individuality rare in Aeschylean tragedy – there is still no injury done to the subordinate relation of 'character' to 'plot.'

If it is the masculine aspect of Clytemnestra which has been prominent in these initial impressions, it is the female element which she displays in her speeches of welcome to the King and in her symbolic victory over him in the 'carpet scene.'[63] The culmination of the contest between Clytemnestra's assertiveness and the Chorus' ill-advised doubts about the over-credulous nature of women comes in Clytemnestra's scornful remark to the Chorus after her belief in Agamemnon's victory has been vindicated by the Herald ('and someone said sneeringly ... that it was typical of a woman's heart to be too easily buoyed up!' 590–2). But the Queen swiftly blends this triumphant assertiveness into the role she is now to play:

> And so, I kept making my sacrifices and, in accordance with women's custom, one in one place and one in another kept raising the glad cry of praise throughout the city ... (594–6)

In the message which she now sends her husband through the Herald (600–14), thought and language play over various aspects of female sexuality, suitably chastened to fit the apparent situation: first, the properly conjugal ('How might I best receive my revered [$αἰδοῖον$] husband ... ? For what is sweeter for a wife than to open the gates to her man home from the wars?' 600–4); next, the chastely faithful (' ... with love's seal unbroken through all the length of days,' 609–10); finally, the adulterous (' ... delight ... from other men I know no more than dipping of the bronze' [611–12] – a striking expression which, in its metaphorical overtones, leads us from Clytemnestra's past adultry to her coming butchery; once again, Clytemnestra's language, even in protesting her innocence, declares her guilt). Before she speaks again (in the presence of Agamemnon himself), Clytemnestra has, in all probability, stood silent not only through the rest of the second episode and the second stasimon but also through the Chorus-Leader's cautionary welcome to Agamemnon and the King's reply.[64] Such stage facts provide a salutary reminder of the highly conventionalized nature, allowing as much scope for rhetoric as for direct communication, of these speeches of the Queen: in such theatrical circumstances, it is less difficult to accept the failure of both King and Queen to address each other directly at the beginning of their opening speeches. We have already seen dramatic reasons why the King should address the state (including the Chorus) before he addresses his wife. In the case of the Queen, too (once the conventional acceptability of this procedure has been recognized), there is much to be gained from an oblique form of communication with her husband by addressing her opening remarks to the citizens. She can, in a sense, 'talk at' the King, saying things about her years of grass-widowhood which will mean one thing to the Chorus (who know much), another to her husband (who knows nothing), and a third to herself (who knows all). Moreover, the Queen's gradual shift from oblique to direct address to the King in this speech (855–913) contributes powerfully to the seemingly casual but all-important request to Agamemnon which marks its climax.

In her opening passage (855–76), addressed ostensibly to the Chorus, the Queen returns, with dangerous irony, to her earlier theme of conjugal fidelity:

> Citizens, ... I am not ashamed to tell you of my husband-loving [or 'man-loving'] ways [τοὺς φιλάνορας τρόπους]: for, in time, timid modesty [τὸ τάρβος] declines in us mortals! (855–8)

But this theme soon recedes as murderous images of nets and wounds (all projected in an ostensibly innocent context) begin to crowd Clytemnestra's inner vision at the actual sight of her victim. Thus she reports the alleged 'malignant rumours' (itself an ambiguous expression in the circumstances) which plagued her while Agamemnon was at war:

> If this man of mine had received as many wounds as rumour reported of him, he'd be more riddled than a fishing-net to hear them tell it! (866–8)

Once embarked on these images of Agamemnon wounded in battle, Clytemnestra cannot let them go. Her power of imaginative rhetoric feeds on her real and passionate expectation of *seeing* the King so mutilated (the gashed bath-robe will soon replace the fishing-net), till she pictures him as triple-bodied to accommodate the ever-growing report of wounds and, following him to the very grave, describes the triple cloak of earth he'd need for burial.

The second passage (877–86) gives the Queen's explanation of Orestes' absence at the court of Strophius the Phocian and is addressed to the King himself, though we become aware of this transition only as gradually as we become aware of the new subject of her discourse.

> For these reasons, our child, surety of our joint troth, is not here present, as were right ... Orestes, I mean. Be not surprised at this. (877–9)

The possessive pronouns (for an awful moment we think that Clytemnestra may be speaking of Iphigenia) make the transition to the direct address of the imperative (μηδὲ θαυμάσῃς τόδε) to the King himself.

In the third section (887–94) of her speech, the Queen turns, this time with direct and personal references (ἀμφί σοι, repeated, 890, 893) to extravagant claims of worries for the absent Agamemnon. Again there are subtle overtones of private irony:

> ... seeing in my dreams of you more sufferings than the time which slept with me [could have encompassed]. (893–4)

Surely the point of this unique conceit, 'the time which slept with me'[65] for 'the time while I slept,' is meant to suggest Clytemnestra's secret memory of another, adulterous, bed-fellow.

Finally, in her peroration, Clytemnestra abandons the more direct form of address to the king for a series of flattering and highly rhetorical apostrophes. Several of these involve simply excessive images for masculine protection of home and country ('saving mainstay of the ship, firm post for the lofty roof,' 897–8), but they include as well a brilliant sequence of naturalistic 'relief' metaphors ('land appearing for the despairing mariner,' 899; 'fine weather after storm,' 900; 'fresh water for the thirsty wayfarer,' 901), destined to reach a savage climax later in the play.[66]

'Let envy be absent!' (φθόνος δ' ἀπέστω, 904). The panegyric breaks off with the conventional ending (in which, however, there is still a note of irony)[67] when suddenly, after the most formal part of her oration, the Queen utters her only word of personal endearment, as she bids the King descend:

> Now, dear one [φίλον κάρα], for my sake descend from your chariot, but, master, sacker of Troy, set not your foot upon the ground. Servants, why this delay ... ? Let there be forthwith a path with purple strewn so that, all unexpectedly, Justice may lead him to his home. (905–11, in part)

Agamemnon initially forbids both the spreading of the purple carpet and the 'grovelling clamour' (χαμαιπετὲς βόαμα, 920) which accompanies such performances. He gives the expected, conventional reasons for refusing such honours: abhorrence of the manner of the barbarian despot (919–20) and fear of inspiring divine envy by usurping honours due only to the gods (921–5). It is not possible to give a rational explanation of why, under pressure from Clytemnestra, he completely changes his mind (though he declares he will not, 932), for the simple reason that the dramatist is not, I think, concerned to give us one. There are, however, two or three indications in the words of both Agamemnon and Clytemnestra as to the way in which we are led to look upon this dénouement.

Before the brief debate with Clytemnestra, Agamemnon describes the state of mind which would be forfeited if he accepted the Queen's invitation to tread the purple carpet.

> To be of sound mind [τὸ μὴ κακῶς φρονεῖν] is the greatest gift of god. (927–8)

But Agamemnon has, as the Chorus has told us long before, already departed from this happy condition, at Aulis,

> when he took on the yoke of necessity, breathing the impious changing winds of the mind, impure and unholy, then he committed himself
> to ponder [φρονεῖν] the deed of utter daring. (218–21)

It is Agamemnon's *lack* of 'sound-mindedness' (for all his protestations) which Clytemnestra now proceeds to exploit. First we should note her superb refusal even to argue the matter in terms of conventional Greek morality which the King has advanced (919–25). Indeed, the barbaric aspect of the deed ('What do you think that *Priam* would have done?' 935) and the acknowledgment of the human envy it will induce (937 and 939) are actually used by Clytemnestra to *support* her demand. Agamemnon attempts (though it is a losing battle) to present the conventional moral view: 'Nay, mighty is the strength of the people's voice' (938).

But the crucial allusion in Clytemnestra's utterances comes at v 933. 'But would you not, in a moment of fear, have vowed to the gods so to act [ie 'to tread the purple']?' The question contains, surely, an oblique reminder of the sacrifice of Iphigenia. Indeed the allusion seems the chief justification *for* the question, since (as editors have pointed out) a vow to the gods to do something offensive to them has a certain *prima facie* improbability about it.[68] The Queen's thoughts, without ellipsis, would seem to run like this: 'You say you won't do this deed, because it would offend the gods and civilized men, because it would ruin your fair renown? And yet (remembering Aulis and how you acted there), if you had been in a desperate plight which you could escape only by vowing to perform such a deed as this, wouldn't you have so vowed? – just as you paid to Artemis *her* heinous price?' And Agamemnon's reply, 'Yes, if one [like Calchas at Aulis] with full knowledge of the matter prescribed this rite ... ' (934), seems to indicate that he blandly takes her point.[69] The argument does not, of course, *persuade* Agamemnon; the King continues to resist, but the dramatist has had Clytemnestra introduce the allusion early in the exchange to alert us to the fact that, as at Aulis (or perhaps as a result of Aulis), Agamemnon will, in the end, continue to make the wrong – and fatal – moral decisions.

This being the case, the actual way in which the King's capitulation comes about is of dramatic, rather than moral or psychological, concern. Much has been made, in the preceding two choral lyrics, of the power of Temptation (*Peithô*) which Helen has, consciously or otherwise, exercised so totally over Paris. Later in the play, after the catastrophe, the Chorus is to make a sinister link between Helen and Clytemnestra as the agent of the daimon's destruction of the twin strains of Tantalus (Agamemnon and Menelaus) and the rest of the trilogy will continue to stress the essential 'male-versus-female' aspect in all its struggles. Thus it is fitting that this purely symbolic defeat of Agamemnon, in the 'carpet scene,' should be effected in the end by a simple piece of female seduction. Agamemnon, while still resisting, has called the Queen's contentiousness 'unwomanly' (940). Immediately, Clytemnestra 'plays the woman': 'It is fitting for powerful ones to let themselves be conquered' (941) and 'Yield: for if you yield *willingly* to me, you show your power' (943). Agamemnon succumbs.[70]

Thus the force of this scene, the theatrical centre of the play, is almost entirely symbolic. As Xerxes' 'outrageous' bridging of the Hellespont is a symbol of his real *hybris* in contravening the *moira* of the Persians by his attack on Greece, so, too, Agamemnon's treading on the purple serves as a spectacular, on-stage symbol of his hybristic deed at Aulis, his real outrage against gods and men.[71] This and the symbolic on-stage victory of Clytemnestra over her husband, anticipating the bloody victory to follow, are the main purposes of the scene. Hence the importance of the three features of the scene just indicated: Agamemnon's ironic emphasis on sound moral judgment as saving him from such rash actions; the Queen's equally ironic veiled reminder that he *had* so acted, in the necessity of Aulis; the (purely theatrical) emphasis on feminine *Peithô*, as the means whereby the trick is turned. It has been argued by some critics[72] that in this encounter Agamemnon is deprived of his wits, maddened, as at Aulis, by a Zeus-sent *atê*. I would prefer to regard it as a sort of continuation of the *atê* which Agamemnon has already drawn on himself by his own fatal decision at Aulis, a view supported, I think, by the ironic reminders, just cited, about Calchas and about similar outrageous decisions taken in fearful circumstances. But as far as *this* scene is concerned, the distinction between the two views is not, perhaps, essential, provided that it be recognized that what is important is the decision, inevitable and fatal, and the deed itself.

This symbolic view of the scene is well borne out by Clytemnestra's words as the King begins his fatal walk along the purple way into the palace. In her vivid imaginings, the streams of purple from the boundless sea (ἔστιν θάλασσα – τίς δέ νιν κατασβέσει, 958) have already become the streams of Agamemnon's royal blood,[73] soon to flow from his mortal wounds, the 'dipping of clothes' (εἱμάτων βαφάς, 960) echoing the sinister χαλκοῦ βαφάς which we have already noticed at v 612. The idea of trampling on the rich 'inexhaustible' stores of the house's wealth, which she so gladly countenances in this case, recalls Agamemnon's earlier more terrible plunderings of the household and clashes ironically with the new series of 'protective nature images' ('shade from the scorching dog-days ... heat in winter ... in summer, delicious cool.' 966–71) with which the Queen now graces Agamemnon as home-coming lord of the house. But as the King enters the palace, she no longer restrains her call to Zeus τέλειος (973), 'Zeus, the fulfiller,' to avenge the deed of *hybris* which has taken place before our eyes.

As the King enters the palace, the Chorus breaks into an appropriately fearful lyric, fluttering (ποτᾶται, 978) and buzzing (βρέμει, 1030) with unanswered questions and unnamed terrors. Appropriate, too, is the image expressing this fear, 'a seer unbidden and unpaid ... ' 979, for Cassandra, seated in majestic silence, will break forth into prophetic chants as soon as Clytemnestra leaves the stage. Rational assurances – 'Much time has passed since Aulis ... ' (983 ff),[74] 'With my own eyes, I've seen him safely home!' (988–9) – are of no avail: 'Confidence sits not [ἵζει, 982: a nice, settling word, to contrast with ποτᾶται, 978] at the mind's throne' (980–3), and the 'dirge of the Erinyes,' which the Chorus' inner heart keeps singing, provides a piquant anticipation of the grim realities to come.

The second strophic pair (1000–34) expands on such disasters as are feared ... on their causes, their remedies, and (in the second antistrophe) on the kinds of woes which have no remedy. As in the coda to the second stasimon, there is here a faintly Solonian reminiscence in the sequences of 'weal and woe' (good health with disease, νόσος, as its neighbour, 1003–4; prosperity, πότμος εὐθυπορῶν, and the hidden reef, 1005–7). But the contrast between 'blood once shed,' for which there is no remedy, and the dangers of mere wealth, which prudent jettisoning can cure (1008–21), is, like the imagery in which it is encased,[75] surely Aeschylean.

The lyric ends with a consolation as cryptic as its fears:

> If it were not so, by the will of the gods, that one established lot [*moira*] restrained another [*moiran*] from overstepping, then my heart, getting the better of my tongue, would spread abroad these fears. (1025–9)

The passage is cryptic in the extreme and has been variously interpreted.[76] Does it mean that the Chorus will keep their peace because they believe that the usurpers' careers will inevitably be curtailed by another's *moira* (in this case, Orestes'), just as Agamemnon's *moira* has been curtailed by them? Or because they believe that Agamemnon's *moira* must be curtailed by Clytemnestra's, just as Iphigenia's was curtailed by Agamemnon's? The Chorus do not elucidate but return to their dark muttering, their 'minds on fire' and powerless to conjure profitable hopes.

6 Fourth episode, including first kommos (the 'Cassandra Scene') (vv 1035–1330)

All through the portentous scene between Clytemnestra and the King, Trojan Cassandra ('gift of the army, blossom most choice of all plunder,' 954–5) has been seated in the background on her chariot. After her victory over Agamemnon, Clytemnestra turns to deal with his royal mistress, but, though language has been her great weapon heretofore, it breaks on the silence of Cassandra. Obsequious irony ('Even Heracles, they say, endured the broth of slavery,' 1040–1); sinister invitation to the festivities ('Kine for the sacrifice stand ready ... ' 1056–7); finally, outright threat ('she's mad and knows not how to wear the bit till in blood she foams away her strength,' 1064–7): all this evokes only the apologetic twitterings of the Chorus. From Cassandra, nothing – till the enemy, bested for the only time in the play, has left the stage.

Part lyric instrument, part dramatic personality, Cassandra stands midway between the Chorus and the other dramatis personae in her effect on the imagination of the audience. The mighty choral odes preceding the entry of Agamemnon have darkened the stage with shadows, but so far these shadows have been thrown by the more immediate past of Agamemnon, Iphigenia, and Troy. It is left to Cassandra, Apollo's prophetess, to reveal the primal curse from Atreus' crime, the precise horrors of the immediate future, and, in a few prophetic flashes, the whole sequence of suffering still to come. Process, cause, and consequence are seen in a single timeless moment and no voice but Cassandra's could so convey this whole.[77] Yet Cassandra is a human sufferer as well and it is from this fact that the scene derives its poignancy. She is at once passionate ally of Agamemnon,[78] outraged victim of Clytemnestra, and passive instrument of Apollo's mantic power. Hence, the anguish of her futile warnings is strangely blended (a blend which is at the heart of Aeschylean pathos) with the cold resignation born of certain knowledge of what must come to pass.

Cassandra's utterances fall into two main parts: the *amoibaion* (1072–1177), in which her wild lyrics are answered first by iambic trimeters and then (1121 ff) by excited dochmiacs from the Chorus; then a series of plain speeches (1178 ff) in iambic trimeters, interspersed by stichomythic passages with the Chorus. But, just as in the *amoibaion* with the Chorus, Cassandra's lyric utterances gradually become more controlled by the introduction (from v 1082 onwards) of some iambic trimeters, so too the Chorus-Leader, who begins soberly in trimeters (1074 f), becomes affected by Cassandra's words and manner and (at vv 1121 ff) abandons trimeters entirely for (mainly) excited dochmiacs.[79] Again, in Cassandra's passage of 'plain speech' (1178 ff), in which she attempts more sober explanations and prophecy, the staid iambic trimeters are eventually interrupted by more excited dimeters (vv 1214, 1216) and by other, verbal signs of excitement (eg, v 1256) as fresh visions of past and coming violence assail her conscious mind.

Cassandra's lyrics have three main themes: the primal curse arising from Atreus' crime; the imminent murder of Agamemnon; finally, her own slaughter, interspersed with visions of past Trojan glory. These she deploys in a complex, if unconscious, pattern, but it is a quality of her ecstatic, inspired state that she can sweep on, without rational 'connections,' from one crucial moment to another in these past and future horrors. Throughout this part of the scene, Cassandra's rapid dance movements, accompanying the excited rhythm of her lyric cries, must have formed a major part of the total theatrical effect. Some hint of the variety and extravagance of these movements is given in the wondering comments of the Chorus-Leader, who likens her now to a hunting-dog tracking down bloodshed (1093-4), now to a god-driven maniac (1140).

Cassandra opens (1072 ff) with lyric exclamations of horror at Apollo (a shock to the Chorus, for what has Apollo to do with lamentations?) whom she names as her destroyer (1080-2).[80] This theme, abandoned a few verses later, anticipates the prophetic images of Cassandra's own doom which are to complete the lyric part of her own utterances. In between (1085-1129), Cassandra's songs provide a series of vivid, disconnected reports of Apollo's mantic invasion of her senses. First comes the recognition of the house by the reek of carnage, the blood coursing over the floors and finally 'the witnesses themselves' (1095), the slain children of Thyestes, 'bewailing their roasted flesh eaten by their father.' This much the Chorus recognize: 'No prophets are needed on that score!' (1099; cf 1106).

Now the visions move to Agamemnon's murder:

> Alas! what is she planning? ... A great evil she plots, unbearable to her kin, unholy. And help stands far away.[81] [1100, 1102-4] Cheering her husband with her bathing – how am I to tell the end? – Hand after hand reaches out – [1108-11] Ah! horror! what new apparition is this? Some net of Hades? But the wife is the net, the coadjutor in the murder [1114-17]. Look! Look! Keep the bull from the cow! Capturing him in the robes, she smites him with her black-horned weapon! ... [1125-8]

The quick, kaleidoscopic succession of details, Cassandra's own horrified reactions to them, and the macabre imagery in which symbol and fact blend into one – all these devices greatly enhance the sense of immediacy, of action going on before our eyes, with which Cassandra's visions are conveyed.

(The most striking instances of this blending of symbol and reality appear in the related images at vv 1116 and 1126-8. The first of these ['but the wife *is* the net!'] sustains the 'net imagery' so prominent in the Chorus' treatment of the justice of Zeus enveloping Paris and Troy [357-61]. Here again the 'symbol' and the 'symbolized' blend [as we have seen them do when the Atreidae are 'blamed' for the portent of the feasting eagles (135-8) which represent them], for Agamemnon actually *is* slain by the confining bath-robe which becomes a net when riddled with weapon-thrusts. With this we may also compare Clytemnestra's own anticipation of the same murderous reality in her fanciful image for the reports of Agamemnon in battle: 'more wounded than a net, to hear them tell it!' [868]. This same device of blending symbol and reality is repeated again in the difficult and daring image at vv 1126-8. 'Keep the bull from the cow!' is obviously symbolic language. In the next sentence, however, whether we take μελαγκέρῳ ... μηχανήματι ['with black-horned instrument'] with τύπτει or with ἐν πέπλοισιν ... λαβοῦσα, the preceding bovine image becomes inextricably involved with the literal details of the murder.)[82]

As for the Chorus, they profess (perhaps truthfully)[83] not to understand these visions of coming violence. They respond, however, to the passion if not the sense of Cassandra's outburst, shifting from staid iambic trimeters to free-wheeling dochmiacs (1121 ff, 1132 ff) under the impact of her lyrics. In their movements, too, they would now begin to follow the frenzied dances of Cassandra.

In the final stanzas of her songs (1136-72), Cassandra returns to the theme anticipated in her initial outcry against 'Apollo, my destroyer!' The ease with which the abandoned thread is recovered is indicated by the singer's question (casually addressed to Apollo without naming him): 'Why have you led me hither? For nothing but for death!' (1138-9). Prophecy replaces visions, then lamentations prophecy. The tone becomes more poignant (the Chorus likens it to the nightingale's song) and iambic lines begin to intrude on the dochmiacs,[84] as Cassandra's consciousness of self returns and her thoughts turn inward to her own fate and backward to other days, on the banks of the Scamander. For memories of Troy now blend with the images of death (1156-61; 1167-72); the marriage of Paris with the family disasters (1156); the native Scamander with the rivers of Hades, soon to be seen (1157; 1160-1); Priam's vain sacrifices with the streams of her own blood, soon to be shed (1168-72). This juxtaposition, in the two halves of Cassandra's lyrics, of her own and Agamemnon's death, and of the destinies of Priam's and Agamemnon's houses, is no idle vagary. The cry to Apollo the destroyer (of Cassandra) anticipates the cry to Apollo the Healer (of Argos) later in the trilogy. Zeus' justice on Paris has served, in the first stasimon, as a paradigm for the justice of Zeus on Agamemnon,[85] just as Helen's temptation of Paris, in the second stasimon, anticipates Clytemnestra's luring of Agamemnon in the 'carpet scene'. Helen, too, is the beginning of Agamemnon's doom (as the Chorus will remind us later, 1455 ff) as Paris is of Cassandra's. And now, in Clytemnestra's sacrifice, the blood of Cassandra and Agamemnon will flow together.

The second and longer part of the 'Cassandra episode' is composed in iambic trimeters (ie both Cassandra's and the Chorus-Leader's parts are dramatic, not lyric, in form) in a structure well suited to the three themes which it develops. Three speeches from Cassandra, each of increasing length, are each followed by four lines of comment or question from the Chorus-Leader and a passage of stichomythia between him and Cassandra; two final prayers from Cassandra (one to the citizens, one to the gods), followed by a conventional clausula (1327–30) on human fortunes, complete the scene. Cassandra's three speeches provide sharp contrasts with one another in content and mood and in the speaker's attitude toward the citizen Chorus. The first two speeches deal, respectively, with the two separate strands of the family curse, the guilt of Thyestes and the guilt of Atreus, and their effects. The first speech (1178–97) is strong and clear in style and spoken with the explicit intent (1194–7) of convincing the Chorus of the speaker's credibility. The second speech (1214–41), spoken under the influence of fresh visions from Apollo, approaches the vivid and frantic manner of the earlier lyric utterances; here, revelations of the coming fulfilment of the curse blend, in the second half of the speech, with passionate revilings of Clytemnestra; at its close (1239 ff), Cassandra expresses scornful unconcern as to whether she is believed or not. In the third speech (1256–94), inspired by yet another onset of Apollo, the vision still concerns the murderous Queen but this time her victim is Cassandra herself. In this speech, however, the power of the vision is brief, and Cassandra, in her own person, turns her attention first to the god who has destroyed her and then to the man who will avenge both Agamemnon and herself. The speech (unlike the earlier two speeches) ends with a passage of self-communion (1286–94) in which the Chorus is ignored.

It is time now to take a closer look at these three speeches and at their motivation in their dramatic context.

> No longer will my prophecy speak like a bride from behind her veils.
> Rather, clear and fresh, it will blow toward the dawn, so that, like
> a mighty wave, a woe far greater than the one I mention now will break
> in the light of the rising sun. (1178–83) [Thus does Cassandra contrast
> her own fate with Agamemnon's more dreadful one.]

In this striking image, where the freshness and brightness of wind, water, and sunlight blend with the threatening power of the waves, Cassandra gives clear expression of her purpose: her words will be both clear and terrifying and her aim the persuasion of the Chorus that she speaks the truth. Thus she adapts an image which the Chorus have used earlier of her mantic powers:

And running with me you will bear me witness as I sniff out the track
of ancient ills. (1184–5; cf 1093–4)

The 'track of ancient ills' leads Cassandra first to the 'revel band'
(κῶμος) of kin-Erinyes who cling to the house and who have become
more brazen since drinking human blood (see 1186–90). This is, of
course, another reference to the slaughter of Thyestes' children, but
the new feature of the revelation is the emphasis on the prior presence
of the Erinyes and the following account of the primal woe (πρώταρχος
ἄτη) which first brought them to the house:

Seated about the ancient dwelling, they [the Erinyes] sing their song,
the primal guilt [πρώταρχον ἄτην]; each in turn, they spit upon the crime
against a brother's bed, hating the one who defiled it. (1191–3)[86]

The salient feature of this passage is, then, the emphasis which it
gives to the adultery of Thyestes, rather than to the resultant slaughter
of Thyestes' children by Atreus, as the πρώταρχος ἄτη, the first cause
of the family curse and of the successive visitations of the Erinyes.
This emphasis is, perhaps, explicable in immediate dramatic terms as
due to Cassandra's loyalty, clearly evident elsewhere,[87] to Agamemnon's side, and in larger thematic terms as bearing on the fate of
Aegisthus, the son of Thyestes, who may hence be thought to inherit
the hatred of the Erinyes along with the adulterous and treasonous
character of his father.[88] And by extension it increases the prejudice
against Clytemnestra, the adulterous wife of the King.

Have I gone astray? or, like a keen archer, have I hit the mark? Am I a
false prophet ... ? Bear witness, on your oath, that I know well the
offences of this house, so old in story. (1194–7)

Cassandra's first intention in this speech appears in these final
sentences and its fulfilment is assured by the Chorus-Leader's answer
(1198–1201). Like Prometheus in the *Prometheus Bound* (824) she is
establishing her credentials as a prophet by her knowledge of past
events known to her hearers but not, save by supernatural powers,
to herself. But of equal or greater importance for the dramatic tension
is this further reminder of the 'revel-rout of Erinyes' actually present
(to Cassandra's special vision) in the palace where Clytemnestra is
welcoming the King.

The ensuing interrogation of Cassandra by the Chorus-Leader is vital both to the logic and to the dynamics of the rest of the Cassandra scene. Having achieved (or so it would appear) the very credibility she sought, Cassandra must now, in explaining her knowledge to the wondering Chorus, explain also why her prophecies never win belief. Apollo as lover bestowed the gift; Apollo, jilted, gave the penalty.

- How then were you punished by Apollo's wrath?
- I could persuade no man of what I prophesied. (1211–12)

Cassandra has made one bid to defeat the divine penalty in the 'plain speech' in which she proves her powers. As if to underline its futility, the divine invasion of her spirit is suddenly renewed (1256 ff) and in the ensuing series of warning visions, she sees the murdered children of Thyestes sitting before the house holding in their hands the severed flesh of which their father tasted.

'For these offences, I say someone is plotting vengeance!' (1223). There follows a savagely embittered description of Aegisthus ('the cowardly lion, the stay-at-home, luxuriating in the master's bed' 1224–5) and of Clytemnestra ('the hated bitch [1228], the lurking Scylla [1233–4], the raging Hell-mother [1235], flattering her husband to his death,' 1229–30, paraphrase). The speech closes abruptly: 'Whether I convince or no, 'tis all the same. The future will come ... ' (1239 ff) Cassandra has remembered the power of Apollo's penalty.

In her third speech, Cassandra concentrates on her third vision, that of her own death. In this prophecy, though the victim is now revealed as Cassandra herself, the interweaving of her fate with Agamemnon's, which we have observed in the lyric treatment of this theme, is effectively sustained in several ways. First of all, the lion image, previously used in connection with Helen and the ruin of Troy (717–36) and with Aegisthus' plotting against Agamemnon (1223–5), now recurs, though in oddly different form:

The two-footed lioness herself, consorting with the wolf, in the absence of the noble [εὐγενοῦς] lion, will slay me, the unfortunate one. (1258–60)

Secondly in prophesying the coming of Orestes as *'our* avenger,' Cassandra again relates her fate to Agamemnon's and, as the following lines (1281–5) clearly show, the vivid account of Orestes as his father's avenger throws the emphasis back on the main theme of the trilogy, the sequence of bloodshed in the house of Atreus. Finally, the treatment of Apollo and his favours (perhaps the most striking feature of this speech) has a significance greater, perhaps, than even Cassandra recognizes. As she foretells her death, Cassandra furiously casts off the insignia of the god (1264-8) and, to the degree that this is possible, appears to repudiate the god himself for his desertion of her. Yet the avenger, whose coming she proceeds to prophesy, will himself be the agent of 'Apollo the Healer,' as the Herald has prophetically addressed him in the second episode (512). The connection between the two servants of Apollo – the one who prophesies the vengeance and will die, and the one who will execute it and live – is hinted at in Cassandra's description of them both as wandering exiles (1273-4; 1282), the one at the end, the other at the beginning of his career.

As Cassandra's fate is linked with Agamemnon's, so both are linked with Troy's. In the detached and suddenly 'private' finale to her speech (1286 ff), it is this realization – that Troy is finally being avenged on her conquerors – which provides Cassandra with her only consolation for Agamemnon's death and hers. (Here, for a moment, we do find an anticipation of Euripides' Cassandra.)

At the end of Cassandra's third speech, there occurs a curious stretching of the dramatic probabilities which we have already noted.[89] The Chorus, who have refused credence and even comprehension to Cassandra's prophecies about Agamemnon's death, now clearly indicate (1295-8) that they fully grasp the prophecies about herself; indeed the Chorus-Leader, in his final exchange with Cassandra, presses on her (eg, 1301-4) the conventional consolations to the doomed. One wonders whether the power of the god's penalty – that no one will believe Cassandra – has disappeared with the rejection of his insignia. It is more likely, perhaps, that the dramatist simply does not care about this inconsistency. The disbelief in Cassandra's prophecies has, perhaps, served its dramatic purpose in providing a reason for the Chorus' failure to respond to Cassandra's warnings and in providing Cassandra with the frustrations which, in turn, affect the changing tenor of her utterances.

Cassandra's prophetic senses, at any rate, remain unimpaired; indeed, they provide a fine theatrical finale to the scene, for, as she begins to enter the palace, she starts back in horror at the 'tomb vapours' (1311) which assail her. Still, Cassandra ends her scene with the power and nobility which she has shown throughout, declaring her readiness for death ($ἀρκείτω\ βίος$, 1314), while calling on man to witness and the gods to fulfil the avenging of herself and Agamemnon.

A brief anapaestic passage by the Chorus (1331–42) serves to separate the Cassandra scene from the actual murders, off-stage, of Cassandra and Agamemnon. The Chorus' comment here is limited to a perfunctory moral platitude concerning the deceptiveness of human prosperity. It provides us, however, with another example of the separation, in Aeschylus, between the (limited) dramatic function of the Chorus, as we have witnessed it in the Cassandra scene, and their conventional role as commentators on the action, for here the basis of the Chorus' comment is their acceptance of Agamemnon's imminent death, despite the confusion and uncertainty which the Chorus-Leader has expressed (1249 ff) about Cassandra's prophecies on the matter.

7 Fifth episode and second kommos (the off-stage murder and its aftermath) (vv 1343–1576)

During the actual murder of the King, whose off-stage cries clearly announce his mortal wounds, the dramatic and conventional roles of the Chorus again meet in a brief and (to the modern reader) mildly embarrassing confrontation (1346–71). Dramatically speaking, the Chorus is a group of patriotic Elders who have declared their allegiance to the King (783–809). Hence one or another of these elders (the whole passage is divided between twelve individual choreutae, who speak two verses each) at least makes gestures at sounding the alarm (1348–9), confronting the assailants (1350–1), dying honourably in the face of tyranny (1364–5), and so on. Conventionally, of course, this will not do, and so the poet, using another dramatic device, permits other members of the Chorus to delay matters with advice for and against precipitate action, until the time for action is clearly past when the Queen is revealed (probably by the *ekkuklêma*) standing over the slain bodies of her victims.[90]

In the speeches of Clytemnestra immediately following the murder of Agamemnon and in the ensuing epirrhematic exchange between the Chorus (singing) and Clytemnestra (speaking, later chanting in anapaests),[91] several earlier themes of the tragedy are recapitulated in ways which are both startling and revealing. Of these the most important is the question of an individual's responsibility for a consciously chosen deed of violence which may also be seen as the fulfilment of the will of Zeus or of a family curse. Another is the reassertion, in more explicit form, of the parallel roles of Clytemnestra and Helen as priestesses of destruction (*Atê*) in the house of Atreus.

In her first speech, Clytemnestra asserts in the strongest possible terms her responsibility for, and satisfaction in, the murder of her husband:

I stand now where I struck, as I stand by the deed I have accomplished
ἕστηκα δ' ἔνθ' ἔπαισ' ἐπ' ἐξειργασμένοις]. (1379)

So I acted and I'll not deny these deeds! (1380)

I struck him twice ... and gave him a third blow where he had fallen ... (1384–6)

No other speech in Greek tragedy contains so many (ten in all) and such insistent references to the speaker's responsibility for a deed. Even the immediate motivation of the murder, vengeance for Iphigenia, takes second place to the physical satisfaction, the sheer glorying in personal and well-planned achievement. No hint of any supernatural *force majeure* is allowed to enter yet; indeed this same assertion, defiant and personal, receives still greater emphasis after the first brief outburst (1399–1400) from the Chorus.

I tell you, this is Agamemnon, my husband, now made a corpse by my right hand ... (1404–5)

Yet after a hundred lines of exchanges with the Chorus, this same Clytemnestra is to say, indignantly:

You imagine this to be *my* deed: but don't think of me as the wife of Agememnon [μηδ' ἐπιλεχθῇς⁹² / Ἀγαμεμνονίαν εἶναι μ' ἄλοχον· 1497–9]. Nay, manifesting itself as the wife of this dead man here, the ancient, bitter-avenging curse [ἀλάστωρ] on Atreus ... has offered this man in payment, the lord sacrificed for the children ... victims of times past. (1497–1504)

This is a striking change of attitude in the wife who, a few minutes earlier, was glorying so explicitly in the deed of husband-murder. Let us return to the beginning of the kommos (1407 ff) to see how it has come about.⁹³

In the first part of the epirrhematic exchange, the Chorus sings brief lyric stanzas, mostly in dochmiacs, with Clytemnestra answering in iambic trimeters. The Chorus, aghast at the Queen's crime, first threaten the hatred of the citizens, the people's curse (δημοθρόους τ' ἀράς, 1409): an ironic reminiscence of the warnings of the first stasimon where the people's curse was spoken of as directed against the Atreidae (456-7; cf 450-1) for all the deaths at Troy. And it is back on Agamemnon that Clytemnestra now redirects these curses as she is goaded to her first justification of her crime: Agamemnon 'who, caring no more for her death than for that of a beast, sacrificed his own daughter to charm the winds at Thrace' (1415-18).[94] But in this, her first defence, the Queen still speaks as responsible to herself alone. It is her own deeds (ἐμῶν ἔργων, 1420-1) which she talks about as she warns the Chorus that it is the victor, either herself or the Chorus, who will call the tune (1421-5). The Chorus' answer, as they gaze upon Agamemnon's blood, is to threaten blow for blow (1428-30), and it is this stronger threat which leads Clytemnestra to mention for the first time her allies, supernatural (*Dikê*) and human (Aegisthus): references which are to lead, indirectly, to the gradual depersonalization of her deed.

> By the avenging Justice due to my daughter [μὰ τὴν τέλειον τῆς ἐμῆς παιδὸς δίκην] by *Atê* and *Erinus*, to all of whom I sacrificed this man, Hope, for me, treads not the halls of Fear as long as Aegisthus lights the fires at my hearth ... (1432-6)

In the first part of this sentence, while Clytemnestra still speaks of herself as the doer of the deed, the use of τέλειος with δίκη already suggests that the Justice of Zeus, hardly an abstract force in this play, is at least a coadjutor in the murder. In the second part of her sentence, the Queen mentions Aegisthus, her human ally in murder and adultery, another lead that is to have interesting developments in our theme of responsibility. But for the moment, Clytemnestra's thoughts take another turn. Soon she is off on the track of Cassandra, the second outrage of the King which she daringly converts into gratification, as thoughts of the slain mistress become a fillip, in her savage imaginings, to her own adulterous bed:

> ... and she too, the lover of this man here, like a swan after singing her final death-song, lies there in death and so bestows on me a couch-relish to add to my luxurious delight. (1444-7)

Both Aegisthus and the adultery motif which the Queen has introduced are to be used in the gradual withdrawal of the 'king-murder' from the sphere of personally chosen action to the impersonal sequence of the past: a nice paradox, for both have also provided a part of Clytemnestra's personal motivation. Aegisthus, of course, is to provide a direct lead, through his father, to the curse on the house of Atreus. Adultery now leads the Chorus to think of sister Helen, that other scourge of husbands, for now it sings:

> ... since, for a woman's sake [ie Helen's] our kindliest guardian was subdued and suffered many woes. And by a woman's hand [ie Clytemnestra's] he lost his life. (1451–4)

Thus the Chorus now blames both Clytemnestra and, with increasing emphasis, Helen ...

> ... mad Helen, ... you who have bedecked yourself with this last crowning glory, through blood which cannot be washed away. Then indeed was there strife unconquerable upon the house [ἦ τις ἦν (Schütz) τότ' ἐν δόμοις ἔρις ἐρίδματος], a scourge of husbands. (1455 ... 1459–61)

The close relation between *eris* (Strife) and Helen which this last sentence implies recalls the earlier association of Helen with *eris* (698), and with *Erinus* (744–9); it anticipates also Clytemnestra's view of herself as the disguised embodiment of the ἀλάστωρ (the avenging curse) from Atreus' crime.[95] Looked at in one way, adulterous Helen is linked with adulterous Clytemnestra – and adultery (both Clytemnestra's and Agamemnon's) has at least lent strength to Clytemnestra's murderous blade. But looked at in another way, Helen becomes the instrument of Zeus' justice and the fulfilment of a curse or doom on Agamemnon as (earlier) on Paris and the Trojans. In this role, she has the effect of leading us, in our search for the cause of the present violence, back into the past – to the time before the war, before Iphigenia, before Aegisthus: that is before the personal motivations of Clytemnestra's deed existed.

Earlier in the play (in the second stasimon), Helen has figured as the temptation which led Paris and Troy to their doom; soon afterwards (in the second episode), Clytemnestra appears as the embodiment of that same *Peithô* ('Persuasion, child of fore-counselling *Atê*') which leads Agamemnon to his last (symbolic) act of *hybris*. So, now, in the kommos, the Chorus' introduction of the 'Helen motif' is the turning point in Clytemnestra's journey from vehement insistence to vehement denial of her *personal* responsibility for the murder of Agamemnon. The importance of the moment is marked by a formal change as the Chorus embarks on a formal ode with anapaestic replies from Clytemnestra.

> Turn not your wrath on Helen as the man-destroyer, as if she alone caused many Greeks to perish and worked the sharpest woe. (1464-7)

So Clytemnestra rebukes the Chorus; she means, of course, to turn the blame back on Agamemnon. The Chorus, however, accepting her rebuke, now switches its fury against the ancestral daimon, working on the twin strains of the blood of Tantalus (Agamemnon and Menelaus) through the twin-souled power of women (κράτος ⟨τ'⟩ ἰσόψυχον ἐκ γυναικῶν – ie Clytemnestra and Helen, 1470). This last expression for the daimon-possessed carries an eerie echo of that 'twin-throned, twin-sceptred yoke-of-power from Zeus,' which was the Chorus' opening description (43-4) of the Atreidae: an equipoise symbolizing, perhaps, the struggle between male and female which is to be resolved, on both divine and human levels, only in the final play of the trilogy. Clytemnestra strongly endorses this blaming of 'the thrice-gorged daimon,' though in so doing she unconsciously proclaims her own destruction: 'Ere the ancient woe shall cease, fresh blood[96] will flow!' (1479-80). The Chorus, in turn, push the causation one step further back, to Zeus himself:

> ἰὴ ἰὴ διαὶ Διὸς
> παναιτίου πανεργέτα   (1485-6)

Thus the Chorus has gradually switched from their original emphasis on Clytemnestra's guilt (1407-11, 1426-30), through an ever-receding sequence, to Zeus himself, the cause of all. However, once they return (in the beautiful refrain at 1489 ff) to their grief for Agamemnon, they return to the foul murder by Clytemnestra. But now the Queen, buoyed up by the sequence of the past strife which the Chorus has helped elaborate, is able to reply with her vehement denial of all personal responsibility:

> You imagine this to be *my* deed: but don't think of me as the wife of Agamemnon. Nay, manifesting itself as the wife of this dead man here, the ancient, bitter-avenging curse on Atreus ... (1497 ff)

There is not, of course, any absolute contradiction, particularly for a Greek audience, in this change of perspective which one notices in Clytemnestra. Nevertheless, the element of double determination so common in Aeschylean tragedy appears in unusually striking form when the murderer herself expresses, within a hundred verses, first the personal and then the supernatural explanation of the deed, each in mutually exclusive terms.[97] It is by skilful exploitation of the epirrhematic kommos, an instrument capable of combining lyrical and argumentative effects, that the poet achieves this difficult transition.

After Clytemnestra's extreme statement at 1497 ff, the pendulum begins its backward swing.

ὡς μὲν ἀναίτιος εἶ ⟨σὺ⟩
τοῦδε φόνου τίς ὁ μαρτυρήσων· (1505–6)

'Who will say that you are innocent ... ?' asks the Chorus and in the following exchanges both Chorus and Queen return to the present, the personal and the particular. Clytemnestra reasserts the personal guilt of Agamemnon as her own reason for vengeance (1525 ff)[98] and in her arrangements for the King's obsequies the Queen's own personal venom is back at full strength: she who slew him will bury him, and she for whom he was slain will embrace him gladly, as is right (ἀσπασίως ... ὡς χρή, 1555–6) upon the shores of Acheron.

By the end of this long kommos, the Chorus and Clytemnestra have, surprisingly, reached a sort of bitter accommodation. The Chorus echoes the Queen's gnomic wisdom ἄξια[99] δράσας, ἄξια πάσχων ('sufferings worthy of his deeds...' 1527) with similar sayings of its own (φέρει φέροντ', 1562; παθεῖν τὸν ἔρξαντα, 1564: 'the spoiler spoiled ... the doer suffers'), and with the Chorus' last statement, 'the family is bound to Atê' (1566), Clytemnestra herself heartily concurs. Indeed the Queen's last speech, in which she seeks to make a pact with the daimon, the evil genius of the Pleisthenids, is the one statement in all her utterances which comes close to compromise.

In this extraordinary scene between Clytemnestra and the Chorus, I have concentrated, for the sake of clarity, on the main outlines of the dramatic and thematic development. Of the various other effects (including the metrical changes and development, at which we have only glanced)[100] one in particular should not be overlooked: the overpowering physical impact of the imagery in all matters connected with the murder and its executors, Clytemnestra and the daimon of the house of Atreus.

Something of this impact, which is to be presented with increasing power as the scene progresses, appears first in Clytemnestra's lush description of the deed:

> I wrapped him in a boundless net, as one would fish, an evil wealth of blood (1382–3)

and in her simile, the climax of the 'perverted nature images' observed before, for the *refreshment* which she experiences from that deed:

> and breathing out midst that sharp, bloody butchery, he smote me with a black sprinkling of bloody dew, and I rejoiced in it no less than corn rejoices in the gladdening gift of Zeus' rain, at the birthtime of the buds. (1389–92)

Hard on this savage image follows the Queen's equally macabre conceit of pouring libation over the corpse from the very 'mixing-bowl of evil curses' (1397–8) which Agamemnon had filled for the house while still he lived in it.

This same characteristic imagery of nature perverted recurs in the Chorus' reaction to Clytemnestra. Incredulous, the Chorus suggests (1407 ff) that only the swallowing of some earth-grown root, or of some poisonous sea-draught, could induce such deeds as these. The Queen's hybristic boasting over the corpse is explained, again in physical terms, as a sort of blood-induced madness.

Her mind rages as if with the very blood drops of the event (φοινολιβεῖ τύχᾳ); upon her eyes the flecks of blood (λίβος ... αἵματος) shine clear (1427–8): the repetition of the onomatopoeic word λίβος ('droplet,' here, of blood) is particularly effective.

Clytemnestra's scurrilous description of Cassandra as 'a ship-board lover'[101] anticipates the ghastly but characteristic image for the particular joy (another instance of 'nature perverted') which the Queen feels in her rival's death:

> ... for she has added a new couch-relish to my luxurious delight
> [ἐπήγαγεν / εὐνῆς παροψώνημα τῆς ἐμῆς χλιδῆς] (1446–7)[102]

As the thematic development moves from the *Queen*'s to the *daimon*'s blood-lust and back again, so the recurrent images vary their attachment. The Chorus describes the daimon, the family curse, as standing over the corpse like a carrion-bird (1472–3). Clytemnestra picks up the image with her account of 'the thrice-gorged daimon'

(1476-7) who 'in its belly nourishes its passionate thirst for blood' (1478-9). The Chorus' phrase 'insatiate [ἀκόρεστον] of dread misfortune' (1483-4) completes this series of physical descriptions of the daimon's appetite.

Toward the end of the kommos, the Chorus' relentless emphasis on blood increases, with the depiction of Ares 'forcing his way through streams of kin bloodshed to requite the clotted blood of children slain' (1509-12) and finally with the climactic image hinting at bloodshed still to come in future generations:

> I fear the house-destroying beat of bloody rain ... Justice is being sharpened on other whetstones of Fate for yet another deed of woe. (1533-6)

8 Exodos (the 'Aegisthus scene') (vv 1577-1673)

The uneasy truce between Clytemnestra and the Chorus is, however, abruptly broken by the entry of Aegisthus. The closing scene of the play provides a fitting reminder of the other aspect of the blood feud, the vengeance for Thyestes' family, now completed from Thyestes' side but to begin again in the next play as Agamemnon's children take up the unending duty of requiting blood with blood. The tone is set by Aegisthus' opening verses. 'O kindly light of the day which brings us justice!' For Aegisthus, less perceptive than Clytemnestra and the Chorus, the issue is clear, the conflict over: the slain Agamemnon lies wrapped 'in the woven robes of the Erinyes,' having paid the penalty for his father's deeds of violence. The bulk of Aegisthus' speech sets out (for the first time explicitly) the tale of Atreus' awful banquet and the resultant curse of Thyestes. (It is to be noted that Aegisthus, not surprisingly, suppresses mention of Thyestes' adultery, the occasion for Atreus' vengeance on him: Cassandra, however, has already reminded us of Thyestes', as of Aegisthus' own, adultery [1191-3; 1223-6, respectively] and of the fact that the Erinyes bestow their lethal interest on familial adultery as well as on familial bloodshed [1192-3].) Even Clytemnestra, in the preceding kommos, has shown some awareness of the recurrent danger of blood for blood. Aegisthus, on the other hand, sees himself simply as the coadjutor, with Clytemnestra, in placing Agamemnon 'in the coils of justice' (1611), and that, for him, is the end of the matter.

It is left to the Chorus, then, to redouble the threats which they have already made (unsuccessfully) against Clytemnestra. Indeed they now turn all their fury on the outsider (1612–16, 1625–7, 1633–5), adding scorn (which they could not do in the case of Clytemnestra) for his 'womanish role' and even threatening him with the 'stoning-curses of the people' (1616). Not till the Chorus invoke the hope of Orestes as avenger (1646–8) does Aegisthus call out the guard against them – a nice touch of anticipatory irony on the poet's part.

The only real power on the scene, however, is Clytemnestra, and it is she who easily checks further violence. Aegisthus has been required to lead us back, for the sake of the trilogy's development, to the theme of the ancestral curse and the blood-feud. Once his small role has been fulfilled it is Clytemnestra who effects the uneasy diminuendo with which the action of this play concludes.

NOTES

1 ξένιος Ζεύς (Ag 61–2).
2 In Homer's *Odyssey* (the most relevant passages are *Od* 1.35–43; 3.234–312; 4.511–47; 11.405–61), Aegisthus is usually presented as the murderer of Agamemnon (after seducing his wife, Clytemnestra, during the King's absence) in what appears to be a simple take-over of the latter's royal domain. Clytemnestra appears mainly as the accomplice in this murder, though she is said to have slain Cassandra (*Od* 11.405–39). (In two passages, it is true, the shade of Agamemnon accuses her, in addition to Aegisthus, as his murderer [*Od* 11.453; *Od* 24.199–200]; this may, perhaps, be explained as an indignant exaggeration on Agamemnon's part or possibly as the intrusion of a later version.) At *Od* 3.234–5 Athena names Clytemnestra along with Aegisthus as responsible for Agamemnon's death 'by guile.' The vengeance of Orestes on Aegisthus is mentioned at *Od* 2.193–200 and at *Od* 3.306–10; in the second passage his vengeance on Clytemnestra as well seems at least implied, though with a curious reticence about the actual matricide. Some ambiguity also surrounds the actual location of Agamemnon's palace in the *Odyssey*: at *Od* 3.304–5, it is clearly at Mycenae, but at *Od* 4.514 ff (where it is Aegisthus and not Clytemnestra, as in the *Agamemnon*, who has set a watch for the King and lures him to his doom) it seems to be in Sparta.

Concerning the other constituent elements in the myth (the sacrifice of Iphigenia by her father Agamemnon, the prominence of Clytemnestra as the avenger of this sacrifice, the operation of the family curse from Atreus' murder of Thyestes' children) we cannot tell when they were first worked into one continuous whole. The fact that Agamemnon's sacrifice of his daughter does not appear in the Homeric poems does not mean that this motif was unknown at the time of their composition. For indications of early treatments of this human sacrifice to Artemis, and of its possible significance, see Lloyd-Jones 'Artemis and Iphigeneia' and Solmsen 'The Sacrifice of Agamemnon's Daughter in Hesiod's *Ehoeae.*' For an account of the literary evidence, much of it fragmentary, of the myth in Hesiod, Stesichorus and Pindar, as well as in various graphic representations, see the excellent study by Robbins, *'Pindar's Oresteia and the Tragedians.'* See now also A.J.N. Prag *The Oresteia, Iconographic and Narrative Tradition,* which appeared too late for proper consideration here.

3 In *Iphigenia at Aulis,* Euripides takes some pains to express the conflicting impulses, mixed motives, and the 'psychology' of Agamemnon in his dilemma over the sacrifice of Iphigenia; see, for example, the Prologue and the second debate with Menelaus (vv 471–542).
4 Note the Chorus' repeated emphasis on the liberation of the House, once the usurpers are overthrown and the true heir is reinstated; see *Cho* 800 ff, 819 ff, 961–73.
5 Jones *On Aristotle and Greek Tragedy* pp 82–111 insists that the House of Atreus is the dominant concern of the *Oresteia* from the very beginning. Now it is true that the House of Atreus is undoubtedly the unifying element in the trilogy as a whole, and, by his insistence on this fact, Jones does valuable service in correcting the too-intensive concern of some critics with the motives, the temperament, and even the 'psychology' of Agamemnon. Nevertheless, one feels that Jones' view is rather more severely exclusive in this matter, particularly in the case of the first play, than is the poet's, and his emphasis seems, in the end, to detract from the thematic development of the trilogy, at least as I have sought to describe it: the gradual and successive shifting of focus, first from individuals to the 'house,' then from the House to the *Polis* (the οἶκος writ large, in more contemporary terms). For further criticism of Jones' views stemming from his exclusive emphasis on the 'House,' cf below, n 71.
6 This aspect of the style of the Chorus in *Agamemnon* is well discussed by Kitto *Greek Tragedy*[2] pp 69–70. Too prosaic an approach to the Chorus in this play, as if it were a *narrator* of all it feels it can safely say of the past, has led other critics to some curious inferences. For examples, see below, note 15 and also section iii, ad fin, of appendix 1 to this chapter.
7 In order to facilitate this overall view, various points of interpretation

have been relegated to the notes and, in the case of the parodos, to an appendix, where the most contentious issues are reviewed.

For a somewhat different approach to the role of the Chorus in this play, see the interesting recent study of Gantz, 'The Chorus of Aeschylus' *Agamemnon*.' Gantz, quite reasonably, treats the Chorus in this play as very much the voice of the community; possibly he overestimates the *dramatic* importance which the poet attaches to this role when he suggests that 'the Argive elders [ie the Chorus], in their role as spokesmen for society, assume co-responsibility with the 'actors' ['characters'?] – Agamemnon, Klytaimestra, Aigisthos – for the continuing chain of bloodshed illustrated in the first play.' (See pp 68 ff.) In this connection, cf Rosenmeyer's discussion of the 'choral voice' in Aeschylus (*The Art of Aeschylus* pp 164–8), to which further reference will be made later. (Cf below, chapter 3, n 48.)

8 I have followed Sidgwick in taking the genitives in the expression quoted from vv 70–1 as causal and as having a double meaning: 'rejected sacrifices' (ie 'which will not burn') of the Trojans, and (the hidden anticipatory significance) Agamemnon's sacrifice of Iphigenia. See Sidgwick's note ad loc in his edition of *Agamemnon*. See also Fraenkel's edition, II, and that of Denniston and Page, notes on vv 69–71, for other versions and discussion of the text of this passage.

9 I believe, with Denniston and Page and others, that the Queen has entered unannounced and is actually present supervising the sacrificial fires in the background as the Chorus questions her. It is, however, a debatable point. On the whole question of Clytemnestra's entries and exits in the first half of the play, see below p 24 and n 49 and appendix 2 to this chapter.

10 The subtle anticipation of this later scene is heightened in the present passage (94–6) by the expression πελανῷ μυχόθεν βασιλείῳ ('the royal stores of oil within the palace'), for here, as in the scene where Clytemnestra spreads the purple tapestries for Agamemnon's feet, the emphasis is on the rich stores of oil within the palace (μυχόθεν), and the sinister union of πελανῷ ... βασιλείῳ anticipates the later symbolism of Clytemnestra's squandering of the royal purple (ἔστιν θάλασσα – τίς δέ νιν κατασβέσει; 958) for Agamemnon's last entry to the palace. Cf also Lebeck's treatment of the sequence of thought and imagery connected with πειθώ (persuasion) in the first stasimon *The Oresteia, A Study in Language and Structure* pp 40–1).

11 I read μολπᾷ δ' ἀλκᾶν σύμφυτος αἰών (lit, 'My age is suited to song of valorous deeds'), Denniston and Page's emendation of v 106.

12 'The people's possessions' are actually described as 'the herds [κτήνη]

in front of the city walls' – if, with Fraenkel and others, we accept
the reading πρόσθε τὰ (VFTr); πρόσθε will then govern πύργων. For
the minor interpretative difficulty which leads Denniston and Page
to follow M's reading προσθετὰ (and so to be saddled with an almost
unintelligible sentence) see their note ad loc. The three (or four?)
words quoted above do, perhaps, provide a minor crux but not, I
think, one which seriously affects the interpretation of the passage as
a whole.

13 The traditional reason given for Artemis' anger was that Agamemnon
had angered her by shooting a deer in her sacred grove and had
then boasted that he surpassed Artemis in hunting. See appendix 1,
section i, to this chapter, where a fuller discussion of the whole
problem of the 'the anger of Artemis' in the *Agamemnon*, and of
a selection of scholarly views on it, will be found.

14 On the provenance of such refrains in Aeschylus, and on the possible
significance of the 'sorrow/joy' sequence of the present trilogy, see
Moritz 'Refrain in Aeschylus' pp 194 ff, and references (especially to
Haldane and Sheppard) there given.

15 Dawe, failing to detect a clear anticipatory reference to the crisis at
Aulis at vv 140–59, would transpose the 'Hymn to Zeus' (vv 160–83)
to follow the full treatment of the situation at Aulis at vv 192–217. (His
further inclusion of vv 184–91, actually the beginning of the 'Aulis
passage' as it now stands, on the grounds that certain expressions in
it should logically follow, rather than introduce, the account of Agamemnon's dilemma, provides an egregious example of scholarly failure
to appreciate the difference between lyrical and logical or even 'historical' treatment of a subject.) See Dawe 'The Place of The Hymn to
Zeus in Aeschylus' *Agamemnon.*' Dawe's main argument has, in my
opinion, been well refuted by Bergson 'The Hymn to Zeus in Aeschylus' *Agamemnon*' and, in anticipation, by Fraenkel, *Agamemnon* 1,
113, both of whom argue for a clear reference to Aulis at the end of
Calchas' words quoted by the Chorus at vv 140–59.

Different views on various points in the interpretation of the 'Hymn
to Zeus' passage will be considered below: see notes 16, 17, 18 and
appendix 1, sections ii and iii, to this chapter. For a recent and
ingenious reinterpretation of the whole passage (160–83), see now
Smith *On the Hymn to Zeus in Aeschylus' Agamemnon*. As I have indicated
in my review of Smith's book, this interpretation differs radically
from my own, though it has not been possible in a brief review to
summarize all of Smith's detailed arguments on various crucial points
in the passage.

16 This is Fraenkel's translation of a passage which, as we shall see, has been variously interpreted.
17 This passage, too, has been variously construed and interpreted depending, to some extent, on the reading selected. See appendix 1, section ii, ad fin, to this chapter.
18 Cf Solmsen *Hesiod and Aeschylus* pp 163 ff. For other, less optimistic, views of 'learning through suffering' in the 'Hymn to Zeus,' see section ii of appendix 1 to the present chapter.
19 I do not agree with the view of Onians, *Origins of European Thought* p 54, that the expressions at *Ag* 187 and 219 are not really metaphorical but simply express, in fairly literal terms, the archaic Greek association of thinking and feeling with air, breath, etc. Most of the passages (many of them are Homeric) on which Onians bases arguments about the Greek view of the physiology of thinking and feeling are drawn from sources considerably earlier than Aeschylus, or else from relatively idiosyncratic 'scientific' theories, such as those of Diogenes of Apollonia. Moreover, granted that there may be a certain subliminal influence of scientific on poetic ways of thought and expression, poets are not normally concerned with precise physiological formulation in their lyrical expressions of emotion and anguish.
20 See appendix 1, section iii, to this chapter.
21 Agamemnon's failure to mention the will of Zeus in connection with his mission against Troy is a clear indication that he makes his decision here for 'human reasons,' not because he feels compelled by Zeus to continue to Troy at all costs. The point is important, and several critics, including Kitto (*Form and Meaning in Drama* p 5) and Gantz ('The Chorus of Aeschylus' *Agamemnon*' p 75), have made it. It might perhaps be argued that Agamemnon's use of the word θέμις at v 217 in connection with the desire (of the allies? see next note) to consummate the sacrifice of Iphigenia conveys an impression of supernatural justification of this desire. θέμις is certainly a word loaded with authority and traditional right, though an examination of its uses in Aeschylus will indicate that it does not *always* imply divine authority; cf, for example, *Ag* 98, *Suppl* 136.

See also Winnington-Ingram *Studies in Aeschylus* pp 79–81, who, in arguing strenuously for the human motivation of, and responsibility for, Agamemnon's sacrifice of Iphigenia, rejects the further argument that these acts were, purely and simply, supernaturally determined by the curse on Atreus for his offence against Aegisthus: 'This amounts to saying that some original offence was (presumably) deliberate and humanly motivated, whereas the events which flow from it are supernaturally determined ... which is not quite plausible' (p 81). Nevertheless, we may, I think, allow to the effect of the family curse a certain disposition to disaster. See below, pp 13-14 and n 23, and references there given.

22 A verbal, or rather syntactical, difficulty in the reading of the mss at v 216 has resulted here in a slight uncertainty about the precise meaning. Editors (including Denniston and Page) who believe that the adverb περιόργως (the mss reading) cannot be used to intensify the preceding adverbial dative ὀργᾷ ('with passion most vehemently': there are no precise parallels) emend (after Bamberger) to περιόργῳ σ⟨φ'⟩, where σ⟨φ'⟩, 'they,' referring loosely to the alliance, will be subject of the infinitive ἐπιθυμεῖν ('to desire'). Editors (including Fraenkel) who accept the difficult adverb περιόργως must supply an indefinite subject ('one') for the infinitive; this, perhaps, adds slightly to the complicity of Agamemnon but not substantially, since he appears in any case to concur with the 'public' view, both in word (note θέμις : "tis right'), and subsequently in action, the sacrificial deed itself.

23 On the 'vulnerability' of Agamemnon, and of other tragic figures in Aeschylus, cf Edwards 'Agamemnon's Decision: Freedom and Folly in Aeschylus.' See below appendix 1, section iii, 'The Guilt of Agamemnon,' to this chapter.

24 See appendix 1, section iii, to this chapter.

25 See Lloyd-Jones, 'The Guilt of Agamemnon' pp 191-2; he compares the description of Agamemnon's state at *Ag* 222 f with the Homeric Agamemnon's account of his 'reckless behaviour,' the result of ἄτη sent by Zeus, at *Il* 19.86-8. Cf also Dawe 'Some Reflections on *Atê* and *Hamartia* pp 109-10, who, unlike Lloyd-Jones, distinguishes (as I have done) between Agamemnon's rational decision and the frenzy required to carry it out.

26 See below, chapter 2, section 3, especially p 113.

27 Thus vv 231-4 have been given a quite different interpretation by Lloyd-Jones, 'The Robes of Iphigenia,' quoted with approval by Page in his note ad loc. Lloyd-Jones takes πέπλοισι περιπετῆ (233) *actively* of Iphigenia 'falling around *her father's* robes,' and παντὶ θυμῷ as 'with all *her* heart,' modifying this supplicatory action of Iphigenia's (and so avoiding what Page calls the 'grotesque' use of this enthusiastic expression to modify Agamemnon's order to his stewards). However, the difficulties which Lloyd-Jones' translation encounters, particularly in the matter of the word-order of the Greek, seem greater than the slight grammatical difficulty of taking περιπετῆ passively (for which see Fraenkel's defence, ad loc) which it removes, and even the alleged

interpretative advantage urged by Page is surely bought at too dear a cost to the sense of the whole sentence. After the vivid expression 'like a goat above the altar (v 232, in Agamemnon's indirect command), it would surely be impossible for the audience to think of Iphigenia down on the ground (before being lifted up) falling about her father's robes, particularly when the phrase πέπλοισι περιπετῆ follows immediately on the vivid image just mentioned.

28 Dover 'Some Neglected Aspects of Agamemnon's Dilemma' p 66, on the other hand, believes that the Chorus are reacting against 'the pitiable and repulsive event' resulting from Agamemnon's decision, as well as the state of mind which induced it, but not against the King himself. But it is surely hard to separate the two so clearly. See appendix 1, section iii, to this chapter.

29 Once again, it may not be until the third play of the trilogy that the advance in wisdom is to be achieved – if we may regard τοῖς ... παθοῦσιν ('those who have suffered') as referring to the whole house of Atreus. On the other hand, in view of v 249 ('the [prophetic] arts of Calchas were not unfulfilled') τοῖς παθοῦσιν may refer either partly or exclusively to the Trojans who have suffered for Paris' injustice.

30 'Within what time-span' (the Chorus has asked, v 278) 'has the city been captured?' 'Within this very night, I say, which now gives birth to this day's light!' (τῆς νῦν τεκούσης φῶς τόδ' εὐφρόνης λέγω, 279) is Clytemnestra's answer. She has previously prefaced her first announcement of the victory with the cryptic expression 'Fraught with good news, as the proverb goes, may the dawn be which now issues from its [kindly] mother Night!' (μητρὸς εὐφρόνης πάρα, 264–5). These two references to Night as εὐφρόνης must surely, in view of the 'benevolent' role attributed to Night here and at the beginning of the first stasimon (355), give the expression more than its conventionally euphemistic sense; that is to say, the poet adds a special punning emphasis to the conventional, deprecatory euphemism. (Schneidewin's suggestion, quoted by Fraenkel, that εὐφρόνης at v 265 echoes εὔφρων at v 263, seems relevant in this connection; Fraenkel is surely too severe in rejecting it.)

31 In the parodos, 'one who hears on high – Apollo or Pan or Zeus? – sends [πέμπει] a late-avenging Erinus on the transgressors' (55–9). In the parodos again, 'Zeus *xenios* sends [πέμπει] sons of Atreus against Alexander' (60–2). In the first stasimon, Ares 'sends' (πέμπει, 441) home to Argos dust instead of men. So, too, in the three passages cited from Clytemnestra's speech, the same verb is used in connection

with the god-sent beacon fires. (Thus, in Clytemnestra's mouth the
use of 'Hephaistos' in this context seems to acquire an overtone,
at least, beyond its common, metonymical use for 'fire.')

32 Cf Clytemnestra's later savage prophecy (1555 ff), after the murder
of Agamemnon, that the slain Iphigenia will gladly (ἀσπασίως) meet
her father in Hades and 'will kiss him, throwing her arms about him,'
just as the bereaved Trojans here embrace their dead kin.

33 I read ἐγρηγορὸς at v 346 and follow Page's view of the passage, as
against Fraenkel's. Fraenkel's objection to ἐγρηγορὸς, that it 'cannot
but force the thought in a direction contrary to that so clearly indicated by the surrounding uncorrupt lines,' seems to me a gratuitous
denial of the possibility of disingenuousness in Clytemnestra's expression of her 'fears' about Agamemnon and the victorious army.

34 The first of the meanings given above to κόσμων (356) is favoured by
Headlam and by Thomson, in their notes ad loc (Thomson compares
Aesch PV 24); the second meaning given to κόσμων is favoured by
Fraenkel, who well compares Pindar Ol viii.82, where κόσμος (as the
scholiast there suggests) clearly refers to the glory of the victory
just announced – for which (as here) due credit is given to Zeus. I see
no reason why one should not accept the double reference, a feature
not uncommon in Aeschylean epithets (cf, for example, ἄδαιτον,
Ag 150). κτεάτειρα, in the same image, also, as a ἅπαξ λεγόμενον,
presents some difficulty. It may suggest merely 'the possessor'
(= ἡ κεκτημένη, Thomson), which would fit the first meaning, or it
may suggest 'one who has *won*' (Fraenkel relates it to κτεατίζω).
Fraenkel's translation, 'thou hast won us possession of great glories,'
actually suggests something of both meanings. 'Bestower' (Lattimore)
provides a sort of shorthand expression of this and suits the second
meaning, suggested above, for the whole expression.

With reference to the association of Night with the victory-news,
compare also the Chorus' gloomy comment at the end of the ode:
'I anxiously await some news cloaked in night' (τί ... νυκτηρεφές, 459–
60). Here (as Lebeck has shown, *The Oresteia, A Study in Language as
Structure* p 43) the context clearly suggests not only a reference to
the news of victory but also vague fears about Agamemnon's
own fate.

35 The fact that *Cho* 505–7 are also attributed (Clem Alex *strom* 2.141.23.)
to Sophocles has led some scholars (eg Lloyd-Jones in the note to
his translation, ad loc) to doubt their authenticity here. Surely the place
of the image expressed in these lines in the image sequence outlined
above helps, at least, to remove the doubt.

36 Glyconic codas occur at 381–4; 399–402; 416–19; 433–6; 452–5; 471–4. Kranz *Stasimon* pp 131–2 notes that this *metrical* kind of choral refrain occurs in the great song in praise of Argos at Aesch *Suppl* 630 ff and in the hymn celebrating the deeds of Heracles at Eur *HF* 348 ff, as well as in this present choral ode, *Ag* 367 ff, celebrating the fall of Troy; Kranz concludes that the structure (not, of course, including the antistrophic arrangement which belongs to tragedy) is that of an ancient sacred hymn.

37 ἀθίκτων χάρις (371): χάρις here appears to refer to that benign quality immanent in sacrosanct things or persons. Fraenkel compares *Medea* 439 (βέβακε δ' ὅρκων χάρις); however, Fraenkel is, perhaps, too severe in rejecting as 'not quite accurate' Wilamowitz' suggestion that the expression stresses 'the charm and attractiveness of what one is not allowed to touch' (Wilamowitz *Aischylos Interpretationen* pp 194 f). While this is not the primary meaning of the passage, Aeschylean practice, as well as the series of associated meanings in which χάρις is to be used in the play, rather encourages such an interpretation as an overtone or second meaning.

38 Cf also Lebeck's apt suggestion (*Oresteia* p 38) that the metaphor of treading on 'loveliness forbidden to the touch' (371–2) 'reveals the symbolic content of the carpet scene and prepares the mind beforehand for its underlying significance.'

39 πέφανται δ' ἐκτίνουσ' ἀτολμήτων ἀρὴ
πνεόντων μεῖζον ἢ δικαίως, φλεόντων δωμάτων ὑπέρφευ
ὑπὲρ τὸ βέλτιστον. (374–8)

With some trepidation, I follow Headlam's text (as reproduced, except for the colometry, in Thomson's edition) and Thomson's version of it in the translation given above. The only emendations are of ἐγγόνους and ἄρη (FTr), the latter a matter of accent and so negligible. Denniston and Page, in following Casaubon's emendation ἐγγόνοις, appear (as their note on the passage indicates) to be affected by their desire to relate all deeds of violence by individuals in this play to the sins of their fathers. As Fraenkel has said, criticizing other pre-Pagian defenders of ἐγγόνοις: ' ... in his [Paris'] case, it is the generation of the guilty themselves, and not their descendants, who have to atone for the transgression.' Recently, Bamberger's correction ἔκγονος for ἐγγόνους has been adopted by Jean Bollack, who translates vv 474–6: 'On a bien vu qu'elle était issue / de ce qu'on ne doit pas oser, le défaite des hommes dont le souffle était plus grand / qu'il n'est juste' (Jean Bollack *Agamemnon* 1, *deuxième partie* pp 370–1). See also his note, ibid pp 393–8.

40 Cf also the excellent notes of Thomson and of Fraenkel on *Ag* 385-6. A similar explanation of *Peithô* as the child of *Atê* is well expressed recently by Edwards in 'Agamemnon's Decision' p 28.
41 Fraenkel's translation. For discussion of the much-disputed technical details of this passage, see his notes ad loc.
42 The elliptical quality of the syntax at vv 393-5 contributes to the 'immediacy' with which the images are felt by the hearer or reader: often in the most brilliantly figurative or symbolic passages of Aeschylus (cf also *Ag* 49-60 and *Ag* 111 ff), it is difficult to separate the image or the symbol from the thing compared or the thing symbolized.
43 For passages comparable for their delicate sensuous imagery, at which Aeschylus excels when it is called for, compare *Ag* 690 ff and *Persae* 541-7 (where Persian brides are pictured mourning their young husbands). Aeschylean imagery was not limited to the more obvious physical effects such as the battle scenes parodied by Aristophanes, *Frogs* 403.
44 Lloyd-Jones' translation of δημοκράντου δ' ἀρᾶς τίνει χρέος (δημοκράντου is Porson's emendation of δημοκράτου, FTr). Fraenkel well explains this difficult line: 'the uttering of the curse is to be imagined as having happened in the past, possibly during the early stages of the war; it is here treated as equivalent to the contracting of an obligation. The obligation to pay is redeemed at the moment when the stored up resentment of the people finds voice in the φάτις σὺν κότῳ [which Fraenkel – like Klausen and Hermann, whom he follows here – takes as the subject of τίνει]: this is the first step towards revolt, thus the φάτις brings about the payment.' Nevertheless, v 457 (and the subject of its verb) is at best obscure, and certainty seems impossible.
45 See Fraenkel's defence of the reading εἰ τι θεῖον ἐστι ψύθος for the last clause in this sentence.
46 Cf Aesch *Persae* 93-4.
47 On this point, cf the agreement of Fraenkel (II. 246-9), Denniston and Page, in their note to vv 475 ff, and Kranz, *Stasimon* pp 132 ff (cited by Fraenkel), though these critics differ concerning the degree and the justification of this epode's inconsistency with what precedes it. More elaborate (unnecessarily so, in my view) 'psychological' reasons for the Chorus' sudden doubts are suggested by Dover 'Some Neglected Aspects of Agamemnon's Dilemma' p 68, and by Winnington-Ingram 'Aeschylus' *Agamemnon* 1343-71' pp 23 ff.
48 πιθανὸς ἄγαν ὁ θῆλυς ὅρος ἐπινέμεται ... : I have followed Fraenkel and Lloyd-Jones in taking πιθανός as active (its usual force at this

date). The majority of editors take both πιθανός and the verb as passive and give a different meaning to the puzzling expression ὁ θῆλυς ὅρος. Denniston and Page, for example, tend to favour Weir Smyth's translation (in the Loeb edition): 'Over-credulous, a woman's mind has boundaries open to quick encroachment.' Possibly at least some of the ambiguity is intentional on the poet's part.

49 There is much controversy as to whether Clytemnestra (according to the ascription of the mss) or the Chorus-Leader (in the view of some editors and commentators) speaks vv 489–500. On this point (and on the whole vexed question of Clytemnestra's entries and exits in the first half of the play) see appendix 2 to this chapter.

50 Cf the similar triplicity of the Messenger's doom-laden speeches at *Persae* 353–432, 447–71, 480–514. In the speeches in *Persae*, however, the incident reported in each speech has its moment of optimism, its 'rude awakening,' and its catastrophe. Cf Reinhardt *Aischylos als Regisseur und Theologe* pp 80–3, on the 'Herald scene' in the *Agamemnon*; he observes that what is played up in the Herald's speeches as the greatest of victories turns out to be the greatest of calamities, a hollow victory. Reinhardt further connects this double aspect of the scene with the dual characterization of the Herald himself, in which the personal and poignant thoughts of the soldier and returning native contrast with the exaggerated metaphorical language of the official announcer of victory.

51 This speech is discussed below, pp 34–5.

52 Ἰλίῳ δὲ κῆδος ὀρ/θώνυμον (699–700): one of Aeschylus' most apt puns, for κῆδος can mean 'marriage-bond' or 'bond of sorrow.'

53 The possible ironic overtones in these expressions with regard to the marriage of Helen and the sacrifice of Iphigenia have been discussed by Knox, *Word and Action* 27–38, esp pp 27, 31–2. Knox provides interesting comments on the 'lion imagery' throughout the play; however, I find it difficult to agree with his suggestion that we should apply the 'lion-cub image' (and its sequel) in this passage closely to Agamemnon and even to Clytemnestra, as well as to Helen.

54 Denniston and Page (in their note to 744 ff) argue, on the contrary, that the subject of παρακλίνασ' ἐπέκρανεν (744) is the Erinys itself, not a personification of Helen, and (taking παρακλίνασ' as transitive, 'as usual'), that the sentence means 'she [the Erinys] turned from its course, and accomplished a bitter end of, the marriage.' 'What is being compared [they have argued earlier in this note] is *the lion-cub's career as a whole* with *the whole set of circumstances for which Helen was*

responsible, not specifically *the lion-cub* with *Helen herself.*' Cf also Lloyd-Jones 'Agamemnonea' pp 103 ff, who agrees with Denniston and Page on the subject of παρακλίνασ' and on the application of the image but suggests further that παρακλίνασ' might have the (again transitive) meaning 'having laid beside each other' (as at Theocritus 2.44 and *Anth Pal* 5.2) with Paris and Helen supplied as the objects. These seem to me to be desperately ingenious and erudite solutions to almost non-existent problems (the second one in particular requires a good deal of supposition on the part of the audience). Fraenkel, who accepts the intransitive use of παρακλίνασ', remains the better guide concerning this image: 'As the lion showed itself in the end (735) as ἱερεύς τις ἄτας, so Helen appears finally as Erinys' (Fraenkel, II. 347). De La Combe, in his recent comment on this passage (*Agamemnon* 2, 86–7), qualifies the identification of Helen and the Erinys (in order to meet Lloyd-Jones' objections) as follows: 'Il est plus exact de dire que l'arrivée d'Hèléne est l'occasion du déchaînement de deux forces aussi contraires qu'Eros et l'Erinye, dont la strophe décrit les actions spécifiques' (p 87)

55 Text and translation of vv 768–70 are uncertain in some details and this translation is probably only an approximation of the meaning; cf editions.

56 See Denniston and Page's note to *Ag* 757–62. Cf also Lloyd-Jones' note, ad loc, to his translation of *Agamemnon*, where the same view is expressed. Cf also the following note.

57 It is true that Solon fr 1.7 ff and fr 5.9–10 (both cited by Denniston and Page and by Lloyd-Jones in this connection) do give some support to the view that the passage at *Ag* 705 ff reflects Solonian views; it is true also that Solon fr 3.7–9, quoted by Denniston and Page, describes ὕβρις as inability to control κόρος (great wealth) and the result of this inability as ἄτη. Nevertheless, some distinctions also seem possible. In the first place, disaster in Solon always occurs in connection with wealth, and this is not so either at *Ag* 758–71 or at the other comparable passage at *Ag* 1008–21 – where, indeed, the dangers of 'blood once shed' are contrasted with the *avoidable* dangers of excessive wealth. In the second place, although *Ag* 758–62 and Solon 1.7–32 imply that impious deeds (again, in Solon, unjust acquisition of wealth) affect future generations, the Solonian passage suggests that the *innocent* descendant may be punished for ancestral injustice, whereas the Aeschylean passage states that *further impious acts* are generated. Moreover, there are passages in Solon (eg, fr 1.63–70) where Fate

(Μοῖρα) appears to distribute the gifts of good and evil fortune indiscriminately, disaster to the good and good fortune to the evil, and this too seems to run counter to the present Aeschylean passage.

58 Cf *Ag* 1412–1577, esp 1412 ff, 1468 ff, 1497 ff, and my discussion of these passages below.

59 Cf the references, especially to Pindar, in Denniston and Page's note to *Ag* 757–62.

60 θάρσος ἑκούσιον, v 803, FTr, here taken, as Murray, Headlam, Thomson, and others take it, as referring to Helen. However, it is a difficult expression and may be corrupt, as many other editors (eg, Fraenkel, Denniston and Page) have thought. On the other hand, Ahrens' conjecture θράσος ἐκ θυσιῶν as interpreted by Denniston and Page ('restoring *courage through sacrifices* [eg, of Iphigenia] to dying men') provides more difficulties, in the context, than it resolves.

61 See for example the comments of Sidgwick, Verrall, and Headlam (all of whom Fraenkel rebukes in this connection) in their notes ad loc. Fraenkel, however, (in his numerous comments on the 'Agamemnon scene') seems to me to exaggerate the King's pious and 'gentlemanly' qualities. Grossmann (*Promethie und Orestie*, p 230) is closer to the mark when he speaks of a certain respect which Agamemnon's bearing wins from us in his final hour; for the rest, Grossmann emphasizes, as I have done above, the tragic irony of Agamemnon's 'blindness' in this scene.

62 Some critics would reduce the element of 'character' or 'dramatic personality' in Aeschylean tragedy rather more drastically; see, for example, Dawe 'Inconsistency of Plot and Character in Aeschylus' pp 21–62 (Dawe does not, however, deal with Clytemnestra in *Agamemnon*); Lloyd-Jones in the Introduction to his translation of *Agamemnon* pp 6–8. Cf also my review of the latter in *Phoenix* 25 (1971), 273, where this point is discussed. For a less extreme view of the subject, see Easterling 'Presentation of Character in Aeschylus.' On the other hand, some recent studies still tend to exaggerate personal and 'psychological' elements in Aeschylean characterization, eg (in connection with the *Oresteia*), Grossmann *Promethie und Orestie* pp 223–41, passim; Winnington-Ingram 'Clytemnestra and the Vote of Athena.'

63 Consideration of the role of Clytemnestra in *Agamemnon* is related to the larger question of 'male-female conflict' in the *Oresteia*, which has been much discussed by certain critics; see below, chapter 3, appendix, section iii.

64 See appendix 2 to this chapter.

65 Fraenkel and Denniston-Page compare Pindar *Pyth* 9.23 ff but there

it is not 'time' but 'sleep' itself which is called a 'sweet bedfellow'; there, too, there is a faintly sexual connotation in that sleep is the only bedfellow of the virgin Cyrene. Cf also de Romilly's comments on the psychological significance of such personifications, in *Time in Greek Tragedy* pp 43–4.

66 Cf vv 1389–92, discussed below.
67 Compare Clytemnestra's exclamation here with Agamemnon's sincere expression of fear on the same point, when he is being tempted to walk on the purple tapestries, at v 921.
68 See, for example, Denniston and Page at the end of their note to v 933–4. For the literal meaning of these verses (though not for the interpretative overtones here suggested) I am indebted to Fraenkel's excellent note and his references (especially to Kennedy and Headlam) ad loc. I also follow the majority of modern editors in reading ἐξεῖπεν, Auratus' correction of ἐξεῖπον (FTr) at v 934.
69 Easterling 'Presentation of Character in Aeschylus' pp 17–18 makes a similar observation concerning Agamemnon's (though not concerning Clytemnestra's) veiled allusion to Aulis in this exchange.
70 I follow Weil's and Murray's (OCT) reading at v 943. In general, scholars (too numerous to cite individually) have tended to go to extremes in their interpretations of this scene. Too exclusive an interest in Clytemnestra's victory in the 'male-female conflict' has sometimes distracted attention from the acutal deed to which Agamemnon is lured. On the other hand, the impiety of that deed has itself been exaggerated in other studies, as if it were for *that* that the King must die. Among recent critics, Lebeck *The Oresteia* pp 74–8; Easterling, 'Character in Aeschylus' pp 17–18; and Taplin *Stagecraft* 311–12 have best expressed the symbolic and allusive, as opposed to the actual, significance of the deed. And all have drawn attention to the suggestive images conjured up by this scene, especially that of 'trampling with the foot,' which, as Lebeck has observed (p 74), is 'throughout the trilogy ... a metaphor which describes the crime of sacrilege.'
71 This interpretation has been advanced by several critics; it is, on the other hand, strenuously rejected by Jones: see his scathing references to Thomson, Finley (of whose book, *Pindar and Aeschylus*, he approves in general), and Kitto in this connection (Jones *On Aristotle and Greek Tragedy* pp 85 ff and n 2 to p 85). Jones may be right in suggesting that Agamemnon's fear of *hybris* here springs from his sense of the outrage at so defiling 'fine embroidered work' (923, cf 949); nevertheless, by dismissing the other effects and overtones which we have noted in this scene (eg, at 932–3) as 'psychologizing' and 'spiritualizing'

the quarrel involved, he seems to be more guilty than those he rebukes of rejecting what is clearly in the text.

72 Cf Lloyd-Jones 'The Guilt of Agamemnon' pp 196–7 and Dawe 'Some Reflections on *Atê* and *Hamartia*' pp 109–10. The irrational aspect of the deed (Agamemnon gives reasons for not obeying Clytemnestra's request and then, despite his affirmation that he will not change his mind, 932, promptly does so) makes such an explanation tempting. However, the text gives no indication of a specific onset of *atê*, unless it be taken as a form of *atê* to be seduced by Persuasion (here Clytemnestra's base persuasion), elsewhere called 'the child of *Atê* (386).

73 Cf Goheen 'Three Studies in the *Oresteia*' pp 119–20; Lebeck *Oresteia* p 81 (who refers, note 7, to Goheen in this connection).

74 The precise text and meaning of 983–5 are uncertain and have been much disputed; for a good sampling of editorial opinion, see editions of Sidgwick, Fraenkel, and Denniston and Page. However, it is clear enough (see in particular Fraenkel's note) that the Chorus are speaking of the casting off of the mooring-ropes at Aulis – and seeking to reassure themselves that the troubles at Aulis are now buried in the distant past.

75 Cf *Septem* 767 ff, to which Denniston and Page also refer. There the same image of jettisoning wealth from an overloaded ship is used, but there the contrast is made with the fulfilment of family curses, which (unlike dangers of excessive wealth) 'pass not away.'

76 Sidgwick, Thomson, and Denniston and Page render the passage much as I have, though with slightly varying interpretations. Fraenkel's rendering differs considerably: 'And did not established destiny prevent my portion from winning more from the gods ... ' (see also his note to 1025–9); but this protasis seems to go obscurely with the apodosis and moreover it would be surprising to find *moira* used in two very different applications ('destiny in general' and 'my particular lot') in the same clause, without any indication that this is the case. Nor does the text give us any indication that, as Lloyd-Jones claims, it is Agamemnon's rights as a king which, the Chorus mean, restrain their rights as subjects from exceeding their due. But perhaps any decision as to the identity of the *moira* involved is open to the same charge of subjectivity.

77 Darius in the *Persae* is, in a sense, the dramatic forerunner of Cassandra in the *Agamemnon*. Like Cassandra, he is the one whose special supernatural vision enables him to trace the connections between the remote past (the doom overhanging the royal house of Persia) and the present and future disasters. Darius, of course, also indicates

the guilt of Xerxes himself as the immediate cause of the doom descending on him (*Persae* 742-52, 782-3). The equivalent blaming of Agamemnon by Cassandra would be inconsistent with her attitude to the King (see following note) in this play; besides, this aspect of Agamemnon's fate has already been dealt with by the poet.

78 Cassandra's loyalty to Agamemnon stands in sharp contrast with Euripides' Cassandra in *The Trojan Women* (see *Tro* 356-64), whose chief consolation in becoming the spear-bride of Agamemnon is that she will contribute to his ruin. In *Agamemnon*, Cassandra's desperate attempt to warn the Chorus of Clytemnestra's murderous intent ('Keep the bull from the cow ... ! 1125-6) seems evidence of her peculiar loyalty. It is possible, of course, to regard both this passage and her later hostility to Clytemnestra as Agamemnon's murderer as simply the reflection of Apollo's hostility, but this seems unlikely. Her expressions, especially in the later iambic passages, seem to reflect a very human animosity against the Queen. But even this limited degree of 'characterization' of Cassandra is (as I seek to indicate in my treatment of this scene) a matter of dramatic convenience.

79 On the complex metrical plan of this *amoibaion* and its relation to the themes of Cassandra's utterances, see Fraenkel's subtle discussion, pp 487-8 and especially pp 539-40, including his quotation of Weil's appreciation of the formal structure of the scene and its significance.

80 Ἄπολλον·Ἄπολλον· / ἀγυιᾶτ', ἀπόλλων ἐμός. (1080-1): a grim Aeschylean pun which defies translation.

81 It is tempting to take this as a reference to Orestes (as the Scholiast thought) and so to add another dimension to Cassandra's prophecy at this point. Modern editorial opinion, however (cf Fraenkel's and Denniston and Page's notes), derides this view.

82 Sidgwick and Denniston-Page take μελαγκέρῳ ... μηχανήματι with τύπτει; Wecklein and Fraenkel take it with ἐν πέπλοισιν ... λαβοῦσα. If we accept the latter construing, we actually get an image of Clytemnestra holding out the robe 'on arms extended in front her *like the horns of a cow*' (Denniston and Page's paraphrase of Wecklein's construing, with which, however, they do not agree).

83 The Chorus understand all Cassandra's utterances about the past of the house of Atreus (1105-6, 1242-4) but claim lack of understanding about Cassandra's visions and prophecies of the coming murder (1112-13, 1119 ff, 1130 ff, 1245). This acords with Apollo's punishment of Cassandra (1212), though it is odd that the Chorus *do* follow Cassandra's prophecies about her own death (1162-3, 1295 ff, 1321). Perhaps in the case of the unapprehended prophecies about Agamem-

non's death, the poet is exploiting Apollo's penalty to Cassandra in order to assist in the conventional non-participation of the Chorus in the action. At the same time, their pity for Cassandra's coming fate helps reinforce the pathos of the scene.
84 At vv 1138–9, 1148–9, 1160–1, 1171–2.
85 Reminiscence of this passage is reinforced by Cassandra's use of the 'net image' for Clytemnestra's murder of Agamemnon (1115–16), as the Chorus used the net image in the second stasimon (at vv 357–61) for Zeus' reduction of Troy for Paris' misdeeds.
86 I take δυσμενεῖς (1193) as nominative and εὐνὰς ἀδελφοῦ as 'the adultery of a brother's bed,' ie 'adultery with a brother's wife' (as it must be), as object of πατοῦντι. Cf Denniston and Page's note ad loc.
87 Cassandra's loyalty to Agamemnon appears not only in her attempts to warn the Chorus of his danger but also in her scorn for Clytemnestra and (1224–5) for Agamemnon's supplanter, Aegisthus, as well as in her omission of any reference to Agamemnon's sacrifice of Iphigenia in relation to his coming doom. Cf Mazon *Eschyle* II p 7. Note also the poignant reference to Agamemnon as 'my master' (1225–6).
88 Surprisingly little attention has been paid by the commentators to this emphasis by Cassandra on the adultery of Thyestes as the πρῶταρχος ἄτη: see Fraenkel's note to v 1193 and his references to Bruhn and Méautis; as Fraenkel indicates, many commentators take the slaughter of Thyestes' children as the initial deed of infatuation. Wilamowitz, in the Introduction to his translation of *Agamemnon, Griech Trag* ii.4 (quoted in Fraenkel's note) does comment on the 'mention' of Thyestes' adultery here but refuses to allow it the prominence which Cassandra's words would suggest. Even Fraenkel, who criticizes Wilamowitz for not recognizing that the adultery is set down as the πρώταρχος ἄτη, does not quite do justice to Cassandra's emphasis, suggesting that 'for the Erinyes the murder was of greater moment ... but that in the conception of the poet both [adultery and murder] form a single complex of guilt.'
89 Cf above, note 83.
90 On the question whether this interior tableau was shown by means of the *ekkuklêma* (a revolving platform), as the majority of scholars believe, or by means of other arrangements, such as the use of a mute scene shifter, see Taplin's discussion, *Stagecraft*, pp 325–7.
91 Earlier editors use the term 'kommos' for the latter part of this exchange (1448–1576). More recently, editors tend to describe the whole passage as an 'epirrhematic composition,' since they restrict the term 'kommos' to entirely lyrical duets, usually expressing lamenta-

tion, between Chorus and actor(s).

A part of the following discussion of these passages is drawn from my paper 'Interaction between Chorus and Characters in the *Oresteia*'; see esp pp 324-30.

92 μηδ' ἐπιλέχθης does, it must be admitted, provide difficulties, though not, perhaps, as insuperable ones as Fraenkel suggests. The most serious of these, μηδέ following a positive clause, may be removed, without substantially changing the sense of the passage as a whole, by adopting Scaliger's suggestion, τῃδ' ἐπιλεχθείς, without a stop after the preceding verse ('You ... thinking of it in this way, that I am the wife etc. ... '). Denniston and Page approve of this in their note.

93 Critics often pass over this difference in perspective on the part of the Queen. Smythe, for example, speaks of Clytemnestra's 'ferocious joy' at 1384 ff, and then imagines her to 'snatch joyfully' at the thought of being the evil daimon of the house, without making any distinctions between the attitudes expressed in the two passages. (See Smyth, *Aeschylean Tragedy* p 170.) Winnington-Ingram ('Clytemnestra and the Vote of Athena' pp 134-6) does recognize that Clytemnestra 'changes her ground' here, though his analysis of the passage runs along somewhat different lines from the one to be suggested in the present discussion. Cf also Bremer *Hamartia* pp 127-8, who does speak of Clytemnestra moving, in this kommos, 'to a diametrically opposed position,' though he does not indicate how she reaches it.

94 On vv 1409-37 as a whole, cf Zeitlin 'The Motif of the Corrupted Sacrifice in Aeschylus' *Oresteia*.' She comments well on the ironic juxtaposition of 'sacrifice' and 'curses' in the Chorus' statement at 1409, which Clytemnestra exploits at 1413 ff, by turning the people's curses back against Agamemnon for *his* sacrifice.

95 Cf Fraenkel's comparison, in his note on v 749, of the identification of Helen and the *Erinus* (which he accepts) at 749 with Clytemnestra's vision of herself as the ἀλάστωρ, appearing in the figure of Agamemnon's wife.

96 ἰχώρ, 1480, is an extraordinary word for 'blood,' in the context. Perhaps it should be given the Hippocratic sense of 'impure discharge, pus'; so Lloyd-Jones in his translation and note to v 1479.

97 Possibly the ambiguous treatment of Clytemnestra's guilt sheds some light on the celebrated question of Agamemnon's responsibility at Aulis.

98 Mazon, in his Introduction to *Agamemnon*, pp 7-8, finds the chief significance of Clytemnestra's confrontation with the Chorus to lie in the two ways in which the murder of the King is viewed.

99 Hermann's emendation of ἀνάξια, 1527.
100 The iambic scene (1372–1406) in which Clytemnestra gives her first triumphant vaunts over the dead gives place at 1407 ff to epirrhematic exchanges in which the Chorus sings and Clytemnestra answers, first in the iambic trimeters (1412–25, 1431–47) of dramatic speech, then, when the Chorus embarks on its formal ode (1448 ff), in anapaestic chants (1462 ff, 1475 ff etc, until the end of the kommos).
For metrical analysis and comment (beyond this simple indication of the increasing emotional tension of the passage) of the epirrhematic part of this scene, see Kranz 'Zwei Lieder des *Agamemnon*' pp 312 ff and Fraenkel III, 660–2. Note especially Fraenkel's observation on the effect of the repeated *ephymnia* in the central part of the ode to mark the *thrênos*, or lament, for the King in which the Chorus here indulges.
101 Such must be the approximate sense of Clytemnestra's expression at 1442–3: ναυτίλων δὲ σελμάτων ἱστοτριβής (codd): ἰστοτριβής (Pauw), whether or not we accept Pauw's correction. Recently, a regular spate of articles has appeared defending ἱστοτριβής as an obscene pun, or possibly an accepted piece of metonymous nautical obscenity for a woman 'servicing' a man or men. See Koniaris 'An Obscene Word in Aeschylus' and William Blake Tyrrell 'An Obscene Word in Aeschylus,' who reach similar conclusions by slightly different routes. (There is, however, a nice technical distinction in their interpretations: on the whole I prefer Koniaris' view that the term in the context means 'sailors' harlot'; even if Cassandra's activity, in Clytemnestra's fevered imagination, is regarded as limited to Agamemnon, she might well employ, if she is capable of such expressions at all, a generic term of abuse.) Cf also Borthwick "ΙΣΤΟΤΡΙΒΗΣ: An Addendum,' who notes (in addition to further support for the obscene sense of the word in question) that Young, in 'Gentler Medicines in *Agamemnon*' p 15, has already provided the same explanation of the word as have the two scholars cited above and had cited the same passage in Strabo (8.6.20) as does Koniaris in support of his explanation.
102 I agree with Fraenkel that the subject must, in the context, be Cassandra and not Agamemnon and that there is no linguistic reason for changing the text. I also agree with Lloyd-Jones that the apparent grossness of the thought – viz, that the pleasure of having killed her husband's concubine should heighten her own sexual satisfaction – is insufficient reason for rejecting this meaning. Fraenkel's objection

that the expression is too coarse for the regal Clytemnestra ('she nowhere makes explicit mention of her own adulterous behaviour') is hardly borne out by the suggestions of *double entendre* which we have noted in her language earlier.

APPENDIX ONE TO CHAPTER ONE

Problems in the parodos of the *Agamemnon*

i The anger of Artemis

Few of the alleged problems in the *Agamemnon* have occasioned so much outright disagreement and contradiction between the critics as that of the 'anger of Artemis' as it is treated in vv 131–55 of the parodos. Perhaps only the 'guilt of Agamemnon,' a question closely connected with Artemis' anger in the play (but which I shall try, so far as possible, to treat separately), has caused more critical ink to flow. Critical discussions (with bibliographical references) of numerous conflicting views on both text and interpretation will be found in Fraenkel's Commentary; for more recent discussions see John J. Peradotto's article, 'The Omen of the Egales and the ΗΘΟΣ of Agamemnon.' There would be little point in reviewing all of this material again. Instead, I propose to state the problem as it has appeared to the critics and to indicate, with comments of my own, a selection of the more interesting or, in some cases, influential answers and interpretations which have been advanced. My own view of the passage has already been indicated, in simplified form, in the preceding chapter.[1]

The issue of Artemis' anger in the *Agamemnon* first arises in the form of a prophetic warning appended by Calchas to his favourable interpretation of the omen of the eagles feeding on the pregnant hare.

> Only may no ill-will from the gods threaten the great army-curb forged against Troy. For unsullied Artemis in pity begrudges the winged hounds of the father their feast on the tender mother-hare seized before her hour of delivery. (131–7)

That Artemis' anger will be directed against the Atreidae and their expedition is clear both from the first sentence quoted above and from Calchas' subsequent prayer to Apollo that Artemis may not send adverse winds delaying the fleet, hastening on another sacrifice ... (148 ff). The question most frequently raised with regard to the passage is why Aeschylus suppresses the traditional 'reason' for Artemis' anger (Agamemnon's boasts, on shooting a deer, that he was a better archer than Artemis)[2] and the issue most hotly debated is just what we *are* to understand as the reason for Artemis' anger in our text.

Fraenkel has, in my opinion, supplied the best answer to the first question:

> From the point of view of Aeschylus it was all-important that nothing but Agamemnon's deliberate decision should appear as the primary cause of his sufferings, $\pi\rho\omega\tau o\pi\acute{\eta}\mu\omega\nu$. That effect would have been impossible if the king had first, by a comparatively minor offence, brought upon himself the revenge of Artemis and had consequently been forced to sacrifice Iphigenia. In that case the moral dilemma which Aeschylus wanted to be the fountain-head of Agamemnon's fate would have been degraded to secondary importance. By a bold stroke the poet ... eliminated the act of Agamemnon which had incensed the goddess.[3]

If this were all that Fraenkel said on the matter, one could almost agree with him. Certainly the reason he gives for the avoidance of any moral issue, or even of any offence on the part of Agamemnon calling for divine retribution, *before* the all-important dilemma at Aulis, seems eminently sound: unlike many learned critics, Fraenkel does not let his learning blind him to essential questions of tragic motivation. But Fraenkel is surely wrong in denying that the poet supplies *any* reason for Artemis' anger (the anger itself is, of course, necessary to motivate the dread dilemma at Aulis). Here Fraenkel appears simply to reject (along with many other critics, before and after him) the plain, if somewhat extraordinary, explanation given by the poet for the divine ill-will against the Argive expedition: that, in pity, she resents the feast of the winged birds of the father upon the pregnant hare. Fraenkel rejects both the literal meaning of this statement (at least as the explanation of Artemis' anger which the poet means us to accept) and the more 'sophisticated' interpretation (first attributed by Fraenkel to Conington) that this really means that Artemis hated the future destroyers of Troy, whom the eagles represent: the latter 'easy shifting of responsibility' Fraenkel simply regards as unworthy of a play involving serious moral issues. Fraenkel cannot of course deny the existence of the explanation given in the text; instead, he ducks its implications by attributing it simply to a misunderstanding on Calchas' part. The *real* explanation of the portent as far as the sacrifice of Iphigenia is concerned is, according to Fraenkel, that given by Blomfield: that this portent is not so much the *cause* as the symbol or image of the sacrifice soon to be consummated by the Atridae. Now it may indeed be this *as well* (I shall return to this point) but clearly for Calchas it is an actual cause of Artemis' wrath and I do not think we have the right to reject one part of Calchas' prophetic utterance while accepting the rest of it. (Fraenkel himself rightly rejects the view that Aeschylus expected the audience to supply for themselves the traditional explanation of Artemis' anger on the grounds that we are not entitled to supply what the poet does not himself mention: a similar rebuttal might be urged against the view of Blomfield he supports.)

Several scholars have, however, adopted the interpretation (cited from Conington by Fraenkel) that Artemis' anger at the eagles' feast really means anger at the sack of Troy by the Atreidae, though that interpretation has been defended and developed in different ways. The case against what Fraenkel has called the naïve interpretation (that Artemis hates the Atreidae simply because the eagles whose feast she hates stand for the Atreidae) has been put most strongly by Lloyd-Jones:

> This interpretation seems to me to rest on an intolerable confusion between the world of the portent and the world of the reality it happens ... to symbolize. The eagles and the hare belong to the world of the portent; that portent symbolizes an event which is to happen in the real world. The eagles stand for the Atreidae; so it is natural to infer that the hare must stand for some figure or figures belonging to the real world. We can hardly avoid understanding that it stands for the Trojans and their city. So [Calchas] must mean that Artemis abhors the coming destruction of Troy which the Atreidae are destined to accomplish.[4]

The logic of this almost convinces one, but there are, I think, two difficulties in the way of accepting it. The lesser of these difficulties is that no reason is provided by the poet or by Calchas for Artemis' championing of the Trojans. Lloyd-Jones supplies this reason from the *Iliad* and 'the whole poetic tradition in which Artemis together with her brother Apollo appears as a loyal partisan of Troy against the defenders.'[5] This explanation is in danger of offending against 'Fraenkel's rule' (above) about not supplying traditional explanations which the poet does not himself supply. However, the stronger objection to Lloyd-Jones' most logical explanation is that it renders vv 140-4 of Calchas' utterance – lines which appear to expand on, even to expound, Artemis' hatred of the eagles' feast *on the pregnant hare* – redundant and even irrelevant. Now these verses themselves contain more than one uncertainty in text and meaning (which I shall discuss later), but however we resolve these uncertainties they still deal *exclusively* with Artemis' delight in, and kindly attitudes toward, the young of wild things and they do so in relation to her acceptance of, or demand for (or possibly to her deprecated resistance to), the fulfilment of the action symbolized by the eagle portent. Whether we take that 'action' to be the sacrifice of Iphigenia or, as I think (as far as *Calchas*' meaning here is concerned), the sack of Troy, the reason for Artemis' attitude and so, originally, for her 'anger' is still expressed exclusively in terms of her love of the young of wild animals. These verses, then, support the 'naïve interpretation,' however unacceptable it may be to logical critics, and say nothing at all about Artemis' attitude to the Atreidae's sack of Troy, considered in and by itself.

Peradotto's variant of Lloyd-Jones' view that Artemis is angry with the Atreidae in anticipation of their destruction of Troy does, it must be admitted, avoid some of the difficulties which we have found within the latter scholar's argument. 'It is not,' Peradotto assumes, 'as an arbitrary partisan of Troy, but as a patroness of innocent youth and fertility that Artemis recoils from the indiscriminate predation which she knows a war under the Atreidae will be.'[6] However, there are obvious objections to this interpretation also. Peradotto has gone to some pains to remind us (with references to the archaeological evidence of the Artemis cult at Brauron) of the goddess' concern for 'fertility, pregnancy, youth, innocence'; nevertheless (as Fraenkel cites T. Pluss as noting) 'it is not young human beings that are mentioned [in connection with the destruction of Troy, v 128] but cattle and wealth'.[7] Peradotto seeks to meet this objection by arguing (feebly) that the young must implicitly be included in the total destruction of Troy which Calchas forecasts and that this inclusion is made explicit (but not, unfortunately, until the next ode!) at v 359.[8] Secondly why (once again) does Calchas expend four verses (140 ff) connecting (in some way) the cause (or, as some think, the effect) of Artemis' anger with her love of young *wild* things, if all that arouses that anger in the first place is the destruction of young *human beings* (along with everything else) in the destruction of Troy? The ingenuity of classical philology lands us, indeed, in some strange dilemmas.

Among the many wrong leads which the critics (some of them, at least) have given us about the anger of Artemis is that of taking Artemis and her 'motives' too seriously. Even Kitto, usually so sensible a critic, offends in this respect. *His* Artemis (who, like the Artemis of the critics just discussed, is angered at the coming destruction of Troy) wants to teach Agamemnon a lesson: 'If he must do this [ie wage a bloody war] let him first destroy an innocent of his own – and take the consequences.'[9] This *may* be what *we* think of the situation in which Artemis lands Agamemnon, but there is no hint in the text that Artemis thinks this way – or even that she thinks at all. Fraenkel is surely right in reminding us that her chief function, in the play as in the myth, is to provide Agamemnon's awful dilemma (and in the *play*, that is her *only* function).

Yet another (and perhaps more fruitful) approach is the attempt on the part of recent critics to understand the vexed passage (131–44) in terms of poetic symbolism, for a poetic symbol can, of course, stand for many different things (including 'contradictory things') at once. Lebeck gives perhaps the best (certainly the most terse) expression of this view:

> The language of Calchas' prophecy merges portent and thing portended, turning the moment into a mirror where present, past and future stand reflected ... In Calchas' prophecy Artemis requires payment for a transgression of which the omen is a symbol ... Tender toward all helpless young, she yet turns harsh, her anger roused, and claims a cruel fulfilment of the portent.[10]

If I read Lebeck's elliptical account of the matter rightly, she is saying that the omen of the predacious eagles stands both for the sack of Troy by the Atreidae (which, like many other critics, Lebeck appears to think is what angers Artemis) *and* for the sacrifice of Iphigenia (the 'punishment' or at least the 'price' which she exacts, in advance, for Agamemnon's conquest).[11] Now this duality is, I believe, true as far as the poetic overtone of the passage is concerned. Clearly the poet must mean *us* to think of both events when we receive the image of this portent in the mind's eye ... and, indeed, the *simile* (at 49 ff) of the eagles (the Atreidae) crying for vengeance over the nest robbed of their young (Helen) also carries this double significance and prepares us for the present passage. Where I part company from Lebeck here is in her implication that this is Calchas' meaning also. Calchas has just told us (126 ff) that the omen means the sack of Troy by the Atreidae; τούτων ... ξύμβολα: 'the things portended by these events' cannot now mean *for Calchas* (without any warning from him of a second meaning) the sacrifice of Iphigenia. Prophets may speak in riddling language but a prophet would not, I think, give a clear interpretation of a portent and then understand a quite different meaning (which his hearers are left to intuit) when he speaks of the fulfilment of that portent. It is for this reason that I would maintain that the second, dreadful significance (the sacrifice of Iphigenia) which hovers behind both the portent and Calchas' 'portentous' word (... ξύμβολα ...) is a poetic overtone which the audience is expected to pick up, not a part of Calchas' prophecy. (The sacrifice *does*, of course, become a part of Calchas' fear of the *effects* of the omen on Artemis.)

Of recent editors and commentators on the *Agamemnon*, Page is one of the few to accept (as I do) the 'naïve' explanation of Artemis' anger – namely that she is angry at the cruel feast of the eagles and angry at the Atreidae because they 'are' the eagles.[12] Page, however, takes this 'irrational' cause of the beginning of Agamemnon's troubles simply as part of a whole 'irrational' sequence, the first part of an inevitable doom visited on Agamemnon (who is, allegedly, as helpless and guiltless at Aulis[13] as he was in offending Artemis in the first place by the gods. This view of the reason for the lack of any 'reasonable motive (through some deed of Agamemnon's) being supplied for the anger of Artemis conflicts sharply with Fraenkel's, namely that Artemis' anger is deprived of any morally significant relation to Agamemnon's action so that the moral issue may begin where it belongs dramatically: with the dilemma at Aulis. My own view is, as I have indicated, the same as Fraenkel's except that I think we must accept (as Fraenkel does not) the 'irrational' reason for Artemis' anger with the Atreidae given in the text. In the play (as in the myth) Artemis' anger provides the crucial dilemma at Aulis with which, in the play, the significant action begins. Moreover, as we have seen, the portent of the eagles' feast presents to the mind's eye of the audience a single image embracing the fateful successions of vengeful predations, each answering the other, with which the past, present, and future of the action are concerned.

There are two linguistic points in the meaning of vv 140–4 which have been much debated in the various interpretations discussed above. Those who, like Page, believe that τούτων ... ξύμβολα ('the things portended by these events') refers at this point to the sacrifice of Iphigenia, which they see Artemis as here eagerly seeking, face an obvious difficulty in the *concessive* meaning of τόσον περ κ.τ.λ., in the preceding clause: if Artemis' love of helpless young things is thought to *cause* her vengeful anger demanding the sacrifice of Iphigenia, one can hardly say '*in spite of* such love, she demands etc.' For this reason, Denniston and Page understand πέρ in its less likely meaning, in this construction, as a purely *intensive* particle: 'being, as she is, so well disposed to all young animals she demands fulfilment of what this act portends.' (Denniston and Page cite Denniston *Greek Particles* pp 481 ff in general support of this interpretation of πέρ as intensive here; this is surprising in view of the fact that on p 485 of that work Denniston appears to take πέρ at *Ag* 140 as concessive.) We have already seen how difficult it is, in the context of this prophecy, to understand that by 'the things portended' (the fulfilment of which Artemis is here represented as asking) Calchas could possibly mean the sacrifice of Iphigenia. This difficulty would surely be increased by the necessity of having to interpret πέρ as intensive, in the accompanying circumstantial expression, in order to suit that meaning.

The second word which provides difficulty, this time to two other interpretations of the passage as a whole (131–44), is αἰτεῖ (indicative: the reading of the manuscripts) at v 144. Those who think that 'the things portended' mean (as Calchas has already indicated) 'the sack of Troy' and that Artemis is angry with the Atreidae either because of the feast of the eagles (who represent them) or because of the sack of Troy (which the whole omen represents) must find it difficult that Artemis is here represented as actually *asking* for that conquest by the Atreidae. This difficulty is not, I think, as great as the ones facing the other interpretation of τούτων ... ξύμβολα. Several 'solutions' to the dilemma have been suggested. The simplest, that of Blomfield, suggesting αἴτει, imperative, requires only a change of accent (a matter of 'editor's choice'); this Fraenkel rejects for the not quite compelling reason that Calchas would hardly address a prayer to Artemis ('Ask, O fair one')[14] when immediately afterwards (146 ff) he prays to Apollo to intercede with his sister. Lachmann's reading αἰνεῖ (which Fraenkel approves) certainly provides the best sense to the sentence ('The fair goddess, though so kindly to the tender young etc. ... yet *consents* to the fulfilment of the portent') by only a slight change in the text; it is probably the most acceptable solution. (αἴνει, imperative, Gilbert's suggestion followed by Sidgwick and Headlam, involves, as well as the change of accent and the same text change, the difficulty of the consecutive prayers to the two divinities which Fraenkel has urged against Lachmann's αἴτει, imperative.)

The importance of the 'anger of Artemis' passage, and of our interpretation of it, for our view of the play as a whole explains (if it does not entirely justify!) the amount of critical ink which has been spilt on it. On the one hand, as we have seen, certain aspects of that interpretation are directly related to the topic which we have soon to review: the 'responsibility' of Agamemnon. (According to one interpretation, the passage purposely postpones that issue till the proper dramatic moment, at Aulis; according to another, it is but the first in a sequence of texts exonerating the King from all responsibility in an absurd, god-plagued universe.) On the other hand, the passage alerts us, even at this early stage, to the crucial importance of the sacrifice theme which is to run through the trilogy. The very terms of Calchas' fear of Artemis' anger (' ... hastening on another sacrifice, lawless and inedible [ἄδαιτον], a fashioner of strife, clinging to the race, which fears not the husband,' 151–4) lead us to look backward from the coming sacrifice of Iphigenia to Atreus' grim sacrifice of Thyestes' children and forward to the series of sacrificial murders still to come. That these 'violent deeds of bloodshed are treated not as murder but as ... ritual slaughter' has been well illustrated in Froma Zeitlin's detailed treatment of this theme in the *Oresteia*, a treatment which properly takes its start from a discussion of the present passage.[15] One of the most fruitful features of this realization lies in the explanation which it provides for the persistent recurrence of sacrificial language (sometimes in obscure contexts) throughout the trilogy.[16]

ii 'Knowledge through suffering' in the 'Hymn to Zeus'

I am aware that the optimistic view of the 'Hymn to Zeus' (*Ag* 160–83) and of the doctrine of 'learning through suffering' presented in the foregoing chapter is not a currently fashionable one; the reader should be warned (if such warning is necessary) that it may be too optimistic a view and that Aeschylus may not have intended so far-reaching an application of the potential 'learning.' A much more restrictive view of the matter is expressed in Denniston and Page's notes on the passage.[17] Here the editors decry the belief that anything 'profound' is intended in the whole passage. The emphasis on Zeus' power as the 'triple-thrower' is intended, they argue, only to underline the fact that he is powerful enough to teach a man a lesson (there seems to me something of 'over-kill' in this aspect of their interpretation) and the lesson of 'learning through suffering' is to be equated simply with δράσαντι παθεῖν: 'the doer will suffer' (ie 'If you break his [Zeus'] law, he will teach you to mend your ways by inflicting punishment'). The editors further reject the view (in default, allegedly, of evidence from the plays) that 'moral or spiritual enlightenment is forged (for the sinner) in a furnace of suffering.' Less understandably, they also reject the interpretation that others may learn from the 'sinner's' downfall. However, in restricting the 'lesson' to the 'sinner' (their expression, not mine), Denniston and Page seem to me to involve themselves in at least a minor contradiction. On the one hand they say of Agamemnon, 'what he learns from this [ie from his doom at his wife's hands] is hard to see.' Yet a moment later they insist that '179 ff. strongly suggest that it is the sinner himself who is to 'learn through suffering''. The effect of this discussion seems to me to trivialize Aeschylus' 'doctrine,' so portentously introduced in the 'Hymn to Zeus,' and this indeed seems the intent of the editors, for they ask, 'Is it [ie the 'doctrine' concerned] not merely that popular piece of worldly vision, *experientia docet*?'

Fraenkel, like Denniston and Page, regards the essence of the *phronein* (understanding) which men may achieve by suffering as 'an insight into the everlasting principle of δράσαντι παθεῖν'[18] (ie that the doer of dreadful deeds will suffer). However, he appears to attach more significance to this reflection, in its context, than do Denniston and Page. This grasp of 'the ultimate cause of fate and suffering' he regards as the central idea of the 'Hymn to Zeus,' which, in turn, he calls 'a corner-stone not only of this play but of the whole trilogy.' (We have already observed that Fraenkel regards these reflections of the Chorus as occasioned by 'the point of utter *amêchania*' reached in 'the account of events at Aulis.') Thus it is hard to believe that Fraenkel would, in Agamemnon's case, limit this hard-won favour from the gods to the moment when the King reels enmeshed in Clytemnestra's fatal web of destruction; at any rate he does not explicitly deny, as Page does, that the insight may extend to those who observe the occurrence of δράσαντι παθεῖν, and he hints, though somewhat vaguely, at possible future applications of the doctrine later in the trilogy.

Both Fraenkel and Denniston and Page refer to a similar view concerning suffering and learning implicit in the words which Herodotus has Croesus say at 1.207.1, and Dover[19] quotes at least simplifications of 'the doctrine' in passages such as Hesiod, *Op* 218, παθών δέ τε νήπιος ἔγνω ('the fool learns, once he's suffered'). It is possible that what Aeschylus has the Chorus express in our passage does not go further than such gnomic utterances, though I have suggested that I think it does. But even if it does not, the difference between Denniston and Page's and Fraenkel's recognition of this traditional background is that for the former it leads to disparagement ('merely that popular piece of worldly wisdom,' note to v 184 ff), whereas the latter seems to recognize that poetic greatness can lie in giving fresh demonstrations, immediate and tragic, to age-old truths.

One further difference of opinion (starting from what looks like a mere detail of controversy over mss readings and their interpretation) should at least be mentioned in this connection. In the text of this chapter, I have translated vv 182–3, 'There is, somehow, a grace-that-comes-by-violence [reading χάρις βίαιος, after Turnebus] from the gods seated on their dread bench of the helmsman.' This passage has, however, been variously construed and interpreted (see editions), to some extent in accordance with the reading selected. The most radical differences from the version given above will be found in a recent article by Maruice Pope.[20] Pope rejects Turnebus' emendment βίαιος for βιαίως of the mss; more importantly, for the interpretation, he reads ποῦ interrogative, with M and V the oldest mss, instead of που enclitic (FTr and most editors), so that for Pope the statement becomes a rhetorical question ('where is there favour from the gods who, using force, sit on the dread bench of the helmsmen?'), implying, in the context, that one looks for such favour in vain. I have attempted elsewhere[21] a rebuttal (consonant with the views expressed in the preceding chapter) of Pope's interpretation and its implications for the play and, perhaps, for the trilogy as a whole.

iii The guilt of Agamemnon

The question whether Agamemnon had any real choice or responsibility in the decision to sacrifice Iphigenia is (like the question about Artemis' anger) a major area of disagreement in the interpretation of the play. It has been reactivated in recent times by the authoritative arguments of Page and Lloyd-Jones[22] against the view that Agamemnon has any significant measure of freedom in the fateful dilemma at Aulis. Their arguments may be summarized (with some inevitable simplification) as follows:

(i) Since Agamemnon was sent against Troy by Zeus, he cannot give up the expedition without disobeying Zeus.

(ii) The sacrifice is right (θέμις, 217, ie divinely sanctioned) in the view of the army; the army commanders will perform the sacrifice in any case, even if Agamemnon refuses. (It is Page, pp xxiv, xxvii, and note to v 214, who insists particularly on the latter point as affecting Agamemnon's 'freedom.')

(iii) The language at vv 218–23, particularly the expressions ἀνάγκας ἔδυ λέπαδνον ('he took on the yoke-strap of necessity,' 218, on which Page in particular insists) and παρακοπά ('madness,' 223, on which Lloyd-Jones dwells) clearly emphasizes the King's lack of freedom.

For many (including the present writer) the first of these points has been answered in advance by E.R. Dodds' sane and simple acceptance of 'over-determination' (human decision paralleling divine causation) in Aeschylean tragedy: thus Dodds accepts that a man (viz, Agamemnon) can be fulfilling the will of Zeus and at the same time committing an act which he believes to be his own choice, for his own reasons – and for which he may justly suffer.[23] Dodds also agrees with Snell[24] that (as I, too, shall argue later) even a man 'who takes on the yoke-strap of necessity' might have refused to do so.

However, the subsequent strongly expressed denials by Page and Lloyd-Jones of Agamemnon's 'freedom' or responsibility at Aulis have reopened the question and have resulted in a series of studies, most notably by Hammond, Lesky, Peradotto, and Edwards,[25] seeking to rebut or modify these denials in one way or another. Since, in any such recurrent debate, there must be much overlapping of arguments, I shall simply set down what appear to be the best reasons for qualifying, at least, the 'deterministic' views just summarized and limit further bibliographical references to points of particular indebtedness or disagreement. (Dover's study of Agamemnon's dilemma, to which reference has already been made, opens up a somewhat different line of inquiry and must be treated separately.)

With regard to the first of Page's points, there is, of course, no question of Zeus actually commanding the Atreidae to attack Troy as Page implies. Clearly they have their own reasons for waging this 'war for a woman's sake,' as the Chorus' references to criticisms (including their own) of the Atreidae on this very point indicate (see vv 456 ff, 799 ff). That the war is definitely part of Zeus' scheme of things as well, cannot, of course, be doubted in view of the Chorus' frequent allusions to the retribution exacted by Zeus ξένιος upon Paris and the Trojans (60–2, 362 ff, 367, 748): Peradotto in describing such passages as merely 'a religious interpretation of the Chorus' does them perhaps slightly less than justice. But Agamemnon in his own statement of his dread dilemma at Aulis (where he might be expected to make any possible extenuation for the awful choice he eventually makes) makes no allusion to his role as agent of Zeus ξένιος. Only when he has returned home victorious does he speak of the gods as having sent him (πέμψαντες, 853) to Troy in the first place. In the same speech he speaks of the gods as μεταίτιοι ('sharers', 811) with himself in bringing the Trojans to justice: a passage which vindicates Lesky's reference to 'a mutual and often indissoluble fusion' which he finds in Aeschylus as in Homer between freedom and divine intervention.[26]

Peradotto is surely right in his comment that there is 'little, if any, substantiation in the text' for Page's insistence (on the basis of vv 214 ff) that even if Agamemnon spares Iphigenia, the other commanders will not.[27] Besides (and this seems to me the more important point to make here), even if it *were* true that the other commanders would carry out the sacrifice against the King's will, this fact could not reasonably be regarded as *forcing* the King's decision, as Page suggests. The result, the death of Iphigenia, would, of course, be the same, but, from the standpoint of personal guilt and personal pollution of the King, it makes a great deal of difference whether he orders the sacrifice himself or refuses (at whatever cost to his military position) to order it.

With regard to the first of the 'linguistic arguments,' that the celebrated 'harness of necessity' which Agamemnon dons at v 218 further emphasizes his lack of free choice, I have already argued that Agamemnon may here be accepting simply the military necessity of the deed and all that must now follow from it for himself and his family if (as commander-in-chief) he executed it.[28] ἀνάγκη is not, in any case, quite so absolute a word, its circumstances not always so divorced from all possibility of human freedom, as Page would suggest. Note, for example, Euripides, *Phoenissae* 999 ff, where Menoeceus says it would be shameful indeed if free men, who were not bound by any constraint from the gods (κοὐκ εἰς ἀνάγκην δαιμόνων, 1000), should stand their ground ... while he (who was so bound by the oracle) should flee ... Lesky offers another interesting example, from Aeschylus *Suppliants* 478 ff, where there is room in Pelasgus' dilemma for personal and responsible decision as well as the pressure of ἀνάγκη and Ζηνός ... κότος ('necessity' and 'the anger of Zeus').[29]

The second of the 'linguistic' arguments mentioned above is that the words τάλαινα παρακοπὰ πρωτοπήμων ('dread madness, primal cause of woe') 'imply that Agamemnon is mentally deranged' and so bereft of the power of choice.³⁰ Lloyd-Jones compares Agamemnon's 'apology' at *Iliad* 19.86-8, for his reckless behaviour in provoking Achilles, in which he claims that 'Zeus ... put cruel *Atê* in my mind.' In the present instance, Lloyd-Jones argues, Zeus, determined that the fleet shall sail, enforces his will 'by sending *Atê* to take away his [Agamemnon's] judgment so that he cannot do otherwise.' (The identification of *Atê* and παρακοπά does seem to be justifiable in that παρακοπά does indicate the knocking aside of the wits which is precisely what occurs in *Atê*, a state of divine possession.)³¹ This is, perhaps, the most difficult argument to cope with in seeking to salvage Agamemnon's 'freedom' in the present context. In Aeschylus, even more than in Homer, the commission of any deed fraught with terrible consequences for the doer seems inconceivable without *some* element of divine infatuation. We have seen this in the case of Xerxes' fatal invasion of Greece in the *Persae*,³² in the case of Eteocles' self-destructive decision in the *Septem*,³³ and we shall see it again in the *Choephori* where Orestes will need the supernatural goads supplied in the 'great kommos' before he actually carries out the matricide.³⁴ However, in the case of both Xerxes and Eteocles in *their* plays, we should also note the element of human decision (driving ambition in the one case, military responsibility in the other), and certainly we shall find no difficulty in discerning the same element of personal decision in Orestes' speeches at *Choephori* 246-63 and 297-305. The same combination of personal decision and madness or supernatural compulsion is (as I have sought to establish) present in the case of Agamemnon's sacrifice of Iphigenia in the *Agamemnon*. However, the element of personal decision is not, perhaps, as important in the *Agamemnon*, since it is with the deed itself (already in the past) and its consequences for Agamemnon and for the whole house of Atreus³⁵ that we are here concerned.

Whether, as I have argued earlier, we seek to separate the 'free' (if dilemma-ridden) decision of Agamemnon from a kind of Fury which must possess him before he executes it or whether we regard the ambiguous blend of personal motivation and supernatural possession as essential to Aeschylus' view of any inconceivably awful decision must, in the end, be left to the reader's own responses to the poet's words.³⁶ Relevant to these two attempts to modify Lloyd-Jones' more intransigent position on the issue of Agamemnon's freedom is the 'compromise' (if I may so describe it) suggested by Mark Edwards.³⁷ Edwards' attitude to Agamemnon's responsibility at Aulis is similar to that of Lloyd-Jones, except that he replaces *Atê* by *Peithô*

(Persuasion) as the demonic power affecting Agamemnon's mind at the crucial moment. Comparing Agamemnon's situation to those of Xerxes and Eteocles, to which we have already referred, he finds each of these tragic figures to be in the grip of a divinely imposed temptation ('passion,' *erôs*, even, in the case of Eteocles, *Septem* 688); once he yields to it, *Atê* moves in to 'carry the disaster through to the end.' (It is along these lines that Edwards explains the difficult passage at *Ag* 385–6, where *Peithô* is called the 'child of fore-counselling *Atê*,' for *Peithô* is the agent of *Atê*, who has planned the destruction beforehand and then seizes the victim once he has succumbed to *Peithô*.)[38] An essential point in Edwards' exposition is the emphasis on the element of *vulnerability* attaching to each of these tragic figures: to Xerxes 'because of the great prosperity of Persia coupled with his own youthful impetuosity';[39] to Eteocles, because of the curse of Oedipus; to Agamemnon, because of the curse of Thyestes on the house of Atreus. For Page and Lloyd-Jones, the family curse in *Agamemnon* is the beginning of an inevitable sequence of events in which Agamemnon is, as it were, locked, from the start. Edwards' view of it as supplying a vulnerability, a predisposition, abetted by *Peithô*, to fatal choices, allows more significance to that momentous decision. (Edwards, rightly in my view, agrees with those critics who have argued that the audience has already been made aware, at this early stage in the play, that the crime of Atreus is weighing upon the King'.)[40]

Dover's treatment of Agamemnon's dilemma[41] seeks a new approach to our problem by replacing the assumptions that Aeschylus himself could have given an answer to the question of Agamemnon's 'freedom' or lack of it, and that he made this answer available to careful students of his play, with 'an alternate trio of hypotheses':

> first, that Aeschylus was well aware that in real life we cannot know the extent to which an agent was able to choose whether or not to commit a particular act; secondly, that in *Ag.* 104–257 he has portrayed realistically the manner in which people respond to the commission of an extraordinary and disagreeable act by a respected agent, and thirdly, that the aspect of Agamemnon's predicament which made the most powerful impression on his audience is an aspect to which modern interpreters of the play have seldom alluded even by implication.[42]

Stated in these general terms, the first two of these hypotheses (the third still remains to be expounded) strike one as reasonable, but some of Dover's arguments in support of them seem to go somewhat beyond the hypotheses themselves. Thus in discussing the Chorus' response to the 'extraordinary and disagreeable act' by the 'respected agent,' Agamemnon, he warns us against following the 'Christian and liberal tradition' that no individual should be unjustly punished or sacrificed as a means to an end. Dover skilfully illustrates the difficulty which the ancient Greeks (like sophisticated moderns) had in assigning guilt or responsibility, by such celebrated dramatic debates as that over Helen's adultery at *Troades* 945 ff and 987 ff and those over husband-murder and matricide, respectively, at *Agamemnon* 1468 ff and *Choephori* 910 ff; he concludes that the Greeks tended to assert or to deny responsibility depending on whether they were attacking or defending the person concerned. Dover then argues from this that all we can expect from the Aeschylean Chorus in this case is to find 'their treatment of the sacrifice of Iphigenia characterized by caution, doubt and ambivalence in everything that concerns responsibility for it as an *act*, contrasting with unambiguous revulsion from it as an event.'[43] At this point, the critic proceeds to include in his illustrations of the expected 'caution and ambivalence' in the Chorus' treatment of the whole 'sacrifice episode' such alleged omissions as the lack of explanation of Artemis' anger, the lack of reference to the alternative legend of Artemis' rescue of Iphigenia, and the lack of information as to whether the adverse winds actually changed after the sacrifice. It is hard to see how some of these allegations of 'omission' can be substantiated; with regard to the last, for example, the Chorus does tell us 'the arts of Calchas were not unfulfilled' (249) and with regard to the first, reasons *are* given for Artemis' anger, however inadequate *we* may find them. However, leaving this point aside, it is still more difficult to see what bearing these alleged obscurities in the Chorus' treatment have on the question of Agamemnon's 'responsibility.' This difficulty is resolved (though not in an entirely satisfying way) when we discover that in Dover's view the 'rightness' of Agamemnon's decision is somehow tied to the accuracy of Calchas' interpretation of the omen and the efficacy of the sacrifice (ie, the procuring of favourable winds). It is in this context that Dover interprets both the Chorus' and Agamemnon's prayers, 'may the good prevail!' (at vv 159 and 217 respectively): 'Agamemnon, too, (ie like the Chorus at v 159) hopes but does not know that the consequence of obeying Calchas will be good.'[44] (This, it appears, is the allegedly neglected aspect of the situation referred to in the third of Dover's hypotheses above.) So, too, the Chorus' 'relief' in contemplating the power of Zeus (at vv 160 ff) is taken to refer to their relief in recognizing that it is Zeus alone, not men, who decides how things will turn out, not to any optimism residing in the recollection (clearly stated at vv 176 ff) that Zeus has 'laid it down that knowledge comes through suffering,' and that, in this way, understanding comes to men, however much they may resent that suffering (cf 180–1). The surprising pragmatism of Dover's interpretation appears in his conclusion on this passage: 'Zeus has so constructed the universe ... that we cannot understand whether we are taking the right course until we have experienced the consequence of that course.'[45] Once again there is the implication that, as far as Agamemnon is concerned, the rightness or otherwise of his decision to sacrifice Iphigenia depends on its results.

Dover's emphasis on uncertainty as to the validity of Calchas' prophecy (nowhere, as far as I can see, justified by the text of the *Agamemnon*) is complemented by a demonstration, dependent on historical as much as poetic texts, on Greek uncertainty concerning the arts of divination, and their practioners, in general,[46] and the same preoccupation continues to dominate this critic's otherwise helpful account of the celebrated 'yoke-strap of necessity' passage.[47] On Dover's well-documented showing, ἀνάγκη ('necessity') is not an absolute term denoting irresistible compulsion; indeed he suggests that Agamemnon's predicament was beset with various necessities, 'all disagreeable or perilous,' of which Dover regards the necessity 'to subordinate one's own life and that of one's dependants to the common good' to be the overriding one, the one which 'most people with Greek values and presuppositions would regard as dictated by honour, justice and piety.' Dover supports this view with references to Teiresias' rebuke to Creon at Euripides' *Phoenissae* 922 for *not* being willing to sacrifice *his* son for the safety of the city, to Euripides' treatment of the sacrifice of Chthonia by Erechtheus (see fr 50, Austin, 14–21, 37–9), and to the use which Lycurgus (*Leocr* 98–101) makes of this story in addressing a jury. It is questionable, perhaps, whether the audience is expected to join in Teiresias' mild rebuke to Creon in the *Phoenissae*: Menoeceus himself treats his father more gently by waiting until he has left the stage before declaring his own patriotic refusal to avoid his ἀνάγκη (*Phoen* 999). Refusal to avoid such patriotic sacrifice of *oneself* might well have been regarded as the only honourable course by the Greeks (witness not only Menoeceus' martyrdom – and his exculpation of *his* father for seeking to avert it, *Phoen* 994–5 – but also that of Iphigenia in Euripides' *Iphigenia at Aulis*); however, Euripides' own treatment of Agamemnon's decision to sacrifice Iphigenia (including Menelaus' comments on it) reopens all the question of justification and motive (ranging, in *that* treatment, from patriotism down through personal ambition to ignoble fear of reprisal from vassal-kings) with which discussion of the famous dilemma seems to have been fraught from ancient to modern times. Nevertheless, Dover is justified at least in stressing the ambiguity of possible Greek responses to Agamemnon's dilemma. This he expresses well in the terms in which he rejects for the Greek audience Kitto's assurance that the sacrifice of a daughter was 'a price which a man of courage and sense would refuse to pay':

> I feel that many an Athenian in Agamemnon's place would have thought that courage and sense demanded that sacrifice; in Clytemnestra's place, he would have thought the opposite; and in the chorus's, he would have *felt* as they do and would have changed his *opinion* frequently about the claims of courage and sense.[48]

Even so, Dover's earlier assertions concerning the Chorus' 'caution, doubt and ambivalence' about Agamemnon's responsibility (attitudes which would presumably affect the audience's attitude as well) neglect the Chorus' reservations (62; cf 225–6) about Agamemnon's own motives in this war, as well as their horror not only at the sacrificial *event* but also at Agamemnon's choice in his dilemma (219–20). And with Dover's earlier allegations concerning the uncertain accuracy of Calchas' prophecies, and concerning the significance of this for the justification, or otherwise, of Agamemnon, I find it very difficult to agree.

NOTES

1 See above, chapter 1, pp 9–10. For Fraenkel's discussion, see vol II, pp 86–99 of his edition of Aeschylus' *Agamemnon*.
2 Fraenkel, II, pp 97–8, quotes in full Proclus' summary of the relevant passages from the cyclic epic, the *Cypria*. Cf also Soph *El* 566 ff; it seems likely that the further point mentioned by Sophocles, that Agamemnon shot the deer in Artemis' sacred grove, was also in the traditional version which Sophocles was following. A different version (of what antiquity we do not know) is given in Euripides' *IT* 20 ff and 209 ff, namely that Agamemnon had promised to Artemis the fairest fruit of one year's produce, which Artemis now claims to be Iphigenia, 'firstborn offspring of Agamemnon and Leda's daughter Clytemnestra,' *IT*

209 ff. This sounds as if (as Platnauer observes in his note to *IT* 20) Agamemnon had made his rash promise in the year of Iphigenia's birth.
3 Fraenkel, II, p 99.
4 Lloyd-Jones 'The Guilt of Agamemnon' p 189.
5 Ibid, p 190.
6 Peradotto 'The Omen of the Eagles and the ΗΘΟΣ of Agamemnon,' p 247.
7 Fraenkel, II, p 96.
8 Peradotto, 247-8. Lloyd-Jones has argued further (not very convincingly) that κτήνη ... δημιοπληθῆ ('the abundant herds of the people,' 129) really means (in prophet language) 'the herds that are the people.' (See 'Guilt of Agamemnon' p 189 and 'Three Notes on *Agamemnon*' p 76 ff. Even so, they are not specifically '*young* people,' which is what Peradotto's argument requires.
9 Kitto *Form and Meaning in Drama* pp 4-5.
10 Lebeck *Oresteia* pp 21-2.
11 Cf Whallon 'Why Is Artemis Angry?'
12 See Denniston and Page, Introduction, pp xxix ff.
13 This part of Page's view will be considered below, in the next section of this appendix.
14 Editors reading the imperative of the verb must also, of course, take καλά (referring to Artemis) as vocative, not nominative. Two mss readings (MV) actually favour this, since they do not include the article; editors reading the indicative (with all mss) must, of course, include the article with καλά (so FTr).
15 Zeitlin 'The Motif of the Corrupted Sacrifice in Aeschylus' *Oresteia*' p 464. Cf also Zeitlin 'Postscript to Sacrificial Imagery in the *Oresteia* (*Ag* 1235-37).'
16 See, for example, Zeitlin's discussion of προτέλεια, vv 65, 227, 721, at pp 464, 466-7, and of the 'lion-cub image' (vv 717-48), at pp 466-7 of the first of the two articles cited in the preceding note.
17 See, in Denniston and Page's edition, especially the notes on vv 160 ff and 184 ff. Contrast the novel (and much more 'optimistic') view of the πάθει μάθος passage at vv 176-8 in Neitzel's recent study, 'πάθει μάθος – Leitwort der aischyleischen Tragödie?' Neitzel's arguments, with which I regret that I am unable to agree, are discussed briefly below: see note 21 of this appendix.
18 Fraenkel *Agamemnon* II, p 112; see also pp 113-14 for the further citations of Fraenkel's views which follow.
19 Dover 'Some Neglected Aspects of Agamemnon's Dilemma' p 63.
20 Pope 'Merciful Heavens? A Question in Aeschylus' *Agamemnon*.'

21 Conacher 'Comments on an Interpretation of Aeschylus, *Agamemnon* 182–3.' Cf also Neitzel πάθει μάθος pp 283–7, whose reinterpretation of the πάθει μάθος passage at *Ag* 176–8, though it differs radically from any discussed so far, owes at least something to a concern aroused by Pope's pessimistic interpretation. Neitzel considers Pope's construing of vv 182 ff as a despairing question to be the logical consequence of the usual interpretation of vv 176–8, according to which suffering is taken to be part of the 'law' (*Gesetz*) here imputed to Zeus. Neitzel, however, rejects this usual interpretation on several grounds: that it is not repeated, as one might expect, elsewhere in Aeschylus or in ancient comments on him; that it implies (according to Neitzel) that Zeus has nothing in store for men but undeserved suffering, whereas, in fact, even the Chorus ends by agreeing with Clytemnestra that Agamemnon suffered justly for his sacrifice of Iphigenia; finally, that this interpretation is logically unsatisfactory in that it involves an intolerable combination of 'prescription' ('Learn etc') and penalty ('Suffer') for not learning in the same 'law.' These arguments (which, as my own interpretation shows, I do not find irresistible) lead Neitzel to propound the new view that 'Learn' is the law of Zeus, 'Suffer' the penalty for not obeying it.

22 See Denniston and Page, pp xxii–iv, xxvii–viii and nn to vv 213, 214, 218, 222; Lloyd-Jones 'The Guilt of Agamemnon' pp 191 ff. Cf Fraenkel's notes on vv 212, 213, but see also his notes on vv 218, 219, where marked differences from Page's view are to be observed.

23 Dodds 'Morals and Politics in the *Oresteia*' p 26. Fontenrose, a recent defender of the view that Agamemnon is not guilty of offending Zeus, would also do well to ponder Dodds' argument. In his article, 'Gods and Men in the *Oresteia*,' Fontenrose comes to the surprising conclusion that although Agamemnon's 'faults' lead to his doom, his offence and Clytemnestra's vengeance (merely 'allowed' by Zeus, according to Fontenrose) are purely human matters. (See pp 104–5; cf pp 80–4). This view seems to take little account of such passages as *Ag* 1485–6 (... διαὶ Διὸς / παναιτίου πανεργέτα 461–70, 1500–4, where the supernatural aspect of Agamemnon's 'punishment' is clearly indicated.

24 See Dodds, p 26 and his citation of Snell ad loc.

25 Hammond 'Personal freedom and Its Limitations in the *Oresteia*'; Lesky 'Decision and Responsibility in the Tragedy of Aeschylus'; Peradotto 'The Omen of the Eagles and the ΗΘΟΣ of Agamemnon'; Edwards 'Agamemnon's Decision: Freedom and Folly in Aeschylus.' Of these studies, Peradotto's is the most detailed and explicit in rebuttal of Page's arguments. Among the more recent articles on this topic, see

also Tsagarakis, 'Zum tragischen Geschick Agamemnons bei Aischylos'; cf n 26, below.
26 Lesky, p 78. Cf also Tsagarakis, pp 23 ff, who compares Aeschylus' treatment of Agamemnon's dilemma at Aulis with Homer's treatment of Odysseus' dilemma at the island of Thrinacia (*Od* 12.325–38). Here Tsagarakis finds a similar situation: 'choice' against a background of divine necessity (in the *Odyssey* passage, the necessity of dying from hunger if Odysseus and his men obey the gods, or of facing inevitable retribution from the gods if they kill the sacred cattle of Helios for food). The situations are not, perhaps, quite as comparable as the critic suggests, but he does make the interesting point that whereas Odysseus appeals to the gods in his insoluble dilemma, Agamemnon does not. Herein, thinks Tsagarakis, lies the root of Agamemnon's personal failure, of his *hybris* even, namely, that he undertakes to meet this crisis facing the expedition on his own, without seeking the help of the gods whom elsewhere both he and the Chorus regard as his allies (cf vv 813 ff, 362–4, 399–402).
27 Peradotto, p 254. Cf Denniston and Page, pp xxix, xxvii and n to p 214. Lloyd-Jones also puts much emphasis on θέμις (v 214), 'right in the sight of heaven,' in Agamemnon's alleged description of the other leaders' desire for the sacrifice. But even if Bamberger's emendation (⟨σφ'⟩) be sound, Agamemnon's statement may, in any case, be merely a (shaky) assumption on his part. Cf Fraenkel's comment ad loc: 'He knows that the task he has in hand may be necessary but it cannot possibly be θέμις.'
28 See above, chapter 1, p 14.
29 Lesky, p 79. Cf also Dover 'Some Neglected Aspects' p 65, who supports with further useful references his statement,' ἀνάγκη is applicable to any legal, physical or moral force to which resistance is shameful, painful, perilous or for any other reason difficult.'
30 Lloyd-Jones, p 191.
31 Cf also Dawe 'Some Reflections on *Atê* and *Hamartia*' pp 97 and 109, who also agrees with this identification.
32 Cf the Ghost of Darius' comment on Xerxes' deeds, *Persae* 739–42.
33 *Septem* 653–76: the whole of this speech of Eteocles must be read to appreciate the combination of supernatural and individual human motivation of Eteocles' decision.
34 *Cho* 306–465; cf my article 'Interaction between Chorus and Character in the *Oresteia*' where other views of the 'great kommos' in the *Choephori* are also given.
35 Cf Jones *On Aristotle and Greek Tragedy* pp 78–9, who, however, goes

to the other extreme in emphasizing the major importance of the afflictions of the house of Atreus as opposed to those of its individual members.

36 Cf Hammond, pp 44 ff and Lesky, pp 78–85, passim, esp pp 84–5, both of whom argue for some kind of blend of supernatural and personal responsibility in Agamemnon's decision. (Lesky also compares the situations of Eteocles and of Orestes in *Septem* and *Choephori*, respectively.) On the other hand, Jean Bollack has argued recently (*L'Agamemnon d'Eschyle*, 1, deuxième partie, 286–90) that the very submission to divine necessity (which, without qualification, he regards Agamemnon's enforced decision as being) brings with it, in the Greek view, an onset of madness or extreme daring. However, Bollack's reference to Theognis 193–6 (where the situation is very different from that of Agamemnon) does not provide impressive support for his view of the present passage.
37 Edwards 'Agamemnon's Decision.'
38 Ibid p 28.
39 To this reason I would add (though Edwards curiously does not) a further one: the mysterious divine prophecy hanging over the Persians to which the ghost of Darius alludes, *Persae* 739 ff, in the same passage in which he describes Xerxes' excessive eagerness.
40 Edwards, p 23 and n 28.
41 Dover 'Some Neglected Aspects of Agamemnon's Dilemma.'
42 Ibid p 58.
43 Ibid p 61.
44 Ibid p 63.
45 Ibid.
46 Ibid pp 63–4.
47 Ibid pp 65–6.
48 Ibid p 66, n 15. The passage which Dover cites from Kitto is from *Form and Meaning in Drama*, p 5.

APPENDIX TWO TO CHAPTER ONE

The entry of Clytemnestra, with particular reference to the attribution of vv 489–502

There has been considerable controversy over the attribution of the opening lines (489–502) of the second episode and, indeed, over the whole question of when Clytemnestra is on stage during the first 680 lines of the play. I find it difficult to accept the minority view (though it has been supported by several formidable scholars) that the Queen is not present during the Chorus' interrogation of her at vv 83–103.[1] Of this group, Oliver Taplin has given the most detailed consideration to Clytemnestra's movements (as to all other questions of staging) throughout the play. Taplin would postpone Clytemnestra's first entry until her exchanges with the Chorus-Leader at the beginning of the first episode at vv 264 ff; after that he keeps her busy with exits and entries, alternately, at 350 (while the Chorus-Leader addresses her retreating back at 351 ff), at 587 (to deliver her speech to the Herald), at 614 (where she leaves the Chorus and the Herald to complete the second episode on their own), at 855 (where, after arriving some forty-four verses late for the King's arrival home, 'she blocks the way, she occupies the threshold' to speak her words of welcome as Agamemnon is about to enter the palace).[2] At the other extreme to Taplin's envisaging of Clytemnestra's movements is that of Denniston and Page, who prefer to imagine Clytemnestra 'as constantly present, though often in the background' from v 40 or at the latest v 83 down to v 1068 (when she enters the palace to commit the murders).[3] A rough consensus of the more traditional views of editors and commentators[4] would have Clytemnestra enter at v 83 (when she is questioned by the Chorus); exit at v 354 (before the first stasimon but, Taplin to the contrary, *after* the Chorus-Leader's complimentary words to her [351–4] on the speech just completed); enter either at 489 (to speak the lines, 489–500, announcing the Herald's arrival) *or* at 587, or just before (to address the Herald); leave at 614 (after her address to the Herald; some, however, would keep her on right through to the end of the scene with Agamemnon); enter at 855 (to welcome the King); exit at 974 (to commit the murders).

This is not the place for prolonged debate on these issues. The high element of subjectivity in decisions on stage movements may be seen from the two extreme positions of Page and Taplin, each of them based on a clear theatrical conception on the part of the scholars concerned. Thus, Page regards 'the tension and power of the scenes, 503–37 and 615–80, [as] ... greatly enhanced by her presence, and particularly by her silence, throughout.'[5] For Taplin, Clytemnestra's constant and symbolic command of the door leading to the palace is one of the dominating conceptions dictating *his* decisions in this matter. Both conceptions show theatrical imagination; both face certain difficulties, Taplin's from the text (particularly in the case of vv 83 ff; possibly in the case of 489 ff), Page's from the point of view (as Taplin suggests) of normal fifth-century and especially Aeschylean practice. We shall content ourselves here with indicating arguments supporting Page's (and others') choice of Clytemnestra as the speaker of vv 489–503.

The mss indicate Clytemnestra to be the speaker of vv 489–500 with a change of speaker (Chorus) indicated at 501. The mss are, of course, no evidence for the original attribution (Fraenkel, in his note to 501, blames 'the later Middle Ages' for 'the nonsensical introduction of Clytemnestra at 489'). *Paragraphoi* marking a change of speaker (as at 501) 'must [Taplin admits] be allowed some textual authority through continuous transmission, though they are easily corrupted.'[6] Fraenkel dismisses the marking of the change of speaker at 501 as connected with the wrong attribution at 489. Page, in his note to 489 ff, reminds us that some support for two speakers is indicated by σοι at 496 and by the harsh asyndeton at 501, though these points are not compelling by themselves (even with Clytemnestra as speaker at 496, the ethic dative σοι has struck editors, including Page, as clumsy, and there are other 'harsh' asyndeta, besides that at *Ag* 501, in Aeschylus). So far, then, these slight indications that there may have been two speakers involved, with a change of speaker at 501, provide the main support of the mss attribution of 489–500 to Clytemnestra. Its rejection, then, depends on the alleged improbability of such attribution. Taplin's argument that entrance announcements are usually made by the

Chorus may be rejected.[7] Such announcements *by actors* are common in Euripides; there is one such in Aeschylus, at *PV* 941–3 (if *Prometheus Bound* is by Aeschylus, which Taplin, among others, doubts);[8] there may well have been others in the numerous lost plays. (Taplin's further objection, namely to the sharing of an entry announcement between two speakers, also seems negligible; the entry announcement [for the Herald] is completed before v 501.)

However, if Clytemnestra does speak vv 489–500, she has presumably remained on stage during the first stasimon (355–487); otherwise she must have entered unannounced (Taplin would have her exit at v 350) during the epode (475 ff) or else just before the speech at 489 ff. Denniston and Page, as we have seen, keep her on stage throughout the first stasimon and Taplin's arguments against this are by no means compelling. First he has argued that in other cases (eight out of a possible twenty-two) where an actor remains on stage during an ode, 'either the actor is made relevant to the song ... or there is a dramatic consideration which keeps him on.'[9] On examination, however, some of these 'relevancies' and 'dramatic considerations' are no more special than such as may be found for Clytemnestra's presence. It could be argued, for example, that there is an ironic effect gained by having Clytemnestra present in the background as the Chorus sing (460 ff) of 'the gods watching out for those guilty of much bloodshed' and 'of the black Erinyes setting at naught the man who is prosperous without justice.' More cogent still, perhaps, is the fact that at vv 590 ff Clytemnestra herself makes a pointed and sarcastic allusion to previous expressions of doubt about her too-credulous female heart for believing in the beacon-message. The epode of the first stasimon (475–87; note especially 483 ff) is the only passage after the actual description of the beacon-message where such doubts have been expressed: apparently Clytemnestra has heard them. (A somewhat similar argument for Clytemnestra's presence during the first speech from the Herald is made by Denniston and Page, viz, 'that when Clytemnestra begins her speech at 587 *she already knows that Agamemnon has arrived at Argos* [559]' – news which has been imparted by the Herald.)[10] These various dramatic considerations seem to me to outweigh both Taplin's objections to having Clytemnestra present during the first stasimon and his further objection that this would also offend against the normal exit of an actor before a choral ode. (Exceptions to the latter convention are admittedly less common than the presence of an actor during a choral ode. Nevertheless, they *do* occur; Taplin lists seven such instances in extant tragedy, three of them — *PV* 525, *Suppl* 624, *Persae* 622 – in Aeschylus, though in each case Taplin finds 'justifications' of the anomaly.)[11]

NOTES

1 See Fraenkel *Agamemnon* note to vv 83 ff and references there given; Taplin *The Stagecraft of Aeschylus* pp 280–1; recently, Mastronarde *Contact and Discontinuity* pp 101–3. In his argument that Clytemnestra need not be on stage during the Chorus' questioning of her at vv 83 ff, Taplin cites passages in two other parodoi (Sophocles *Aj* 134 ff and Euripides *Hipp* 141 ff) where the Chorus apostrophize characters who are off stage. Neither of these passages offers a reasonable parallel to the one under consideration. At *Ag* 83 ff the Chorus ask the Queen specific and urgent questions about activities (the supervision of sacrificial fires) with which she is, one would judge from the questions, presently engaged, and urgently request an answer (97 ff) in order that their own fears might be allayed. Both the *Ajax* and the *Hippolytus* passages cited are clear cases of apostrophe of an absent person. No questions at all are asked in the long anapaestic passage in *Ajax* (*Aj* 134–71); the questions which do follow at *Aj* 172 ff, like those at *Hipp* 141 ff, are clearly the conventional rhetorical questions which the Chorus often ask concerning the source of their master's or mistress' troubles. The Queen's failure to answer the Chorus' questions has also sufficed to convince Fraenkel and others (see Fraenkel's note to 83 ff) that she cannot be on stage. This argument has been developed by Mastronarde who, while admitting the difference in tone between the Chorus' questions here and in the passages cited by Taplin, argues, in effect, that the very urgency of the Chorus' question makes the Queen's failure to answer the more inexplicable if she *is* present. I would say, on the contrary, that this only makes the Queen's silence the more effective. Characteristically, she bides her time until she is ready to speak – and until the dramatist finds it appropriate, for the parados must be sung in ignorance of the victory at Troy.
2 Taplin *Stagecraft* pp 280–308.
3 Denniston and Page *Agamemnon* p 117, note to 489 ff.
4 Detailed bibliographical references to these views are provided in Taplin's discussion (above, n 2).
5 Denniston and Page, p 117.
6 Taplin *Stagecraft* p 294.

7 Ibid p 295; cf pp 268–9. At *Suppl* 180 ff, Danaus provides the only preparation for Pelasgus' entry at 234.
8 Ibid, appendix D, pp 460 ff. Cf also Griffith *The Authenticity of 'Prometheus Bound'* and (for a summary of the arguments, pro and con, on this matter) Conacher *Aeschylus' Prometheus Bound: A Literary Commentary* appendix 1.
9 Taplin *Stagecraft* pp 288–9; cf pp 110–14.
10 Denniston and Page *Agamemnon* pp 116–17 (note to 489 ff).
11 Taplin *Stagecraft* p 110.

CHAPTER TWO

Choephori (*The Libation Bearers*)

1 Preliminary comment

The action of the *Choephori* ('*The Libation Bearers*') concerns the deed of vengeance on Clytemnestra and Aegisthus, that necessary purification of the house of Atreus which Orestes must perform with Electra to vindicate their father and restore the house to its true succession. Thus the *Choephori* is a sombre and terrifying play, for the vengeance, however justified, involves the deed of matricide, an act more polluting, more certain to call forth the outraged powers which support the laws of nature, than any of the deeds of Agamemnon and Clytemnestra that precede it. Aeschylus was more aware than either of the other Greek tragedians who also treat this theme of this aspect of the vengeance of Electra and Orestes. Thus the *Choephori* is the darkest of the three plays of this trilogy. The *Agamemnon* begins with the King's triumph and end with his bloody overthrow; the *Eumenides* begins with the horror of the Furies' pursuit of Orestes and ends with his vindication, along with a new dispensation of justice to end such blood-feuds. In between, the *Choephori* grapples with the dilemma of an ordained and necessary vengeance coupled with unspeakable pollution. For more than half the play, darkness and horror (the horror both of the deeds which have gone before and of those to come) predominate. Only toward the end is the light of justice and of restoration allowed to overcome this darkness (though there have been a few anticipatory gleams) and, in the final moments, even this light is quenched as the Furies (invisible as yet, save to Orestes) drive the matricide in madness from the scene.

The first half of the play (up to the end of the 'great kommos,' 306–

478, and the series of iambic invocations which follow it) is concerned with marshalling all the motivations and forces (human and supernatural) for the undertaking and execution of the dread deeds of vengeance. These motivating forces come in part from the avengers themselves, in part from the Olympian gods, specifically Apollo, and the laws of retributive justice which they uphold, but most of all from the spirit of the murdered Agamemnon, whose power still sleeps beneath the earth until the invocations of Orestes and Electra can arouse it. Thus, much of the early action of the play is directed *downwards*, to secure the allegiance of Agamemnon and of the infernal powers in general, both as destroyers and renewers of life in the world above.

2 Prologue, parodos, and first episode (vv 1–305)

Hermes-of the-earth, you who watch over the father's realms below, be now my saviour and my ally as I pray to you. For I have come and make my return from exile [κατέρχομαι] to this land. (1–3)

This opening invocation to Hermes χθόνιος and the Aeschylean pun on κατέρχομαι (the literal meaning, 'descend,' blending with the technical and contextual meaning, 'return from exile') give initial emphasis to this downward direction, which is to dominate the action until the actual murder plot begins.[1] Through Hermes, messenger from the living to the dead, Orestes cries out to his father buried in the tomb by which he stands and makes his offerings of two locks of hair, one a 'nurturing lock' to the life-giving river Inachos (river-gods are included among chthonic powers), the other a 'grieving one' to his father's spirit. Thus at the outset, both grief and hope of renewed life are present in the avenger's prayer.

As he speaks, Orestes catches sight of the Chorus of Libation Bearers entering by the parodos at the right side of the orchestra. Do their black robes presage 'some new woe upon the house' (13)? Or are they bringing libations as appeasements (μειλίγματα, 15) to the dead beneath the earth? (Ironically, Orestes will be proved right in both his guesses.) The sight of Electra (whom Orestes instantly recognizes) with the Chorus vindicates for him his second guess. With a cry to Zeus to aid him in his vengeance, Orestes withdraws, with the silent Pylades, to eavesdrop on this supplication at Agamemnon's tomb.

The Chorus, after an initial stanza of conventional lamentation, sing (32 ff) of a terrifying night-time vision, followed by a scream of fear, which has shattered the peace of the women's quarters in the palace. Priestly interpreters, they tell us, have blamed the anger of the slaughtered dead for this apparition and now ('O earth, our nurturing mother!') 'that godless woman' (Clytemnestra) has sent them with this bootless offering[2] as appeasement. The Chorus fear even to tell their tale: 'for what cleansing can there be of blood once shed upon the earth?'[3] The strophe ends with a series of dark, oppressive images:

> O suffering home! O ruined house! Sunless shadows, hateful to men, now cover it entirely – for the master of the house is dead. (49–53)

Gloom answers gloom in the antistrophe (54–65). Awe, instinctive and irresistible, the proper due of Agamemnon's majesty, has been replaced by stark fear of the usurper, Aegisthus. Consolation comes with reflections reminiscent of those of the Chorus in the *Agamemnon*: either soon or late, Justice overtakes prosperity unrightly won.[4]

The last strophic pair recapitulates the theme of 'blood once shed' which grows stiff and will not melt away.[5] Once again the life-giving aspect of earth is stressed ('blood drunk by nourishing earth ... '), a grimly ironic reminder that this process may be reversed by chthonic vengeance, if life itself is violated by man. The irreversibility of bloodshed is thrust home by the startling image of defloration ('when man once violates the bridal bower there is no cure,' 71–2) which interrupts the Chorus' account of the pollution which no purifying streams can wash away. The ode ends with a reminder from the Chorus of their own servile position: they are but captives in the house, powerless themselves to inflict the vengeance which their song has portended. This provides Electra, herself the chief libation bearer, with her cue for speech, for, as we shall see, the young avengers in this play are to rely heavily on the tutelage of the older slave-women.[6]

To each scene in the *Choephori* belongs its appropriate action. The little passage (84–151) between Electra and the Chorus which precedes the recognition scene is easy to underestimate amid the more strikingly dramatic or emotional moments of the play. But we should remember that this *is* the libation-bearing scene (and here we readers do lack the element of spectacle); it is here that the propitiatory offerings sent by the Queen are first turned against her. The ultimate horror of the matricidal intent which underlies this 'perversion' of Clytemnestra's perverse offerings and the steely resolve it will require for execution will, in due course, receive greater emphasis – all the more so for being all but suppressed by the minor key of Electra's first utterances. For what we notice most about this Electra is the gentle and tentative nature of her approach to the grim situation thrust upon her. Her first speech opens with a series of timid questions to the Chorus, culminating in the question whose fearful irony she hardly dares express:

> Am I to ask this, the customary prayer of mortals, that equal requital be given to those sending these offerings, a gift to match their ... evils? (93–5)

So too, in the dialogue which follows, it is to the Chorus that Electra turns for the words she hesitates to say herself:

> – What am I to say? O teach my inexperience!
> – Pray that some god or mortal come against them –
> – As judge, do you mean, or as one who inflicts justice?
> – Say simply, someone who'll take life for life!
> – But is it pious for me to ask this of the gods?
> – How is it not pious to requite one's enemy with ills? (118–23)

Electra begins her libation-prayers with invocations, like those of Orestes – to Hermes χθόνιος, to the powers (δαίμονας, 125) beneath the earth, to Earth itself, 'who bears all things and having nourished them receives again the produce [κῦμα, an effectively pregnant metaphor] of her off-spring.' (127–8: once again the double function of the chthonic powers, to create life and to receive it in death, is recognized, though it is the deathly aspect of the cycle which is here celebrated). The particular form of Electra's prayers continues the tentative, almost innocent, approach we have already noted: 'that Orestes may return with happy fortune' (138), 'that I may be more sober in my counsels [σωφρονεστέραν πολύ, 140] than my mother, and in deed more pious,' and 'that against your enemies, O father, an avenger may appear and justly requite the murderers with murder.' (142–4). Neither the mother nor the avenger is specifically mentioned in these careful prayers and Electra's innocent tones with regard to Orestes and herself must undergo a change before the vengeance will be fulfilled.[7] Nevertheless, the function of the libation scene has been accomplished: Clytemnestra's propitiation of the dead has been transformed to prayers for vengeance on her, an intent which is sealed by the sequence of bitter images of reciprocity (ἴσ' ἀντιδοῦναι ... δόσιν γε τῶν κακῶν ἐπαξίαν, 94–5; ὅστις ἀνταποκτενεῖ, 121; τὸν ἐχθρὸν ἀνταμείβεσθαι κακοῖς, 123; καὶ τοὺς κτανόντας ἀντικατθανεῖν δίκῃ, 144, which we have noted, in various contexts, throughout the scene.

A brief lyric stanza (mixed dochmiacs and iambics) divides the two parts of the first episode as the Chorus add their prayer to the libations at the tomb. They too pray for the coming of an avenger; like Electra, they do not name Orestes as that avenger and so prepare for the 'revelation' of the returning hero in the coming scene.

The artificial and improbable 'tokens' of Aeschylus' 'recognition scene' in this play have been much discussed. The recognition is prepared for and effected by the use of three formal devices: Electra's discovery of a lock of hair like to her own laid on Agamemnon's tomb; the discovery of a footprint nearby which also fits her own; finally, when Orestes appears and declares himself, the showing by Orestes of a piece of clothing which Electra herself had woven for him as a child. Let us be content to accept these three devices for what they are: three formal and perhaps traditional recognition tokens, not intended to be logically 'convincing,' but perfectly well suited to the non-realistic and in many ways symbolic *êthos* of this play.[8]

Two or three further points in Aeschylus' treatment of the Recognition should, perhaps, be briefly noted. The tentative quality which we have noted in Electra's early utterances in this play is maintained in the dialogue with the Chorus in which she presents her first 'evidence' of Orestes: it is the Chorus who is led actually to name Orestes (177) as the possible (if distant) donor of the lock of hair. Electra's further thought that Orestes himself might still be far away (180) and the Chorus' mournful comment on it (181–2) provide, with just the right touch of anticipation, for the minor reversal of Orestes' self-revelation in the second part of the scene. Finally, and perhaps most significantly for our appreciation of the dramatic single-mindedness of this version of the Orestes theme, Orestes indulges in *no* cries of joyful recognition and warns Electra also of the danger of such demonstration: 'For I know that our dear kinfolk (in the palace) are our bitter enemies' (234). Electra is allowed a brief but restrained (iambic) expression of rapture at her brother's return ('O blessed sight, who must for me be father, mother, sister, brother, all in one!') and even this is quickly blended with a prayer for vengeance ('May Power and Justice with Zeus, the mightiest of all, be with you now!' 244–5).[9] Orestes' own answering speech (246 ff) takes its cue from this clausula as the recognition scene blends smoothly into the first preparations for the major action of the play.

The two speeches of Orestes (246–63; 269–305) which conclude the first episode are of considerable importance both to our interpretation of the long kommos which follows and to our understanding of Orestes' own 'motivations' in the action of the *Choephori*. In the first of these Orestes makes his formal appeal to Zeus for aid in the restoration of his father's royal house. Clearly this restoration will involve the murder of the usurpers (obliquely referred to, perhaps, in the ambiguous expression θήραν πατρῷαν, 251 discussed below), but such is the precise economy of this play that we are not yet ready for the actual working-up of Orestes (or of ourselves) to the actual deeds of bloodshed. Rather, the emphasis is on the deprivation of the dispossessed children of Agamemnon: 'starving hunger oppresses the bereaved, not strong enough, as yet, to carry to the nest their father's prey' (249–51).[10] Nor is the Aeschylean Orestes above an appeal to Zeus' own self-interest: the reminder (reminiscent of Eteocles' similarly 'archaic' prayer at *Septem* 271–8; cf 77) that if Zeus fails to restore the children of Agamemnon the offerings which he used to receive from Agamemnon will also remain unrestored. Thus, this prayer from 'the brood of the eagle' (αἰετοῦ γένεθλ', 258: a reminiscence of the regal imagery of the *Ag* 49 ff, cf 114–38)[11] stresses both the weakness of the would-be avengers (as Electra's earlier utterances have done) *at this point in the play*, and the personal or 'selfish' motivation of Orestes (as distinct from familial and supernatural ones) in the coming action.

In the second of his two speeches, on the other hand, Orestes stresses the insistent orders of Apollo's oracle (along with his own confidence in the god's support) to take vengeance on his father's murderers. Indeed the compulsions laid upon Orestes 'if I do not pursue in the same manner, life for life, those guilty of my father's death' (273–4) are recounted in the strongest possible terms: loathsome physical afflictions springing from malignant nether powers (ἐκ γῆς δυσφρόνων μηνίματα, 278) and other penalties (ἄλλας προσβολάς, 283) from the Erinyes of his father's blood,[12] including madness and exile, exclusion from feasts and altars. The full list of horrors included in Orestes' quotation of the Oracle is clearly designed to indicate the weight of supernatural compulsion on the prince and so to exonerate him, in advance, from the unnatural deed of matricide. Orestes may indeed have his own reasons for committing the crime (and these are to be repeated in a moment), but we must also see that, in terms of this compulsion, he also has no real choice but to do it. This compulsion on Orestes from the nether powers is the other side of the coin of Orestes' own use of those powers to aid him in the execution of the murder.

The final passage in this second speech sums up and blends together the complex motivations, personal, familial, and supernatural, which impel Orestes.

> Should I then trust such oracles? Even if I do not, the deed must still be done. For many desires move me toward one end: the commands of the god, my great grief for my father, my own lack of substance and the wish that my most illustrious fellow-citizens, sackers of Troy famed for their spirit, remain not subject to this 'pair of women.' For his [Aegisthus'] is a woman's heart; if not, we'll soon find out.
> (297–305, reading εἴσομαι [Hermann] at 305).[13]

The preliminary action of the play is now completed; the first tentative approaches to the nether powers have been made by each of the major figures involved (by Orestes, by Electra, and, with ironically reversed effect, by Clytemnestra); the Chorus has hymned the awful effects of 'blood once drunk by nourishing earth'; the returned Orestes has been recognized and has formally avowed himself as Avenger. The first stage in the avenging itself now begins with the kommos at vv 306–478, the long song and (on the Chorus' part at least) dance with the Chorus, Orestes, and Electra perform about the tomb of Agamemnon.[14]

3 The 'great kommos' (vv 306–478)

There have been over the years numerous conflicting interpretations of the meaning and dramatic purpose of the 'great kommos' of the *Choephori*. Recent studies (beginning, perhaps, with Reinhardt's excellent discussion of this kommos[15] and ending, for the moment, with Lebeck's work on the *Oresteia*)[16] have for the most part corrected certain extreme arguments which tended to emphasize one feature or another of this passage to the exclusion of all else. Wilamowitz' view[17] that the main function of the kommos was to bring Orestes' inner struggle to the awful decision of matricide has now been properly refuted in several studies. As we have seen in our résumé of what precedes the kommos there is no doubt in the mind of Orestes or of the audience that he has decided, for his own reasons as well as those imposed on him by Apollo, to fulfil the deeds of vengeance. Wilamowitz' extreme treatment of the kommos as a moral struggle for the decision of Orestes led to extreme reactions such as those of Schadewaldt, who, despite his long and complex analysis, tended to subordinate everything in the kommos to its climax, the evocation of the powers of the dead to help in the implementation of Orestes' decision.[18] This view misses something of the real dramatic progression. However right it may be about the end result of the kommos, the uncomfortable fact remains that, as we shall see, much of the earlier part of it is not immediately concerned with calling on the spirit of Agamemnon for vengeance.

Albin Lesky[19] attempted a compromise between these two extreme positions. He rightly sees that the varied songs of the kommos are designed to affect now the spirit of the dead King and now the emotions of his living avenger. But more basic to his argument (and in the end less convincing) is his attempt to distinguish between Orestes' decision before the kommos as one forced on him by Apollo and his decision as a result of the kommos as one entirely integrated with his own will. What goes on outside the kommos, he suggests, is essentially what Aeschylus received from the tradition and is, indeed, all that is needed for the actual plot (Handlung) or action of the play. What is contained within the kommos provides the essential tragic material for this reason:

> Ein Orestes, der blind dem Gebote des Gottes gehorcht, als sein Werkzeug die Tat vollbringt und dann von dem Gotte gegen ihre Folgen geschützt wird, kann nicht der Gegenstand tragischen Geschehens sein, am allerwenigsten in der Dichtung des Aischylos.[20]

The chief difficulty facing Lesky's view, that in the kommos alone is Orestes' human and personal desire for vengeance aroused, is provided, as Lesky himself sees, by the lines (297-305) immediately preceding it. Here, as we have seen, Orestes clearly states his own personal will to vengeance, in accordance with his own desires, even (as he tells us) if he did not believe in the threats of the oracle. Lesky provides strenuous but not quite convincing arguments to discredit the authenticity of these lines; if we do still accept them, he suggests, the best we can do is to regard them as a sort of prelude to what is essentially the material of the kommos – surely rather a desperate effort to preserve the kommos as the only repository of the human aspect of Orestes' decision. Nor, in my opinion, is this aspect of the kommos as prominent as Lesky suggests.

More acceptable, because it is less categorical, is Reinhardt's insistence on 'mourning becomes revenge' ('Klage wird zu Rache') as an observable process of the kommos which is central to its dramatic meaning. His view coincides with that of Schadewaldt in that he recognizes that the question how, not the question whether, the deed of vengeance is to be done remains the main emphasis of the kommos; however, he is subtler than Schadewaldt in his realization that the kommos is at first concerned with mourning which becomes a part of the deed of vengeance as the avengers gather power from one another and from the avenging spirits beneath the earth.[21] Lebeck agrees with Reinhardt in her assessment of the final result of the kommos but she attributes to it more concern than would Reinhardt (or the present writer) with 'the whole process of Orestes' decision,' which she regards as being 'acted out' in the kommos. (The fact that Orestes has already, before the kommos, expressed this decision is dismissed by Lebeck, in this context, on the somewhat dubious ground that such considerations of temporal priority are irrelevant to the discussion of lyric passages.)[22]

In one or another of these studies, the principal meanings of this kommos have no doubt been expressed. What still needs to be discussed is the process: the actual lyric-dramatic development of the kommos by which these meanings are expressed and the interaction between its elements which gradually fuses these meanings into a single climactic act.

After an opening series of anapaests (306–14), the form of the first part of the kommos (314–442) falls into four lyric triads, the first three of which are followed by a series of marching anapaests by the Chorus. The stanzas are sung in strict alternation: Orestes, Chorus, Electra, choral anapaests, etc, till the fourth triad where there is no anapaestic conclusion. Throughout this part of the kommos the Chorus undoubtedly leads and even directs the thoughts and emotions of the other two singers, until near the end where, suddenly, it is the Chorus who loses confidence. In its opening anapaests, the Chorus calls on the Moirai to accomplish Zeus' Justice[23] and intones the ancient story of slaughter for slaughter and δράσαντι παθεῖν (the doer must suffer). The first two lamenting cries from Orestes and Electra (315ff, 332ff) amount to little more than plaintive attempts to reach the shade of Agamemnon. To each cry, the Chorus' reply leads the singer firmly toward the business on hand. Orestes' contrast of the realm of light with the darkness of the tomb (319) is answered by the assurance from the Chorus (324) that even in death the mind lives on; to Orestes' remark that praise-laden lament is a grace to the house (320–2), the

Chorus adds that lament leads to *justice* (330).[24] So, too, Electra's 'tomb threnody' (334-5) is converted, in the euphoric mind of the Chorus, into a victory paean (343) to sound throughout the royal halls. In each case, the poet's emphasis on the Chorus' dynamic redirection of Orestes' and Electra's utterance is made clear by the Chorus' exploitation of the words and images just used: Orestes' tentative offer, σκότῳ φάος ἀντίμοιρον (319) answered by ἀναφαίνεται δ' ὁ βλάπτων (328); Orestes' γόος εὐκλεής (321) answered by γόος ἐκ δίκαν ματεύει (330); Electra's ἐπιτύμβιος θρῆνος (334-5) answered by ἀντὶ δὲ φρήνων ἐπιτυμβιδίων παιὰν ... (342-3).[25]

The avengers, responding but slowly to the Chorus' lead, express (each in turn) an 'impossible wish': Orestes, that his father had been slain at Troy and left a glorious name (348-53); Electra, that not Agamemnon but his slayers had perished as he actually perished, that is, at the hands of their own *philoi*. Again, the Chorus converts these unpromising laments to something more positive. To Orestes' 'impossible wish,' they add: '(even so), illustrious [ἐμπρέπων, 355] are you now among your friends who perished gloriously ... for you were a King ... ': a reminder that, even murdered, the King is still a power beneath the earth.[26] So, too, the Chorus corrects Electra's wishful prayer:

> Fine things you utter, for yours is the power [δύνασαι γάρ, which could imply 'It's easy to wish!' or, possibly, 'you can make the wish come true']. For now, the blow of this double scourge on the earth reaches its mark. Even now are there helpers ... 'neath the earth. ... To the children belongs the vengeance.[27] (374-9, in part)

Thus does the Chorus seek to involve the avengers with the nether powers and to transform their wishful prayers to action. 'Like an arrow,' the last admonition of the Chorus reaches Orestes' ear (380-1): from this point on, the increase in metaphors signals the quickening pace of the kommos. At last the avengers begin to catch the Chorus' fire. First Orestes (382ff), then Electra (394ff), calls on Zeus to send his vengeance. First Electra (394ff), then Orestes (405ff), calls on the powers of the underworld to aid in the righting of injustice. Still the Chorus remains a step ahead, leading the avengers on. When Orestes calls on Zeus to send a late-avenging *Atê*,[28] the Chorus already pictures itself as singing a victorious death-dirge over (specifically) 'the man slain and the woman destroyed' (386-9). In the same passage, it is the relentless will of the Chorus which evokes the poet's strongest image: 'Before the prow of my spirit blows the piercing wind of my resolve' (390–2).[29] And when Electra calls on Zeus, Gê, and the chthonic powers for justice, the Chorus reminds her almost sharply (ἀλλὰ νόμος μὲν ... 400ff) that 'blood once shed ... demands another deed of blood.'

We have observed in the case of the Clytemnestra-kommos in the Agamemnon that toward its end the Queen has almost reversed the attitude to her murderous deed which she took at the beginning. We may note a similar, though less extreme and significant, shift in the position of the Chorus toward the end of the triadic part of the present kommos.[30] As the royal pair is gradually brought to more specific and aggressive prayers for vengeance, the Chorus betrays for the first time its apprehension. Its imagery flutters between despair ('My heart [σπλάγχνα] grows dark as I hear your words,' 413–14) and hope ('then, in turn, hope uplifts me and sweeps away my sorrow, as it dawns brightly upon me,' 415–17) as it ponders the dreadful action to come. Electra's song, on the other hand (a violent contrast to her gentle prayer at vv 140–1), becomes more specifically threatening:

> Fawning there may be but these woes are not to be softened. For savage is our spirit, like a wolf, proof against the fawning of our mother.[31]
> (420–2)

With a sudden change of metre and theme, the Chorus bursts into a violent spate of lamentation, in lyric iambics, which anticipates the direct appeals to the dead King at the end of the kommos. The 'clenched fists, blood-bespatterings and flailing arms' of this passage (423–8) suggest the violent movements of the accompanying choral dance. Electra, now that the dread word μάτηρ has been mentioned (422), can aim her accusations directly at her mother, as she and the Chorus in turn (429ff, 439ff) describe the insulting burial and mutilation of Agamemnon. Orestes responds (434ff) to this goad from Electra with his first clear promise, in the kommos, of vengeance by his own hands:

> πατρὸς δ' ἀτίμωσιν ἆρα τείσει
> ἕκατι μὲν δαιμόνων
> ἕκατι δ' ἁμᾶν χερῶν;   (435–7)[32]

Electra and the Chorus, in turn, apply this goad of shameful mutilation to the spirit beneath the earth:

Hearing these woes of yours, ⟨father⟩, write them on the tablets of your mind. [Electra, at v 450]

Let this tale reach your ears [pondering it] with the soft tread of your mind ... Now, with wrath unblunted, must you return. [Chorus, 451–2; 455]

Thus, with the Chorus still leading, each element contributes to this common arousal (which finally includes the dead King himself) of vengeful emotion. Orestes' final cry, Ἄρης Ἄρει ξυμβαλεῖ, Δίκᾳ Δίκα ('Violence shall fall upon Violence, one Justice shall clash with another Justice,' 461), illuminates the whole antithetical theme of the trilogy; Electra adds her prayer for justice from the gods; the Chorus (after a brief shudder of horror [463] at the kin-violence it has itself helped arouse) sings its own conclusion, first mourning the unbearable deeds inflicted on the house (466ff), then celebrating, in the antistrophe (471ff), the vengeance which the house itself will execute with equal bloody violence.

It is surely wrong to view this kommos either as, simply, an invocation of the spirit of Agamemnon or as, simply, an arousal of Orestes to the deed of vengeance. Certainly it is more the former than the latter, as its climax shows. Nevertheless, the dynamic quality of the kommos and the real dramatic progression which it manifests prevents us from taking any simple view of it. It has been argued that because Orestes has already, before the kommos, expressed his determination to take vengeance, no further encouragement is needed. But there is a difference between logical choice and the emotional impetus which the deed itself requires, and a tragedy which is totally concerned with this awful matricidal vengeance quite properly presents each in dramatically different terms. Moreover, the working up of Orestes and of the spirit of Agamemnon to vengeance is all part of the same operation. This tripartite kommos, with its shifting pattern of lament and urgency, of horror and vengeful imprecation, and with its blend of lyric and dramatic elements, is an ideal instrument for this complex arousal of the living and the dead.

4 Second episode and first stasimon (vv 479–651)

In the three lines of marching anapaests which supply the concluding frame to the great kommos, the Chorus has called upon the 'blessed chthonic powers' (μάκαρες χθόνιοι, 476) to send the children of Agamemnon help for victory. This is the cue for Orestes and Electra to begin their actual goading of the dead King to action in an extraordinary iambic sequence (479–509) comparable, in its vigour, to the almost bullying appeal of the Danaids to Pelasgus in *The Suppliants*. Paradoxically, though it is Agamemnon who is to be avenged, all manner of inducements are showered upon him to arouse his spirit's powerful aid. To the traditional bribe of sacrificial offerings (484–5; compare the similar prayer to Zeus at vv 255–61) are added reminders of past indignities ('Remember the fatal bath, father!' 491; 'Remember the net ... !' 492), and the inducement of restored glory through the reinstatement of his offspring (503–4) is aptly summed up in Electra's vivid 'corks image':

> For children of a hero slain are saviours of his fame, even as corks hold up a fishing-net, sustaining cords which stretch from depths below! (503–7)

One further supernatural element must be provided before the avengers are ready for specific plans. This is the omen, the gods' guarantee about the future such as was provided for the Trojan expedition by the portent of the eagles feasting on the pregnant hare (*Ag* 109 ff). It is for this that the detailed reading of Clytemnestra's dream, already sketched in lyrical terms by the Chorus (32–41), has been reserved, to provide that final touch of divine assurance (for 'dreams are from Zeus') as the spirits of vengeance have now been brought to the brink of action. The Chorus (through its Leader) is the appropriate reporter of the dream which first occasioned the propitatory libations it has carried from Clytemnestra. When Orestes hears the details of this dream (the birth of a serpent to the Queen, its biting of the breast that fed it), he is finally ready for action:

> Now I, the dragon-portent here made manifest [ἐκδρακοντωθείς] will slay her, even as this dream declares! (549–50)[33]

In a play so deeply concerned with *arousal* for the commission of 'impossible' deeds, and with the necessary evocation of supernatural powers, it is to be expected that the practical aspects of its execution will be kept to the minimum. The actual planning, which now ensues, for the murder of Aegisthus (the disguised entry of Pylades and Orestes as Phocian strangers seeking hospitality; the despatch of the usurper by Orestes as soon as – and wherever – he sees him) is simplicity itself; for the murder of Clytemnestra, the main and the only dreadful event, there is, significantly, no plan at all.

The preparatory action of the play is now completed. Orestes is ready but the audience have still to be prepared to accept Clytemnestra as a fit victim of matricide. This function the Chorus now fulfils in the first stasimon (585–651) with a terrifying review of monstrous females of mythology engaged in various deeds of familial violence.

The ode begins with a bold, imaginative description of nature's monsters ($\delta\epsilon\iota\nu\acute{\alpha}$): ' ... dread spawn of the earth, seas teeming with horrid beasts, skies ablaze with fearful, flashing fire ... ' But far worse (we hear in the antistrophe) is the pride of men and especially the passions, capable of anything ($\pi\alpha\nu\tau\acute{o}\lambda\mu o\upsilon\varsigma$), of reckless women, 'partners with the spirits of vengeance which prey on men.'

> For passion, loveless passion [$\alpha\pi\acute{\epsilon}\rho\omega\tau o\varsigma\ \check{\epsilon}\rho\omega\varsigma$], mastering the female,
> defeats the paired unions of men and beasts alike! (599–601)

This grim prelude prepares us for the series of specific mythological horrors to follow: three deeds of female passion involving various forms of familiar murder. In the second and third of these examples (612–22; 631–8), the motives, as well as the lethal females and their familial victims, remind us of Clytemnestra and her deed: greed led hateful Scylla to cut off the fatal lock from her father's (Nisus') head; jealousy caused the ghastly slaughter by the Lemnian women of their husbands (631–4). But the first of the Chorus' three mythological examples, dread ($\tau\acute{\alpha}\lambda\alpha\iota\nu\alpha$) Althaea's deed of vengeance (602–11), suggests more subtle and complex dramatic applications:

> ... death-plot by lighted fire-brand which the dread, child-destroying daughter of Thestius planned, consuming with fire that tawny branch, her son's co-eval from the moment of his natal cry, fresh from his mother's womb ... ' (604–11)

In the myth here allusively treated, Meleager was doomed to die when a certain hearth-log was consumed by fire; Althaea his mother (daughter of Thestius), in fury at her son for slaying her brother in battle, hurled the log in the flames. Thus, while this tale of another familial murderess recalls Clytemnestra, as do the other examples, the relationship of murderer and victim, so starkly emphasized by Meleager's natal cry, also anticipates, in ironic reversal, the coming matricidal situation between Orestes and Clytemnestra.

Murders maternal, filial, and conjugal: in the midst of this grim gallery from myth, the bloody deed of Clytemnestra is (according to the traditional sequence of our text)[34] suddenly obtruded:

> And since I have called to mind these bitter deeds, 'tis not untimely[35]
> that I mention that loveless marriage, hateful to the house, and the
> fell plans of a wife against a warrior husband. ... (623–7)[36]

The final strophic pair (639–51) provides a magnificent coda to these paradigms of horror crying for retribution. As often in Aeschylus, strong metaphors abound to express in concrete form what to us are abstractions. The strophe sets out the general law: the smiting of the impious by the sword of justice. In the antistrophe, the imagery assumes a more immediate relevance ('sword-avenging Fate prepares her weapons,' 647) and the agent of Justice and of Fate, now both subsumed in the figure of the Avenging Curse, is at last specified:

> In time, the famed Erinys, pondering deep, presents to the house a son [τέκνον][37] to pay for the pollution of bloodshed done of old. (648–51)

So much by way of general comment on the first stasimon, at least as it has been received (with numerous textual uncertainties) in the traditionally accepted text of the play. There remain, however, certain problems raised by the Chorus' choice of mythical *paradeigmata* (in relation to ostensible purpose of the ode) and to their arrangement, to which the foregoing summary has not done justice.

To consider the second of these two points first (since it has been the more frequent cause of scholarly concern), it is puzzling that mention of Clytemnestra's deed (which would appear to be the point of the mythical comparisons) interrupts the three exempla. As T.C.W. Stinton has observed, 'When a series of mythical examples is invoked, the point to be illustrated always comes before or after them, or both – never in the middle.'[38] It is for this reason that Preuss, followed by several editors (and supported, rightly, I think, by Stinton) reverses the order of the third strophe (623–30) and antistophe (631–8), so that the third mythological example will precede the reference to Clytemnestra's deed. Various attempts, none I think successful, have been made to defend the traditional sequence.[39] Holtsmark, for example, in an otherwise excellent comment on this ode, has argued that 'the gnomic [585–601] – paradeigmatic [602–38] sequence is designed to prove the validity of the definition of τὸ δεινόν which the Chorus offers (633f.) in support of its tacit exhortation to Orestes to exact vengeance from his mother.'[40] But (as Stinton rightly insists) the point of the mythological series is to invite comparison (in terms of horror) with *Clytemnestra's deed*; it is this, rather than the example of 'impiety punished' (Holtsmark's account of the allegedly climactic Lemnian example)[41] which leads to the justification, at the end of the ode, of the coming vengeance of Orestes against his mother.

The other problem (or, at least, point of inquiry) which has been raised concerning this ode concerns the choice of the first two mythological examples. As Anne Lebeck has well observed, 'since neither is a case of illicit passion [which, as Lebeck has already noted, might have been expected from the preceding antistrophe], or a husband's murder, the resemblance to Clytemnestra's crime is slight.'[42] Lebeck provides a subtle explanation, convincing at least in some respects, of this apparent discrepancy. She suggests that the stories of Althaea and Scylla have a double function or, to use her phrase, are 'operative on two levels.' Besides their immediate relevance as women's crimes against the family, they 'give back a looking-glass reflection of the parallel crimes committed by Agamemnon and Orestes, reversed in such a way that woman's treachery comes to the fore each time.'

> The crime of Althaea [Lebeck continues] is the inverse of that act which Orestes left the stage to commit ... At the same time, since a parent slays a child, the myth is relevant to the murder of Iphigenia by her father. The crime of Scylla exactly reverses the relationship of the previous paradigm ... instead of father slaying daughter, daughter slays father. And, in that it is the murder of parent by child, this myth parallels the murder of Clytemnestra by her son.[43]

Taken together [Lebeck later concludes of the three mythological examples], they play upon the various combinations of kin murder which beset the seed of Atreus.'

I have quoted above what I regard as the more unassailable part of Lebeck's subtle arguments. With regard to her account of the third mythological example, that of the 'Lemnian horror,' 'in which crime follows crime and one generation pays for another's wrongs,'[44] I feel less confidence. Lebeck cites Herodotus 6.138 to remind us that the Lemnian atrocities continued 'when the Pelasgians of Lemnos murdered the Athenian women whom they had carried off along with the children borne them by these women.' But if the Chorus (or the poet) is seeking to recall this latter-day 'punishment' at vv 635–6 it does so most obscurely,[45] and moreover, the later generation which 'pays' is not the offspring of the Lemnian women but the abducted wives of the Pelasgians and *their* children. And Stinton is right to point out that Lebeck's secondary levels of meaning for the three mythological examples do nothing to support the traditional order (which Lebeck has sought to defend) of the third strophe and antistrophe: 'In the highly traditional forms of Greek poetry, the rhetorical pattern of a passage must reflect in the first place its primary surface meaning.'[46]

5 Third episode (vv 652–782)

The two brief scenes which now take place before the murders are as apt in their placing and as skilful in their execution as anything in Aeschylus. In the first, Orestes, disguised as a Phocian stranger and accompanied by Pylades, reports to Clytemnestra the 'death' of Orestes. In the second, Orestes' childhood Nurse, dispatched by Clytemnestra with a message for Aegisthus to return home, is persuaded by the Chorus to adapt the message to suit the plans of the conspirators. Both scenes abound in dramatic irony which must be quietly played, since those who know the truth must keep their excitement well in check. These tense yet low-key dramatic moments provide an effective contrast to the overt excitements of the preparatory action (the long, exhausting kommos, the iambic goading of the dead King to aid in vengeance, the terse exposition of the actual murder-plot). They also provide by their tone (in the genteel hypocrisies of the exchange between 'the Phocian stranger' and Clytemnestra and in the Nurse's homely reminiscence about Orestes as a babe) a grimly ironic contrast to the murders soon to come.

The ironies begin, perhaps, with Orestes' thrice-repeated knocking (τρίτον τόδ', 655) at the door, for any sensitive member of the audience must be aware by now of the significant use of triplicity (and especially of triple blows!) in the *Oresteia*.[47]

> Let someone in charge [Orestes cries] come out – a woman overseer or, more suitably, a man. For in conversation the respect one owes a women [αἰδώς: the word for 'awe/shame' which is later to stick in Orestes' throat as he is about to slay his mother][48] makes one speak obscurely. (663–6)

So 'introduced,' as it were, Clytemnestra – the woman of manly counsels, as she has been called earlier in the trilogy[49] – makes her first appearance in this play. Ironies (unconscious and conscious) answer Orestes' ironies:

> Strangers [she replies to Orestes' plea for shelter], we have whatever hospitality requires – warm baths, soft bedding and the presence of candid eyes. But if you have business requiring more counsel, then that is matter for my husband, with whom I share this realm. (668–73)

The first irony ('Strangers,' as a greeting including her own son) is, of course, unconscious; the second, mention of 'warm baths' as a part of Clytemnestra's hospitality, is, presumably, the poet's and not the Queen's,[50] but it is hard to imagine that the suggestion of women's inadequacy in counsel could pass quite ingenuously through Clytemnestra's lips!

The casual tone of the 'stranger's' message from Strophios the Phocian ('If you happen to be going to Argos in any case, remember, in all decency, to tell his parents that Orestes is dead – don't forget now!') and the throwaway ironies of his clausula ('I don't know if I'm speaking to those in charge [τοῖς κυρίοισι, 'generalizing masculine'], but his parents ought to know,' 688–90)[51] are all expertly handled, giving the lie to those who believe that Aeschylus is above, or else not capable of, the minor details of dramatic polish. The same sureness of touch shows in Clytemnestra's reply. Her speech allows for two kinds of irony: first, the poet's own, when he has Clytemnestra accuse the family curse (τῶνδε δωμάτων Ἀρά) of Orestes' supposed death (692–9); second, Clytemnestra's own, when she pretends grief, in typically rhetorical style, that the only hope of release from the Curse has now perished ('Now set down Hope, the house's only doctor in its mad revelry, as quite deserting us,' 698–9).[52] At the end of the scene, the 'messenger's' conventional regret for his bad news and Clytemnestra's conventional reassurances ('A friend to the house, no less, for all your news!' 708) are similarly exploited for ironic effect, and Orestes gains his entry to the house peacefully, there to await the return of Aegisthus.

A series of choral anapaests (719–29) separates the Orestes-Clytemnestra scene from its complement (in the first murder plot), the scene between the Chorus and Orestes' Nurse.

> O sacred earth and revered funeral mound now covering the royal corpse of that leader of the ships, now hear! ... (722–5)

Thus does the Chorus preserve from the earlier action of the play that awareness of chthonic power on which the success of the action depends. More topically (for the Chorus is about to embark on a special piece of pleading), it calls on Peithô (goddess of Persuasion) to come down to its aid[53] and for chthonic Hermes, a dark ($νύχιον$) and guileful god, to guide the undertaking.

The 'Nurse scene,' unobtrusively 'naturalistic' like the preceding episode,[54] serves several different though related ends. Most obvious, of course, is its function in the plot; the Chorus, here affecting through its leaders the dramatic action to an unusual degree,[55] persuades the Nurse to bid Aegisthus to come home *without attendants*, to hear the news. But the Nurse also provides in her rambling chatter an unconscious commentary on the preceding scene. There we have witnessed Clytemnestra's 'grief' at the news of Orestes' death. Now the Nurse, our only 'inside' witness, testifies to the Queen's secret and unnatural joy ('hiding laughter behind her eyes,' 738–9) ... and so alienates us further from her. Again, in the preceding scene, we have seen a full-grown Orestes deceiving his mother as the first step toward murdering her. Now we hear from the Nurse of another Orestes, a helpless babe, witless and innocent, a slave to its belly, fit only to be nourished like an animal.

The Nurse's real grief for Orestes is born of her nurture of him:

> The various woes of old on this house of Atreus all mixed together, all
> hard to bear, have pained my heart. But never have I endured pain
> like this. The others, though grievous, were bearable, but dear Orestes,
> the exhaustion of my days, whom I received from his mother and
> nourished ... (744–50)

Thus the Nurse provides an element of tenderness notably lacking in the exchange between the real mother and her son. The contrast prepares us, perhaps, for the minimizing of the maternal relationship by Apollo and Orestes in *Eumenides*.[56]

The Chorus-Leader's words at the end of this scene let in the first glint of light in the dark situation. When the Nurse questions the sanity of her new instructions, the Chorus-Leader hints that Zeus may send 'a changing wind from evils' ($τροπαίαν ... κακῶν$, 775): an image which has been used earlier in the trilogy for a crucial change of another kind, and which is to be repeated in slightly different form in the following ode.[57] Hope ($ἐλπίς$), which in the preceding scene has been used only in a savagely ironic sense by Clytemnestra (698–

Choephori (The Libation Bearers) 121

9), now takes on a positive meaning (776-7) as the Chorus-Leader gives the Nurse at least veiled assurance that Orestes, 'hope of the house,' may still be living.

6 Second stasimon (vv 783-837)

A brilliant and difficult ode (mainly in the trochaic metre, well suited to its exhortations) precedes the entry of Aegisthus and the fulfilment of the murder plot. The ode falls into three parts, each part (a strophic pair, divided by a mesode) containing a separate theme. The first part (783-99) is an exhortation to Zeus alone; the second to the household gods (800 ff), to Apollo (807 ff), and to Hermes (812 ff). (Hermes, as we have been reminded at the beginning of this play, is the most 'chthonic' of the Olympian gods, but even Apollo is addressed – 'dweller in the great cavern,' 807-8 – in such a way as to recall the association of his oracular seat at Delphi with the chthonic powers: an anticipation, perhaps, of the Pythia's celebration, at the beginning of the third play of this trilogy, of the peaceful transference of their gift of prophecy to the god of light.) The third part of the ode (819-37), on the other hand, ends with an exhortation to Orestes himself, the third and most essential element in this vengeance shared by Olympian, chthonic, and living human power.

This ode, unlike the preceding stasimon, provides a sudden wealth of imagery, as the Chorus makes final prayers for the success of the vengeance and then begins to anticipate its triumphant fulfilment. In each part of the exhortation, the images are suited to the theme. The prayer to Zeus (which includes, as before, the reminder that Zeus himself will be rewarded – triply so, in fact – for his aid)[58] ends with a complex but vivid metaphor for the danger of madness from which only Zeus can save the matricide:

> Know, then, O Zeus, that the orphaned colt of that beloved hero [Agamemnon] is yoked to a chariot of woe! As he runs, set such rhythm and measure to his pace as will ensure his safety, so that we may see his straining gallop o'er the plain end in success! (794-9)[59]

In the second part of the ode, the prayers to Apollo and to Hermes evoke suitably contrasting metaphors of light and darkness around which so much of the play's imagery revolves. To Apollo, the Chorus pray directly:

that our hero's house may in prosperity look up once more, and that the light of freedom may look on him with friendly eyes, out of her veil, (809–11)[60]

In the prayer to Hermes, a wind metaphor (' ... may Hermes help with favouring wind ...' 812 ff), picking up the optimistic image noted at v 775, is followed by an obscure passage prophesying that Hermes wearer of the cap of darkness (implied at v 818), will, if he wishes, bring to light many secret matters (815 ff). Uncertain as the text is at this point, it is clear at least that Olympian brightness is balanced by chthonic murkiness (though whether the 'dark word' of v 816 is that of Hermes or the Chorus we cannot be sure). This, too, fits the context, for it is in this central passage of the ode that the Chorus has voiced the trilogy's recurrent fear. 'Wipe out with fresh slaughter the blood of ancient deeds!' it beseeches the household gods (804–5). But, like Clytemnestra in her wishful covenant with the family curse at *Agamemnon* 1568 ff, it prays, too, that ancient bloodshed (γέρων φόνος) may not breed yet more bloodshed for the house (806): even in the midst of this prayerfully optimistic ode, the doubt returns, which is not to be resolved until the third play of the trilogy.

In the final part of the ode, the Chorus revives its 'song of the favouring wind' (οὐριοστάταν ... νόμον, 821–2) as it pictures itself raising a victory chant for Orestes. Then, suddenly dramatic, it addresses the hero himself, on the very brink of matricide. Bidding him cry 'Πατρός' ('of the father!') to his mother's cry of 'Τέκνον' ('child!' 829), the Chorus anticipates with a flash of prophecy both Orestes' final exchange with his mother (eg, at vv 924–5) and Apollo's defence of the matricide in the trial scene of the final play.[61] 'Take to *your* heart the heart of Perseus!' it advises (831 f). Like Perseus (though with cause more terrible), he must not look upon the Gorgon whom he slays.[62]

7 Fourth episode (vv 838–934) and third stasimon (vv 935–72)

The two brief speeches of Aegisthus before he enters the palace to meet his doom are again fraught with two-edged irony. Aegisthus' hypocritical lament for the house 'already sore with wounds' (843) anticipates his own imminent condition, while his image questioning the report of Orestes' death (' ... frightened words from women leap skyward soon to die,' 845–6) suggests joy rather than the fearful apprehension he here imputes to Clytemnestra.[63] When the Chorus-

Leader (again unusually 'busy' in Orestes' interests) bids Aegisthus enter and learn from the man himself, Aegisthus complies, with the assurance that *his* 'quick-eyed mind' won't be deceived.

Hard on the Servant's announcement (*thrice* repeated, once again, 875–6) of the murder of Aegisthus comes the dramatic climax of the play, the scene between Orestes and his mother. Clytemnestra enters first. 'The dead are slaying the living, I tell you!' cries the Servant. The Queen's reactions are characteristic. Quickly 'reading the riddle' with no further aid, she declares first her awareness (acceptance even?) of the necessary sequence of events ('By guile we perish, as by guile we slew!' 888), then her readiness to grapple with it ('Bring me an axe, someone, and quickly too!' 889). 'Now let us see whether we conquer or are conquered. For that's the point of evil we have reached!' (890–1). We are reminded of the same brisk alternatives thrown down by Clytemnestra to the citizens after her murder of Agamemnon.[64]

The confrontation between Orestes and Clytemnestra, which now ensues, is the most formal of scenes, and properly so. In the words of Orestes earlier, 'Ares will fight Ares and Justice Justice' ("Αρης "Αρει ξυμβαλεῖ, Δίκᾳ Δίκα, 461), and almost every line in this prelude to the deed of vengeance echoes this precise reciprocity. Aeschylus seems concerned to show, in this way, the deed of Orestes as the inevitable balancing of Justice, free of any taint of personal or passionate involvement, such as rendered the function of Clytemnestra as familial ἀλάστωρ more than a shade ambiguous.[65] To Orestes, on the other hand, only one moment of personal feeling is vouchsafed by the dramatist, and that, too, for the sake of mitigating the personal shame attaching to the matricide. When Clytemnestra claims his mercy in respect for the mother's breast which nourished him, Orestes hesitates (he has not been armoured as we have by the Nurse's revelations about his infancy) till Pylades, speaking his only words in the play, reminds him of his oaths and of the primacy of Apollo's oracle.[66] From this point on, pleas, defences, and threats are all alike precisely parried by Orestes: Μοῖρα for Μοῖρα, gain for gain, betrayal for betrayal, death for death. In a sense, Orestes 'wins' each of these exchanges, but the repeated element of *lex talionis* in his prosecution reminds us that requital in these terms calls for like requital. Clytemnestra's final threat of a mother's vengeful Furies Orestes can parry, but not avoid, by mention of his father's Furies (924–5), an equally dread alternative. Under the 'old dispensation' of justice in this play, Orestes, however justified himself, now becomes as vulnerable as Clytemnestra was, and it is this, as well as the justification and the inevitability of Clytemnestra's death, that the precise reciprocity of these final exchanges is meant to convey.

After Orestes has driven Clytemnestra into the palace to join Aegisthus in death, the Chorus swings into a song and dance of triumph, the free-wheeling dochmiacs, in contrast with the tighter trochaic rhythms of the preceding two odes, sustaining throughout the mood of liberation. The ode begins with a reminiscence of one of the choral themes of the Agamemnon: just as justice, in the long stretches of time, fell on Priam, so also 'the two-fold lion, the two-fold Ares has come to the house of Agamemnon' (Cho 935–8), but now it is Orestes and Pylades who substitute for 'the yoked strength of the Atreidae.'[67] Throughout this song, the avenging powers of the dead, so prominent in the earlier invocations of this play, are left unmentioned. Apollo in the first strophe, Δίκη (Justice), daughter of Zeus, in the first antistrophe, and Apollo, again in the second strophe, are celebrated as the all-powerful helpers of Orestes.[68] The mesodes (942 ff; 961 ff) between the strophes, with sharp imperatives and vivid imagery ('Shout out in triumph ... !' 942. 'Rise from your long sleep, O house!' 963–4) provide a lively contrast to these panegyrics. This emphasis on Apollo as opposed to Orestes' darker allies finds its justification in the final antistrophe. Apollo is the purifying god. Fears of the old bloodshed breeding fresh bloodshed[69] are pushed aside: 'Soon all-accomplishing time will pass through the doors of the house when, by curse-expelling cleansings, it casts out every strain' (965–8).[70] The ode ends with a cheerful image of the Chorus seeing clear horizons 'beneath the smiling face of fortune' (969), as it proclaims again the victory over the usurpers.

8 Exodos (vv 973–1076)

The last scene of the *Choephori* provides a spectacle reminiscent of the final appearance of Clytemnestra standing over the corpses of her victims in the *Agamemnon*. Now it is Orestes who is revealed standing over the bodies of Clytemnestra and Aegisthus: the grim parallel between the two finales is given a further theatrical emphasis by Orestes' display of the blood-spattered bath-robe which had functioned both as an enfolding trap and as a winding-sheet for the murdered King at the end of the first play. We are to see yet another display of crimson robes, equally spectacular but no longer horrifying, at the end of the trilogy.[71]

The scene provides both a finale to the theme of vengeance and a prelude to fresh retribution: the hero's vaunt over the dead gives way to the cries of a fugitive, as Orestes becomes, in the end, the prey of his mother's Furies. In between, Orestes seeks with desperate urgency to justify his deed before the gods and before his fellow-citizens.

Orestes, then, begins strongly, with bitter ironies at the expense of the victims lying before him:

> A fine pair they were before, as they sat on their thrones, and a loving couple they are still ... They swore to murder my poor father and then to die together. They swore well. (975–7)

There follows a long passage describing with lurid imagery the bloody death-robe of Agamemnon which Orestes bids his servants hold aloft. The terms in which this murder-device is described ('a net for beasts, a bath – or coffin? – robe,[72] nay a hunting-net, a snare, you might call it, or else a robe to wrap around one's feet,' 998–1000) recall the net imagery of the *Agamemnon*, both in the earlier passages where the Chorus speaks of the 'enslaving net of destruction' (μέγα δουλείας / γάγγαμον, ἄτης παναλώτου, *Ag* 360–1) cast on Troy and in Cassandra's later descriptions of Agamemnon's net of death ('a net of Hades? aye, but 'tis the wife who is the snare' (δίκτυον ... Ἅιδου; ἀλλ' ἄρκυς ἡ ξύνευνος ... *Ag* 1115–16). So, too, the savage description of Clytemnestra which follows ('a slimy sea-creature, or a viper' (μύραινά γ' εἶτ' ἔχιδν', *Cho* 994) reminds us of Cassandra's terms for the Queen, 'a crawling amphibian or some Scylla lurking among the rocks,' *Ag* 1233–4).

The point of Orestes' descriptions both of his monstrous mother and of her bestial murder-net appears in Orestes' appeal to the Sun God, Helios, to bear witness of his just pursuit (984–9). Just as Orestes' deed is unnatural (the Sun God is, traditionally, expected to abhor unnatural deeds)[73] so to exonerate it he must show how much more monstrous was the deed which he avenged.

A vivid image at the beginning of Orestes' final speech (1021–43) announces the first onslaught of the Furies:

> ... for, like a man driving his team of horses far off-course, I know not where it will end. So, too, my wits, beyond my control, carry me away and overmaster me.[74] Fear sits ready at my heart to sing and dance to the tune of wrath. (1021–5)

Here Orestes begins a dramatic race with madness: a race to plead the justice of his deed, this time to the people of Argos, while yet his wits remain (1026 ff). The appeals to Apollo's orders – and to Apollo's threats – which follow (1029–33), and the hero's preparations to seek Apollo's shrine at Delphi, by the god's command, are further anticipations of the play to come. Just as the preceding ode has thrown more and more of the onus for the deed upon the gods, so too, before the assault of the Furies begins, Orestes as 'human agent' seeks to withdraw still further under the protection of Apollo. The Furies become visibly present to Orestes in the final dialogue with the Chorus-Leader (' ... females like to Gorgons, sable-stoled, entwined with many dragons ... ' he calls them, 1047–9), and finally they drive him from the stage (1061–2).

In the Chorus' clausula (1065–76), 'wind-image' again marks the new change of direction which the trilogy has taken. 'Now this third tempest [τρίτος· ... χειμών', 1066] has blown itself out in these royal halls.' The ending is uncertain, as befits the ending of the second play in the trilogy:

And now, from somewhere has come the third one in the series ...
a deliverer? or am I to say a doom [μόρον]? O when will the fury of destruction be lulled to rest and cease? (1073–6)

NOTES

1 The opening verses of the *Choephori* are missing from the mss, which begin with v 10 in our editions. How many verses are missing we cannot, of course, be sure, though Turyn (*The Manuscript Tradition of Aeschylus* 18, n 22) expresses the view that this Prologue was not a long one. Vv 1–5 are retrieved by two (possibly consecutive) quotations from our play (of which the first, vv 1–3, is given above) in Aristophanes' *Frogs* 1126 ff, 1172 f; vv 6–7 are quoted by a Scholiast on Pindar, *Pyth* 4.146. Aristophanes makes comic play of two ambiguities in the first three verses: πατρῷ' ... κράτη (which *could* refer either to Orestes' father's domains or to Hermes' father's, ie Zeus', powers among the dead) and κατέρχομαι (which the Aristophanic 'Aeschylus' defends as not redundant after ἥκω because it means both 'come' and 'return from exile' in the present context). See (as well as the editions, especially Tucker's appendix I, pp 244 ff), the recent and interesting article by Garvie, 'The Opening of the *Choephori*.' Tucker (in his opening note)

and Garvie believe (with some justification) that there was a statue or some other conventional visual representation of Hermes either at the burial mound (Tucker) or before the palace door (Garvie): cf also v 583 (= v 581 in Tucker's edition) where τούτῳ may refer to Hermes thus visually represented. See also Trendall 'The *Choephori* Painter,' who observes that Hermes is represented in one, and possibly three, of vase depictions of the scene at the tomb of Agamemnon, though this is not, of course, *proof* of his presence in effigy (for which Trendall also argues) in the play.

2 τοιάνδε χάριν ἀχάριτον ἀπότροπον κακῶν ... (42–3). The expression is reminiscent of one of Aechylus' favourite word plays: cf ἄχαριν χάριν at *Ag* 1545; χάρις ἄχαρις, the reading of the mss at *PV* 545, corrected by Triclinius to ἄχαρις χάρις and by Headlam (perhaps rightly) to χάρις ἁ χάρις. In the present passage (*Cho* 42) ἀχάριτον is Elmsley's by no means certain correction of M's reading ἄχαριν (cf Sidgwick's note ad loc).

3 A recurrent theme, of course, in the earlier parts of this trilogy; cf, for example, *Ag* 1017 ff, for one of the most fearsome expressions of it.

4 Again, this is a theme which is prominent, in another context, in the *Agamemnon*: cf *Ag* 750–81. The precise meaning of the present passage (*Cho* 61–5) is admittedly obscure; cf Booth 'Aeschylus' *Choephori* 61–5' for a good summary of various views. Booth rejects the predominant interpretation (paraphrased above) that the passage expresses a sort of temporal declension as to when (in the vigour or in the twilight of life, or in death) Justice will overtake the unjustly prosperous; however, Booth's own interpretation depends on the somewhat dubious sense, in the context, which he gives to ἐπισκοπεῖ (viz, 'helps') in v 61. (Substantially the same arguments about *Cho* 61–5 are repeated by Booth in a later paper, 'The Run of Sense in Aeschylus' *Choephori* 22–83.'

5 Cf Lebeck *The Oresteia* pp 98–101, who marks this image of clotted blood (at vv 66–7), together with the image describing the Chorus as 'frozen' by secret grief (at v 83), as signalling the third in a series of ring compositions encircling the three themes of this ode. However, only in this last instance does there seem to be a clear relation between the topics signalled by the alleged ring composition and the last of the three themes (ritual grief, despair at one's destiny, wish for just vengeance) which the critic describes as comprising the structure of the ode.

6 It is generally assumed (from the Scholiast onward) that the Chorus of slave-women are captives whom Agamemnon brought home from Troy. This is nowhere actually stated (the Scholiast's own inference seems to spring from a gross misinterpretation of ἀνάγκαν ... ἀμφίπτο-

λιν at v 75), and it may seem strange to a modern reader that women captured by Agamemnon should be so keen to assist in his avenging. Against this, however, we must set the fact that Cassandra in the *Agamemnon* also is presented as a staunch defender of the King. As Sidgwick notes (Introduction p xvii), it is a convention of Greek tragedy 'that the household slaves ... should identify themselves with the fortunes of the house' and perhaps this is not much more illogical in the case of Trojan slaves than of any other captives.

7 Cf the interesting comments of Kamerbeek, 'Prière et Imprecation d'Electre,' who also notes Electra's hesitation at making a prayer involving matricide. Kamerbeek observes that at v 118 the Chorus advise Electra to pray for a god *or* a mortal to come and that Electra interrupts with a distinction between 'a judge [and] a bringer of justice.' Kamerbeek finds support in these lines for reading δίκην (M), at v 144 (instead of Scaliger's more generally accepted emendation δίκη), which he takes as subject of ἀντικακτανεῖν (Scaliger) – delayed for the sake of surprise (for Orestes might be expected to be named as the avenger).

8 There would seem to be little point in reviewing the numerous discussions about, attacks on, and tortured 'defences' of the recognition tokens mentioned in this scene in terms of their 'probability,' relevance, authenticity, etc. (Few scenes in Greek tragedy have occasioned as much absurd ingenuity on the part of classical scholars – admittedly, for the most part, of past generations. My own favourite discussion is that of Tucker, who begins by asserting, with magnificent Victorian male chauvinism, 'If she [Electra] is convinced by evidence which, however defective, satisfies herself, she is after all acting as women habitually do' [p lxv of his edition] and then goes on to give a point-by-point 'defence' of the reasonableness of the recognition tokens whose persuasiveness he has previously attributed to Electra's intuitive feminine reactions.) Good summaries of the various scholarly interpretations and arguments for interpolation (particularly with regard to the 'footprint' clue) will be found in Lloyd-Jones 'Interpolations in *Choephori* and *Electra*' and in Roux 'Commentaires à l'*Orestie*' (see pp 42–56 on *Cho* 164 ff). Lloyd-Jones admits the probability of certain minor lacunae in our text (eg, following vv 208 and 229) but resists major excisions with the (to my mind sensible) conclusion that the fifth-century audience would be tolerant of such improbabilities as are involved in the footprint scene, especially if they were a part of the traditional story (p 176). Roux provides elaborate circumstantial and psychological explanations for, respectively, the 'embroidery' and the 'hair' clues (in the latter case, Electra is thought to be already convinced herself and to be pro-

viding corroborative evidence, the fortunate similarity in the colour of the hair, to convince the Chorus); the absurdities of the so-called 'footprint clue' Roux disposes of by arguing that it is not a 'recognition clue' at all: somewhat improbably (in the context) taking μετρούμεναι (209) in the metaphorical sense of 'followed with the eye,' he imagines Electra simply to be describing the direction and termination of the footprints as she paces along beside them. It is an ingenious but not, in the end, convincing explanation, which is not helped by the fact that Electra herself speaks of the footprints as 'a second clue' (δεύτερον τεκμήριον, 205). Further authentication of all of Aeschylus' 'recognition clues' would seem to be provided by Euripides' apparent parody of them at El 520-44.

9 I read σοι at v 245, Stanley's correction for μοι, the reading in M. σοι clearly fits the context better but in rejecting μοι we are not really rejecting a *lectio difficilior*, since the conventional prayer which this couplet expresses would more usually, ie in most contexts, beseech such help from Zeus and Δίκη for the *speaker*.

10 The expression θήραν πατρῴαν (the generally accepted correction of M's θήρα πατρῴα, 251) can mean 'spoil such as their father once carried off,' as several scholars (eg, Tucker, Sidgwick, Lloyd-Jones) take it, or it could mean 'Agamemnon's quarry,' referring to Clytemnestra and Aegisthus. Paley tentatively suggests this second possibility. Tucker (who reads θήρα πατρῴα) takes the secondary meaning to refer to Orestes' 'patrimony.'

11 So also the use, earlier in this speech (at 248-9), of the image of the net in connection with the murder of Agamemnon recalls the use of this image at *Ag* 357 (for Agamemnon's own capture of Troy) and at *Ag* 868 and 1115 for Clytemnestra's disguised, and Cassandra's actual, visions of the net of death prepared for Agamemnon.

12 Ἐρινύων ἐκ τῶν πατρῴων αἱμάτων. The Erinyes are particularly the avengers of familiar bloodshed. It is true that in the next play of the trilogy, the Erinyes avenging the murder of Clytemnestra are to tell Orestes that they did not pursue her for the murder of Agamemnon, 'because she was not kin to the man whom she slew' (*Eum* 605). Nevertheless, the Erinyes of Agamemnon may, consistently with this, force Agamemnon's own kin, Orestes, to take vengeance on his murderer, whether kin or not.

13 The first two sentences in the above quotation have caused some difficulty. Which are the oracles which Orestes wonders if he should trust? Not, surely, the oracle commanding him to take vengeance, for he tells us in the following lines that the deed must be done, whether

he believes these oracles or not, *and then proceeds to include the commands of Apollo* (300) among the compelling reasons for that deed of vengeance. Therefore it seems best to take 'such oracles' (τοιοῖσδε χρησμοῖς) in v 297 as referring to the supplementary oracular warnings just quoted concerning the gruesome penalties which Orestes must face if he fails to take vengeance. Cf also Rivier's interesting discussion of the interpretation and implications of *Cho* 298 in 'Remarques sur la Nécessaire et la Nécessité chez Eschyle.' Rivier argues that πέποιθα in v 298 refers not to belief in the truth of the oracle but to reliance on its support. With regard to the lines which follow (299 ff), he rightly indicates that Orestes' ἵμεροι in the matter of vengeance are not to be considered in isolation from what he knows to be the divine will in the matter. However, here and elsewhere in this article, Rivier tends to deprecate the element of human choice whenever an element of divine constraint is present as well. More acceptable is Lloyd-Jones' formulation of the matter, that the will of Zeus (and, as Apollo tells us at *Eum* 616-18, Zeus is behind all Apollo's mantic utterances) is generally presented as working *through* the human will. (See Lloyd-Jones *The Justice of Zeus* chapter 1, passim, and chapter 4, pp 85 ff.) (The foregoing account of *Cho* 298 ff is drawn from my own earlier discussion of the passage in 'Interaction between Chorus and Characters in the *Oresteia*,' pp 331-2 and n 11.)

14 It seems reasonable to assume that the Chorus marched and danced to accompany the anapaestic and lyric portions, respectively, of their utterances in this passage.

The following discussion of the 'great kommos' is taken from my article 'Interaction' pp 332-9.

15 Reinhardt *Aischylos als Regisseur und Theologe* pp 112-22.
16 Lebeck *The Oresteia, A Study in Language and Structure* pp 93-5; 110-30.
17 von Wilamowitz-Moellendorff *Griechische Tragödie* II, Orestie pp 143-4, 148; *Aischylos, Interpretationen* pp 205-10; cf Reinhardt's discussion (above, n 15).
18 Schadewaldt 'Der Kommos in Aischylos' *Choephoren*.' For the emphasis suggested above, see especially pp 113-15, 335-7. Cf also Lloyd-Jones' note on this kommos in *The Libation Bearers of Aeschylus*, a translation with commentary, p 26. There is, of course, no doubt concerning the importance of the evocation, in this kommos, of Agamemnon's unseen avenging spirit, 'the only truly compelling ghost in Aeschylus [as Rosenmeyer has called him] ... Agamemnon, the punishing power in the tomb, directing vengeance from behind the scene' Rosenmeyer *The Art of Aeschylus* p 267).

Choephori (The Libation Bearers)

19 Lesky 'Der Kommos der *Choephoren.*' See especially pp 118–21 for the conclusions here summarized.
20 Ibid. p 120. ('An Orestes who, in blind obedience to the command of the god, accomplishes the deed as his instrument and then is protected by the god against its results cannot be the subject of tragic experience, least of all in the poetry of Aeschylus.')
21 Reinhardt *Aischylos als Regisseur und Theologe* pp 114–15, 119.
22 Lebeck *The 'Oresteia'* pp 112–14, cf p 120. Lebeck's argument (p 112) that, on the basis of 'the timeless quality of lyric,' we may here disregard the prior decision of Orestes before the kommos is interesting but does not, I think, quite stand up. It is easier to think of similar examples of this sort of sequence in Euripides than in Aeschylus, eg the 'kommatic,' followed by the 'dramatic' death of Alcestis at *Alc* 244 ff and 280 ff; Helen's iambic complaints and threat of suicide at *Hel* 255 ff, followed by similar complaints and threats in a kommatic passage, at 330 ff. However, I know of no other instances in Aeschylus or Euripides in which a series of kommatic exchanges is directed toward a decision which has already been clearly taken in the iambic scene preceding it.
23 Here the Moirai are represented as on the side of Zeus' justice and of the old *lex talionis*. Later in the trilogy, the Chorus of the Eumenides is to associate the Moirai with themselves as παλαιαὶ δαίμονες (gods of the old order) similarly mistreated by the younger gods. See *Eum* 723–8; cf *Eum* 172.
24 I read γόος ἐκ δίκην ματεύει (Murray's emendation of v 330); however, the reading γόος ἔνδικος ματεύει (M) could express a similar idea. Both Schadewaldt and Reinhardt put much emphasis on this verse in their interpretations.
25 'light to compensate for darkness' (319, with punctuation after ἀντίμοιρον, as in several editions); 'the injurer is brought to light' (328); 'lamentation bringing honour' (321); 'lamenatation tracks down justice' (330); 'a dirge at the tomb' (334–5); 'in place of tomb dirges, a paean of victory' (342–3); the Greek expresses the reciprocities more vividly.
26 See Schadewaldt's justified rebuttal ('Der Kommos' pp 325–6) of some editors' desire to emend ἐμπρέπων to ἐμπρέπει (335) and ἔξης to ἔζη (360). It is preferable (except for Wilamowitz' view of the kommos) to have the Chorus addressing the dead King directly here, and this is what the manuscript reading gives us.
27 I follow Dodds' emendation, μέλον for μᾶλλον (M), at v 379, but admittedly we can only guess at the precise meaning of this corrupt line.

28 ὑστερόποινον ἄταν (383). Cf Ag 58–9, ὑστερόποινον ... Ἐρινύν.
29 Aeschylus regularly reserves his 'wind imagery' for crucial turning points in the action or in the decisions of his characters. Cf Ag 187, 219 ff, 1180 ff; Cho 775, 813–14, 821.
30 Cf Thomson's musical analogy: he compares the thematic sequence of subjects, counter-subjects, and restatements in the kommos as a whole with the composition of a fugue (Headlam and Thomson *The Oresteia* pp 37–9).
31 The precise meaning of these lines (420–2) has been disputed. Paley construes as I have, above; Lloyd-Jones (*The Libation Bearers by Aeschylus*) translates, 'for, like a savage wolf, not to be cajoled by my mother is his wrath,' while Sidgwick, Smythe, Lattimore, and others take ἐκ μητρός as indicating the origin of the savage spirit of the speaker. (The word order is surely against the last view.) Perhaps the ambiguity (between the first and second meanings) is intentional. In any case there does seem to be an ironic reminder of Electra's earlier prayer: αὐτῇ τέ μοι δὸς σωφρονεστέραν πολὺ / μητρὸς γενέσθαι χεῖρά τ' εὐσεβεστέραν (Cho 140–1).
32 'She shall pay, indeed, for the dishonour done my father with the help of the gods and by the action of my own hands.' The significance of these lines is underlined by the fact that Wilamowitz, following Schütz, wished to transfer vv 434–8 to follow 455. Left here (in their proper place), they interfere with his view that at this point Orestes was still struggling with his conscience over the mother-murder. See Wilamowitz *Interpretationen* pp 205–10; cf Reinhardt *Aischylos* p 113.
33 As Garvie points out ('The Opening of the *Choephori*' pp 83–4), Clytemnestra's snake-vision was familiar from Stesichorus (fr 42 P) where, however, 'according to the more probable interpretation of the fragment' (supported by some ceramic evidence), the snake was probably equated with Agamemnon himself. Thus Aeschylus may have been the first to have the snake represent Orestes ... 'an Orestes into whom the chthonic *Kratos* of his father has indeed entered' (ibid p 84).
34 There is, however, some uncertainty concerning the sequence at this point; see below, pp 116–17.
35 I read ἄκαιρ' οὐδὲ for ἀκαίρως δὲ: see Stinton 'The First Stasimon of Aeschylus *Choephori*' p 260.
36 The text is again very uncertain from 628 to the end of the strophe.
37 Text and interpretation are uncertain. But if we read δόμοις / αἱμάτων at 648–9 and τίνειν at 650, with most editors, then it seems most reasonable to construe as in the above translation. See Sidgwick's arguments for taking τέκνον as referring to Orestes who enters as the

Chorus ends its sentence, and not (with αἱμάτων) as 'the child of murder in the olden time.' It is quite possible, however, to take αἱμάτων παλαιτέρων as dependent on δόμοις, as Lloyd-Jones does in his translation. However, Lloyd-Jones' switching of the whole construction into the passive ('But the child is brought to the house of ancient murders, to atone at last for the pollution wrought by the famed, deep-designing Erinys') strikes one as slightly tendentious: it tends to place all the active force on the Erinys and none at all on the human avenger (here, τέκνον) – an emphasis which, perhaps, suits this scholar's view of supernatural and the human elements in the trilogy as a whole.

38 Stinton 'The First Stasimon' p 253.
39 Cf ibid pp 253–6, passim. (Lebeck's defence of the traditional sequence will be considered later, in connection with her interpretation of the passage as a whole.)
40 E.B. Holtsmark 'On *Choephori* 585–651' p 215.
41 Ibid p 216.
42 Lebeck 'The First Stasimon of Aeschylus' *Choephori*. Myth and Mirror Image' p 183.
43 Ibid p 183; see ibid p 184 for the following quotation.
44 Ibid p 183, for this and the following quotation.
45 This interpretation would also require an emendation of βροτῶν to βροτοῖς at v 636, as Sidgwick points out: Wilamowitz, followed by Page (OCT 1972) and now by Stinton ('The First Stasimon' p 255), so emends.
46 Ibid p 255. Stinton further supports the sequence for which *he* argues by analysing the formal structure of the ode (up to the concluding strophic pair) as one in which the first priamel (585–601, which we might call the 'gnomic priamel') is illustrated closely and in proper sequence by the second (mythological) priaemel. Then, 'All three examples [of the second priamel] ... converge on Clytemnestra' (pp 255–6).
47 This recurrent triplicity may be seen, to mention but a few instances, in the divine overthrows in the 'Hymn to Zeus,' with Zeus emerging as the 'triple thrower' (*Ag* 170); in the τριγέρων μῦθος (the 'thrice-told' or 'triply-aged tale,' *Cho* 314) which the present Chorus describes as the authority for belief in δράσαντι παθεῖν ('the doer must suffer'); in the three generations involved in the illustration of this truth, at least as far as 'the old order' of justice is concerned; in the trilogy itself in which this τριγέρων μῦθος will finally be aborted by a new order of justice in the third generation. Other instances of triplicity (such as the three recognition tokens in the first episode of the *Choephori*, the three mythological exempla of the first stasimon, and the Chorus' later promise of 'triple repayment' to Zeus for his aid, *Cho* 791–3) *may* be coincidental.

48 Cf *Cho* 899: Πυλάδη, τί δράσω; μητέρ' αἰδεσθῶ κτανεῖν;
49 *Ag* 11.
50 Cf Lloyd-Jones' note, ad loc, to his translation.
51 Cf Lebeck's subtle comment (*Oresteia* p 126) on the secondary and even tertiary meanings suggested here: a parent should recognize her son (to whom she is speaking); 'Or is he, as he claims, a ξένος, his only tie with her that transient residence in the mother's alien body?' (cf *Eum* 660-1).
52 The sense of this sentence, particularly of βακχείας καλῆς, 698, and παροῦσαν, the ms reading for the participle in 699, has been much debated, and some editors find it so dubious that they obelize. The translation given above (essentially the way in which Sidgwick takes the lines) accepts Pauw's emendation of παροῦσαν to προδοῦσαν. If one retains παροῦσαν, then Lloyd-Jones' explanation of 'hope being present' as a legal metaphor (only when a condemned criminal was present could sentence of death be carried out) seems the only (rather desperate) way of explaining it. In any case, I am convinced that βακχείας (whether with καλῆς, ironic, or with the emendation κακῆς) refers to the raving of the family curse; since Clytemnestra has suggested, 691 ff, that the curse has caused Orestes' death, it is consistent that she should now pretend that Orestes was the only hope of defeating the curse, or of saving her from it. This also suits the double irony of the passage (Clytemnestra's and the poet's) since, as far as Clytemnestra is concerned, Orestes is about to embody the family curse, not save her from it.
53 ξυγκαταβῆναι (727): it is true that the word connotes entry into the contest as an ally, but it also suggests a direction *downwards*; Πειθώ is thought of as dwelling above (cf *Ag* 105-6, ἔτι γὰρ θεόθεν καταπνεύει / Πειθώ ...), just as Hermes is the god who will supply guile from below.
54 'Naturalistic,' that is, in contrast to the heroic and supernatural levels on which most of this tragedy operates. The disguised Orestes speaks of 'carrying his own luggage' (675: presumably to allay apprehension on Clytemnestra's part); Clytemnestra, of 'warm baths' (670), the Nurse of a baby's needs ('hunger, thirst and pissing,' 756)
55 Complicity, a negative form of action, is usually the most which is expected of the Chorus in the way of furthering the plot. (The Chorus' attitude in much of Euripides' *Medea* is an obvious example.) In Euripides' *Ion* it is true, the Chorus does reveal to Creousa Xuthos' acquisition of a son, and this in turn triggers a whole sequence of action.
56 Cf *Eum* 606, 658 ff.

57 Cf Ag 219, Cho 821–2.
58 Cho 791–3. Cf the inducements to Zeus in Orestes' prayer at vv 255–63. Note also the recurrent 'triplicity motif' discussed above, n 47.
59 There are numerous uncertainties of text, syntax, and interpretation throughout this ode. None of the versions suggested here should be accepted with confidence in all details without reference to editors' discussions of various problems.
60 This passage has been much emended and debated. The above version is Lloyd-Jones' translation of the text as emended by Dindorf and Bamberger. Others (less well) take φῶς (itself a conjectural supplement to the text) as object, not subject of ἰδεῖν; the pronoun νιν will then be taken as subject of ἰδεῖν and may then refer to 'the house' rather than to the hero Orestes (so Sidgwick and Smythe).
61 I read Murray's emendation 'Πατρὸς' αὖδα (829) for πατρὸς αὐδάν (M), as admirably suiting the sense and supplying the needed imperative. (Possibly the ms reading makes the same point ambiguously, depending on whether one takes the genitive πατρὸς to depend on τέκνον or αὐδάν.) Page's OCT reading 'ἔργῳ πατρός' αὖδα (see his critical note ad loc) would make the anticipation of Eum 606 and 658 ff (where the actual blood relationship of mother and son is questioned) clearer than either of the other readings.
62 Cf Eur El 458–63, where the Chorus describes the depiction of Perseus slaying the Gorgon on the shield of Achilles. Scholars have, I think rightly, related this passage in the Electra with Orestes' own account later (El 1221–3) of veiling his eyes as he slew his mother. (Cf also El 856, where the head of the slain Aegisthus is contrasted with the Gorgon's head.) For a full discussion of the Euripidean passages and their possible connection with the Aeschylean passage above (Cho 831 f) see O'Brien 'Orestes and the Gorgon: Euripides' Electra esp p 17 ff, and his references to other views on the subject.
63 Aegisthus' real fear, presumably, is that Clytemnestra's hopes may have flared up too quickly at the mere report of Orestes' death. One is reminded of the fires and the fire imagery of Ag 92–6 and 281–316; it is ironic that there, too, Clytemnestra's too-credulous feminine optimism has been questioned by the Chorus.
64 Cf Ag 1421–5.
65 For the mixed motives of Clytemnestra and the different aspects of her role as avenger, see Ag 1372–1576 and comments on this passage, above, chapter 1, pp 48–55.
66 Whether the Nurse was also a wet-nurse to Orestes cannot perhaps be established from her claim (ἐξέθρεψα κ.τ.λ. ...) at v 750 ff. Some

editors suspect that a verse is missing after v 750 or 751; if so, this might have made the matter clearer.

On the intervention of Pylades, cf Knox's excellent comment: 'It is the voice of Apollo himself; these three lines seal Clytemnestra's death warrant. Aeschylus has saved up his third actor for this dramatic explosion; further speech from Pylades would be anticlimax, and he says no more ... ' (Knox, 'Aeschylus and the Third Actor' p 42).

67 Cf *Ag* 44 and, for the parallel of 'the justice of Zeus' falling on Troy, cf the second stasimon of *Agamemnon*, esp 355–84. It will be remembered, however, that in that passage the fate of Priam was used as a parallel for what might happen to Agamemnon (see discussion of the first stasimon of *Agamemnon*, chapter 1, pp 17–23. In this connection, we will see that the image, 'the two-fold lion,' in the present passage (*Cho* 938) has weightier significance than perhaps the Chorus itself intends. See the excellent article by Knox, 'The Lion in the House.' Knox has shown the different ways in which the lion imagery has been applied to various characters in the trilogy (particularly in the first play): to Agamemnon, to Clytemnestra, to Helen, to Aegisthus, to Orestes, and, perhaps, to the family curse itself. At *Cho* 938 (to which Knox makes passing reference, p 36), there is, to be sure, some uncertainty (and perhaps intentional ambiguity) as to the reference of the image of the 'two-fold lion.' Some editors and commentators take it, as I have, to refer to Orestes and Pylades, eg, Paley (who refers to the similar view of the Scholiast), Sidgwick, Lloyd-Jones; others, eg, Klausen and Weil, both cited by Paley and Sidgwick, take the image as referring to Clytemnestra and Aegisthus. This is admittedly quite possible, since that pair could stand as the subject of ἔμολε δ'ἐς δόμον τὸν 'Αγαμέμνονος. In that case the further adversative in ἔλασε δ' (or possibly ἔλαχε δ') with the exile Orestes as subject, in the following sentence, would, perhaps, have greater force.

See also the interesting comments of de Romilly on this ode in 'Vengeance humaine et vengeance divine. Remarques sur l'*Orestie* d'Eschyle' p 68. De Romilly finds in the structure of this ode, and particularly in the sentences at vv 935 ff and 946 ff ("Εμολε μὲν ... "Εμολε δὲ ...) an excellent example of the parallelism, observable throughout the trilogy, of divine and human motivation. 'Le sujet du premier verbe ["Εμολε] est un feminin, qui évoque chatiment sous sa forme abstraite et divine; le sujet du second est un masculin et désigne l'agent même de ce chatiment, à savoir Oreste.'

68 Some editors find a reference to Hermes as well, either in implicit apposition to Ποινά (Retribution), in v 947 (since the relative clause

preceding it provides an attribute suitable to Hermes) or even as a textual emendation for Ποινά, allegedly transcribed in error from 936, the corresponding verse of the preceding strophe; see Paley's note ad loc; Paley, I think rightly, rejects both suggestions. See also Lloyd-Jones' translation and note ad loc: he, too, substitutes 'Hermes' for 'Poina' and notes that Hermes, Zeus, Justice, the daughter of Zeus, and Apollo are all praised in this ode – appropriately, since 'Zeus, Apollo and Hermes are all prayed to in the two opening strophic pairs of the Second Stasimon (738 ff ...).' (This strikes me as somewhat forced, since the presence of Hermes in the passage just considered is dubious and Zeus is mentioned in this strophe only as the father of Δίκη [Justice].)

69 Contrast the fearful prayer in the preceding ode: γέρων φόνος μηκέτ᾽ ἐν δόμοις τέκοι ('May the bloodshed of old [which is almost equivalent to 'the family curse'] no longer continue to propagate in the house!' Cho 806). In the present ode, the Chorus sings what it feels (and hopes) is appropriate to the moment of triumph over the usurpers. However, as we have seen from the warnings of the doomed Clytemnestra, and the possible hints of the poet at vv 935–8 in the present ode (cf above, n 67) and as we shall see from the sequel to Orestes' deed at the end of this play and the first half of the next, Orestes himself (and his royal house) is not yet 'out of the woods.'

70 The text, though not, I think, the basic sense, is uncertain in the subordinate clause in 966–8. I follow Page's OCT reading: ὅταν ... ἐλαθῇ (Kayser's emendation of ἐλάσει M, ἐλάσῃ M^s) καθαρμοῖσιν ἀτᾶν ἐλατηρίοις (Schutz's emendation of ἅπαν ἐλατήριον M).

71 On the possible scenic arrangements for displaying the corpses at the end of the *Agamemnon* and the *Choephori*, see chapter 1, n 90 and the reference to Taplin *Stagecraft of Aeschylus* there given; see also Taplin's additional comment on the *Choephori* scene, ibid pp 357–8, with further comparisons and contrasts to the equivalent scene in the *Agamemnon*.

For the point of comparison at the end of the *Eumenides*, see below chapter 3, p 174 and n 90. (on *Eum* 1028 ff) and references there given, especially to Goheen 'Three Studies in the *Oresteia*.'

72 There seems to be a sort of grisly play on words in vv 998–9. νεκροῦ ποδένδυτον / δροίτης κατασκήνωμα. The robe for the bath becomes in actual fact the winding sheet for a corpse, but the further point that, as Lloyd-Jones remarks, in the note to his translation ad loc, 'The word used for "coffin" originally meant "bath"' enhances the verbal effect.

In treating this part of Orestes' speech, I have followed those who transpose 991–6 to follow 1004, so that Orestes' description of the bloody death-robe is not interrupted (only to be taken up again at v 997) by his description of Clytemnestra. Moreover, the latter part of the 'death-robe passage' (an account of the sort of scoundrel who might be expected to make such use of it, 1001–4 in the traditional text) leads easily into the description of Clytemnestra, who actually did so use it. Finally, the last two verses of the speech (1005–6) obviously suit as a conclusion to the sequence about Clytemnestra. These arguments (which occurred to me independently, as they might to any reader once this transposition has been suggested) have already been expressed by Lloyd-Jones in 'Interpolations in *Choephori* and *Electra*' pp 181–4. See also his rebuttal of arguments for excisions (Dindorf, Fraenkel) and other transpositions (Scholefield, Weil) suggested in connection with this problem. The transposition defended above was first made by R. Proctor in a limited edition of the *Oresteia* (London 1904) to which Lloyd-Jones (who reached this decision concerning the passage independently) refers. Page in his OCT (1972) refers to Proctor's and Lloyd-Jones' transposition, as well as to Scholefield's (997–1002) to follow 982); however, though he finds it *vix credibile* that 997–1004 stand in their right place in the received text, he regards neither transposition as satisfactory.

73 Cf Eur *Med* 1251 ff. (There the hopes of the Chorus that Helios might restrain Medea from the murder of her children are, of course, sadly misplaced!)

74 Cf the horse-racing image at vv 794–9, where the Chorus' fears for Orestes anticipate the present reality. See above, p 121.

CHAPTER THREE

Eumenides

1 Prologue, parodos, and first episode (vv 1–234)

The scene is set at Apollo's Oracle at Delphi and the first part of the prologue (an unusually complex one for Aeschylus) is spoken by the Pythia, the priestess of the Oracle. 'Gaia ... Themis ... Phoebe ... Apollo,' in this order, are honoured in the Priestess' opening prayer, as she describes the peaceful transition of mantic power from the chthonic gods which once held Delphi to its present Olympian lord.[1] In the last play, we have seen the alliance of supernal and infernal powers in the execution of Orestes' vengeance on Clytemnestra. In this play, we are to witness the pursuit of Orestes by the Earth-born Erinyes, primeval avengers of unnatural deeds; then their frustration and ultimate appeasement by Apollo and Athena, respectively. And so this initial celebration of Apollo's peaceful 'takeover' of the seat of ancient chthonic power at Delphi anticipates, in ironic fashion, the more revolutionary new order which the Olympians are to establish in the present action. The Priestess' roll of honour continues with Pallas *Pronaia* (an epithet of Athena which reminds us that she too had her shrine 'before the temple' at Delphi) and ends, significantly, with Zeus *teleios*, 'Zeus the fulfiller': it is in accordance with the will of Zeus (as Apollo and Athena are constantly to remind us) that all that happens in this play will be accomplished.

Thus far (to v 33) the Priestess has spoken with no knowledge of the new arrivals at the Oracle and of the dreadful situation which they impose. Now (as we may safely infer from the text) she enters the temple and sees Orestes surrounded by the sleeping Chorus of Furies. She emerges reeling (possibly 'on all fours,' τρέχω δὲ χερσίν,

37) with the horror of what she has seen, 'dread sights to tell, dread sights to look upon.' First she describes the suppliant:

> ... at the shrine I saw a man detested by the gods [θεομυσῆ], grasping the god's seat as suppliant [προστρόπαιον], dripping blood from his hands[2] and holding a freshly drawn sword and olive branch ... (40–3)

then the more frightful vision of the Furies themselves:

> ... women ... and yet not women, Gorgons rather, I would call them ...[save that] they are wingless and black ... abominable, snoring with fetid breath, eyes dripping with a rheumy ooze ... I've never seen the tribe to which this company belongs, nor the land which boasts to breed them scatheless, without groaning for its pains. (48–59, in part)

This, our first and ghastly image of the Erinyes, oldest of the surviving chthonic powers, is probably followed immediately by their revelation through the opened doors of the temple.[3] With it is contrasted the dazzling appearance of Apollo, who now enters, championing the suppliant Orestes and declaring his Olympian hatred of his pursuers ...

> ... these grey and ancient virgins whom no one of gods nor men nor beasts will ever mingle with. For evil were they born, their portion evil darkness and Tartarus 'neath the earth; objects of loathing to me and to the Olympian gods. (69–73)

Apollo's speech closes with the god's first statement of his responsibility for Orestes' matricide ('For I persuaded you to slay the mothering body' 84)[4] and of the remedy:

> Go to Athena's city and sit as suppliant, taking her ancient image in your arms. And there, finding judges of these matters and soothing words [θελκτηρίους μύθους], we will devise the means to cure you of these ills. (80–3)

The final effect of this astounding prologue is the sudden appearance of the ghost of Clytemnestra, come to arouse her sleeping Furies to active vengeance.

> You'd sleep – and yet what good are you asleep? – while I'm dishonoured by you among my fellow-dead and held to blame 'mid them

for those I slew. Bitter charge from them I take while I who suffered
foully for my nearest kin – no one of the gods is wroth on my account.
See these heart-wounds, whence they came, for even in sleep you
keep your sight.[5] Many libations from me have you licked up, nocturnal
feasts served at an hour which no god shares ... Listen as I speak
about my spirit [τῆς ἐμῆς πέρι ψυχῆς]. Take heed, you goddesses of the
underworld; the ghost of Clytemnestra summons you! (94–116, in part)

There follows a macabre 'arousal scene' in which angry mutterings
from the Furies mingle with ghostly sarcasms ('toil and sleep, powerful conspirators indeed!' 127; 'dream beasts you chase, like sleeping
hounds!' 131) from the bitter Queen. The ghost of Clytemnestra (as
might be expected) is the only shade to play such an active aggressive
role in extant Greek tragedy, and nowhere in Greek literature do we
find such a vivid impression of the Erinyes as the personal avengers,
the divine servants, even, of a particular victim of kin-violence.

The prologue of the *Eumenides*, unlike many Aeschylean prologues,
seems both to define a certain nadir, a point of absolute zero, whence
the hero's fortunes can only improve, and to provide some hint, at
least in ironic form, as to how the necessary progression may be
achieved. We know Orestes to be guilty of matricide and we see him
surrounded by the primeval avengers of matricide, their original function being given exclusive emphasis by the goading of Clytemnestra
who regards them as existing solely *as* her avengers. If the old order
of blood for blood and δράπαντι παθεῖν still obtains, as it has throughout the trilogy, then there seems no hope of alleviating the unending
reprisals, of lifting the curse from the house of Atreus – all the more
so in that Orestes' deed of matricide, considered in itself, is the one
most clearly calling for vengeance from the Erinyes.[6] Orestes' deed
is done and even the 'justifications' of the deed have already all been
rehearsed in the *Choephori*. It seems clear, then, that any change from
the situation so theatrically presented in the prologue must relate to
the Erinyes and the operation of their traditional function.

It is in this situation of apparently ineluctable doom that the opening
invocation of the Priestess (as yet unconscious of that situation) has
provided a hint of the solution and a clue to the coming dramatic
action of the play. The Pythia's words have celebrated the peaceful
transference of the ancient prerogatives at Delphi (the sacred umbil-
icus of all future religious and so of all legal authority among the
Greeks) from the chthonic powers to the Olympian Apollo. The prerogative which Apollo has taken over is, of course, the traditional

Delphic function of prophecy (vv 3–8, 17–19), but this transition may presage still more fundamental changes from the old order to the new. We have also heard Apollo speak of finding 'judges' and 'soothing words' (81–2) as a solution for Orestes' ills; what 'judges' and to whom the 'soothing words' will be addressed he does not specify, but his consolation suggests a very different eventual situation from the present one.

If anything is to change, in this situation, then it must be the Erinyes and the older order from which their authority is drawn. Nevertheless, the picture of the Erinyes presented in the prologue (and continued, for the most part, to the end of the first stasimon, at v 396) is one which, on the face of it, seems to offer little hope of progress or of compromise. What is to be the most striking feature of the dramatic development of this play is the extraordinarily dynamic and evolving presentation of the Erinyes and their meaning.[7] And perhaps the major critical error which can be (and has been) made in connection with the transformation of the Erinyes in this play is to look for it exclusively in its most obvious and most striking phase, when Athena wins over the furious Chorus after the acquittal of Orestes. It is not simply to the personal avengers of the spilt blood of Clytemnestra that Athena makes her famous appeal. Much earlier in the progress of the play, the poet gradually modifies this initial and particularized 'vampire' image of the Erinyes by presenting their avenging function as part of the universal order of things, and by endowing it with a certain positive and even 'civilizing' function.[8]

In the parodos (140–78), the song and dance of the aroused Chorus express their frustration at the escape of Orestes from Delphi. Here they are still very much the manifestation of Clytemnestra's outraged spirit of vengeance, as they dance in pain and fury under Clytemnestra's goading:

We have suffered a grievous woe, alas! ... (145)

He has slipped out of the snare! The beast has escaped! (147–8)

A dream-borne reproach has smitten me, like a charioteer, with a hard-gripped goad, here, right in the vitals! (155–8)

... even if he flee beneath the earth, he will never be free! Stained as he is with murderous blood,[9] he'll come to a place where he'll suffer another bringer of fresh pollution upon his own head! (175–8)

Even here, however, there are hints of a broader perspective than the immediate pursuit of Orestes in the plaint, twice repeated (150, 171–2), that a new god is trampling on the prerogatives of the gods of the old order. In the second of these complaints, the Furies link their outrage at Apollo's hands with his outrage against the Fates (Μοῖραι) themselves:

> [Apollo] ... honouring a mere mortal beyond the laws of the gods, destroying the Fates born of old. (171–2)

Later the Chorus is to develop this claim to their ancient prerogative at greater length.[10]

The first, or 'Delphic,' panel of the play ends with a lively scene between Apollo and the Chorus, who are to be the chief antagonists in the second panel, after the *mise en scène* is shifted to Athens. Apollo accompanies his expulsion of the Furies from his shrine ('Out, I bid you! Out at once!') with threats and castigations which set off the contrast between the god of light and his loathsome adversaries. The bright image of Apollo's threat to send 'a winged snake glancing from his golden bow-strings' (181–2) flashes against the dark picture he paints of the Furies, 'vomiting black blood from human prey' (183) and loitering around 'beheadings, eye-gougings ... executions and foul castrations of virile youths' (186–8). Thus we see again that it is the most primitive aspect of the Furies as ghastly avengers (exaggerated, perhaps, by Apollo's own attempts to discredit them by associating them with particularly barbarous practices)[11] that is emphasized in these opening scenes.

The bitter dialogue which follows serves as a sort of rehearsal for the more formal debate of the trial scene to come. In an exchange of some thirty verses, all (or nearly all) of the key issues are touched on: Apollo's responsibility for ordering the matricide through his oracle and for harbouring a blood-polluted man (202–4), Apollo's order to Orestes to seek purification (205); the Furies' outrage as frustrated avengers of kin-murder (208 ff); Apollo's answering fury at *their* denial of just vengeance for outrage to the marriage-bond. 'Pallas [Athena] will oversee the judicial rights [δίκας] of both these claims!' (224). With this conclusion, Apollo prepares us for the removal of the scene to Athens. There will these divine adversaries plead their cases, the Furies driven by 'the mother's blood' (αἷμα μητρῷον, 230), Apollo by the equally pressing claim of his suppliant (ἱκέτης, 232), Orestes:

For dread is the wrath of the προστρόπαιος,[12] among gods even as among men, if I betray him willingly! (233-4)

Two passages in this exchange provide points of interpretative interest and perhaps difficulty. One is the Furies' clear indication (212) that they are concerned only with kin bloodshed, a claim to which Apollo takes equally clear exception (213-24). The other is Apollo's statement that the claims of the marriage bed are stronger than oath and supported by fate and justice (εὐνὴ γὰρ ἀνδρὶ καὶ γυναικὶ μόρσιμος / ὅρκου 'στὶ μείζων τῇ δίκῃ φρουρουμένη, 217-18).

The Chorus' declaration at *Eum* 212 seems inconsistent with what Apollo has told Orestes (at *Cho* 283 ff) about the vengeance which the Furies would wreak on *him* if he failed to avenge his father's murder. The latter Furies are, it is true, 'the Furies from his father's blood' ('Ερινύων / ἐκ τῶν πατρῴων αἱμάτων); nevertheless, there is no avoiding the fact that both *are* Erinyes and so that, theologically speaking at least, there does seem to be a contradiction when Clytemnestra's Furies say that they are concerned only with *kin* murder.

There are several ways of seeking an answer to this difficulty, none of them entirely satisfactory. If one seeks an explanation in terms of ethical ideas as reflected in mythological (or theological) expression, one might say that the *Choephori* passage reflects the earlier conception of the Erinyes (belonging to the days when murder was regarded as a tort to be redressed by the family) as a curse affecting the murdered man's next of kin until he had exacted blood for blood (or blood payment) or until the murderer fled the country; and that the Erinyes of the *Eumenides* reflected the later idea (belonging to a 'guilt culture' as opposed to a "shame culture') in which the Erinyes concentrated on the blood-guilty person.[13] But though this helps to explain the particular concern of Agamemnon's Erinyes in the *Choephori* passage, it does not really explain the exclusiveness of the Erinyes' statement at *Eum* 212. A second, more purely mythological, explanation is needed to justify this 'specialization' in familial blood-guilt. The Erinyes were traditionally thought of as avenging spirits in general (in this role an Ἐρίνυς is almost indistinguishable from an ἀλάστωρ) but more specifically as avengers (or in some cases 'correctors,' simply) of unnatural deeds. This conception finds its mythological justification, at least, in Hesiod's account of the earth-sprung origin of the Erinyes from the blood from Ouranos' genitals, after they were severed by his son Kronos.[14] Aeschylus, then, to suit his dramatic and thematic purposes, adopts this aspect of the Erinyes in the *Eumenides* (or at least in most passages of it)[15] – but not in the *Choephori,* and not exclusively in the *Agamemnon.*

Finally, the Erinyes' avowed limitation (at *Eum* 212 and elsewhere, though not *always,* in this play) may be looked for in terms of the specific dramatic context, which is, of course, totally different from that of *Cho* 283 ff[16] in the preceding play. This view has been well expressed by Owen in his comment on this problem:

> The point is that Apollo and the Erinyes are radically opposed and he [Aeschylus] looks for words relevant to the occasion to express that sharp opposition. Really the only reason they are on Clytemnestra's side is that she has been murdered; with the question of her guilt before that ... they, as avenging spirits, have nothing to do. But the poet has to make an arguable case for it ...[17]

Possibly Owen is right in his further advice that it is 'a mistake to press such details [as the 'inconsistency' in question] ... For the purposes of this play, the Erinyes' cause is bound up with Clytemnestra.' In many ways, this is a sane judgment on the specific problem of the 'inconsistency' concerning the Erinyes' function in the *Eumenides* and earlier in the trilogy. It should be realized, however, that the Chorus' explicit allegiance to the blood-line is here essential to their *raison d'être* (not just a stick with which to beat Apollo) and to the expression of the larger polarities which it is the business of this play to reconcile.[18] Hence it has seemed best to suggest, if only allusively, something of the changing Greek attitudes both to blood-vengeance and to the Erinyes' role in this, at different periods prior to the composition of this trilogy.

The second (and considerably lesser) problem in this initial exchange between Apollo and the Furies is provided by Apollo's curious statement that the claims of the marriage-bed, which are 'fated' and supported by Justice, are 'stronger than an oath' (or, possibly, 'stronger than Oath'; εὐνὴ γὰρ ἀνδρὶ καὶ γυναικὶ μόρσιμος / ὅρκου 'στὶ μείζων τῇ δίκῃ φρουρουμένη, 217–18). This statement is made in the context of Apollo's rebuke to the Furies for ignoring Clytemnestra's murder of her husband while relentlessly pursuing Orestes' murder of his mother. What precisely does Apollo mean? The usual translation given ('stronger than an oath' or 'stronger than any oath') leaves us wondering how this statement helps the point which Apollo is making against the Furies. Both Davies and Thomson have recognized this point in their editions of the *Eumenides.* Davies imagines a lacuna after v 212 in which an allusion was made to Orestes' refusal to take an oath that he did not slay his mother: cf *Eum* 429;[19] Thomson 'explains' the passage by amending: transposing the cases of εὐνή (and its modifiers) and ὅρκος, and reading τίς for 'στί, he is able to derive the meaning 'What contract (oath) is more binding than the marriage-bed, etc ... ?' Neither of these manipulations of the received text seems quite justified by the 'improvements' achieved. The missing reference alleged by Weil and Davies would, taken by itself, be irrelevant to Apollo's argument at this point, and Thomson's emendation really only strengthens, without substantially changing, the meaning which Paley gives to the text as it stands, namely, 'that marriage, though not constituting a blood relationship, is stronger than a mere oath or civil compact, since it is appointed by Fate and sanctioned or protected by justice.' However, Thomson's view of the 'historical significance' of the passage *may* be sound, namely, that, 'while the sanctity of the blood-relation is primitive, the marriage tie was not recognized until much later: in this, as in other respects, Apollo stands for the new order ...'[20]

J.H. Kells thinks that the 'oath' mentioned in this passage refers to the oath sworn by Clytemnestra and Aegisthus (to die together, if they can but kill Agamemnon) at *Cho* 978–9.[21] But again there seems little point, in the context, in saying that the marriage-bed is stronger than this oath; besides, who could deny this obvious truth?

The passage must, perhaps, remain a puzzle. However, before leaving it, we might note two other passages later in the play in which 'oath' and justice are also mentioned. At *Eum* 429 (as we have just noted), the Chorus complains to Athena that Orestes refuses 'to accept or to give an oath' (ie that he had not done the deed), which, according to ancient legal procedure, manslaughter defendants were required to do.[22] Athena rebukes their insistence on the letter of the law by answering, 'You wish to *seem* just [to have the reputation of being just] rather than to act justly' (κλύειν δικαίως μᾶλλον ἢ πρᾶξαι θέλεις, 430), and, when the Chorus ask her to explain this, she replies further, 'Do not, I tell you, seek to defeat justice by means of oaths' (ὅρκοις τὰ μὴ δίκαια μὴ νικᾶν λέγω, 432). As we shall see, Athena's statements here are significant in her development of a new form of justice for dealing with blood-guilt: no longer is the mere fact of commission or non-commission of a deed of bloodshed at issue (the matter with which the *oath* is concerned) but the circumstances and the motive must also be considered. Further, at vv 620–1, Apollo gives this strange advice to the newly appointed human jury which is to try Orestes' case:

> I bid you recognize how strong this righteous defence is and to comply with the father's plan. For an oath is not stronger than Zeus. (619-21)

The oath referred to here may perhaps be the jurors' oath (as Lloyd-Jones indicates in his note ad loc), not (as some editors, such as Davies and Thomson, have thought) the oath of innocence which Orestes refused to take (429). The sanctity of oaths is, of course, one of the most ancient of sanctities (by which even the gods were bound with terrifying penalties attached; cf Hesiod, *Theogony* 400, 783-806). Can Apollo's implication (at both 217-18 and 620-1) be that the new dispensation of Zeus (in the present instance, his championing of the marriage bed) has more weight than such traditional sanctions?

2 Second episode, part 1 (vv 235-53); second parodos (vv 254-75); second episode, part 2 (vv 276-306)

The scene now shifts, the temple in the background now representing the temple of Athena instead of that of Apollo.[23] Two striking features of Orestes' initial addresses to Athena (first to her statue, vv 235 ff and 276 ff, then to the goddess herself, 443 ff) should be noted at the outset. One is that he completely ignores the Furies, a fact to which they themselves take exception (303-4); for this we may find some explanation later. The other is Orestes' emphasis, thrice repeated, and at considerable length (237-9, 276-89, 443-53), that he is no longer a polluted suppliant ($προστρόπαιος$, 237, 445) in need of purification from bloodshed. Some of the details of this claim, which takes precedence over everything else in these three utterances of Orestes, should perhaps be noted. First of all, the repeated use (237, 445) of the technical term $προστρόπαιος$, *negatived*, in Orestes' declarations on this matter draws attention to the difference between his present condition and his condition at Apollo's shrine at Delphi, for there the term or its verbal cognate has been used *positively* four times (41, 176, 205, 234) to describe Orestes' state or suppliant action.[24]

Closely related to Orestes' insistence to Athena on his purified state is his claim to the right *to speak* without bringing harm to those with whom he talks (277-9, cf 448-50) as well as to touch Athena's statue without fear of polluting it (445-6). This again draws attention to the difference between Orestes' present condition (at Athens) and his condition at Delphi (where, except for three verses, 85–7, to Apollo, from whom he seeks purification, he has kept silence) and so to the puzzling question where and how Orestes' purification has been accomplished and clearly established. Most commentators seem satisfied with the view that the purification of Orestes has been completed at Delphi and certainly his clear reference to the actual rite of purification, the 'the cleansings by pig-slaughter at the hearth of Phoebus [Apollo]' while the matricidal pollution was still fresh (281–3), seems to justify this view. However, this purification, if performed at Delphi, must have taken place before the play opens, for Apollo sends Orestes away from Delphi during the Prologue (74 ff, 89 ff). Nevertheless, the Pythian priestess describes the still silent Orestes as προστρόπαιος, θεομυσῆ (god-detested), 'with hands still dripping blood' (40–2) at Delphi; either (as one scholar has argued) the purification by pig's blood is subsequently performed at another shrine of Apollo[25] or else this rite already performed at Delphi has not completed Orestes' purification. Some support for the latter view occurs in Orestes' own further comments on the matter: he refers at vv 238–9 to 'the dulling and wearing away' (literally, 'rubbing off against,' προστριμμένον) of his pollution 'at many houses and on many travelled ways of men.' Orestes has also spoken of 'many purifications' (πολλοὺς καθαρμούς, 277), as if the first one were not sufficient, and he 'proves' his present freedom from taint at Athens by the harmless association (ἀβλαβεῖ συνουσίᾳ) which he has enjoyed with many peoples (284–5). Thus it would almost appear that the purification of Orestes is not instantaneous, with the first performance of the pig's-blood ritual. It includes associations with other men (after this rite) apparently both as a part of the purification and as an indication (when this happens with no harmful effects) as a proof of its success; thus, even when he has reached Athens, Orestes can still speak of the blood on his hand as 'slumbering and dying away' (βρίζει ... καὶ μαραίνεται, 280).[26]

Apart from this insistence on his purified state, two other points of interest may be noted in Orestes' first two pleas to Athena (235–43, 276–98), before the actual arrival of the goddess herself at Athens. First, relying on Apollo's promise (241, cf 81–4), he states with confidence the outcome of his trial (τέλος δίκης, 243) at Athena's house. We shall find this same emphasis on seeking a judgment in the case (κρῖνον δίκην, 468) at the end of Orestes' third appeal, in the presence of Athena. Thus Orestes' relation to Athena is quite different from his relation to Apollo: from Athena, he seeks only justice (242–43; cf 439–40), and, of course, as her purified suppliant (474) protection from the Furies while his case is judged; Apollo, on the other hand (as vv 233–4 have clearly shown), continues to bear responsibility for him as the one who has originally accepted him as προστρόπαιος, and purified him. Secondly (for it is not unknown that appeals for 'justice' be accompanied by appeals for favour), Orestes bolsters his plea to the 'Athenian mistress of this land' for her support by pledging his own land of Argos as a voluntary (ἄνευ δορός: 'unforced') and faithful ally (287–91).[27] This is the first of a series of explicit references to Argos, with, it would seem, contemporary reference to Argive-Athenian relations; it is followed by two guesses as to Athena's whereabouts ('whether she be in Libyan land ... or whether, like a bold commander, she watches over the Phlegrean plain,' 292–6) which would appear to sustain the contemporary political overtones of the preceding passage.[28] We shall note an interesting shift in Orestes' appeal for support after he has learned where Athena has actually been.

Both of Orestes' appeals to the statue of Athena are interrupted first by iambic verses from the Chorus-Leader, then by blood-curdling songs-and-dances from the whole vengeful pack of Furies. The Leader's vivid series of hunting images suggests that the Chorus enter literally sniffing their way along the path of the matricide:

> Here ... this is the clear trail of the man. Follow its silent clues. For, like a hound after a wounded stag, we follow the drops of blood. My breast heaves at my murderous toils ... Now somewhere he's cowering. I gloat with joy at the scent of human blood! (244–53, in part)

(Whatever Orestes may think of the effectiveness of his purification, of the blood on his hands as 'slumbering and dying away' [280], it is clear that the Erinyes do not share his conviction! This difference provides a splendid example of how such physical descriptions can be used in non-realistic Aeschylean drama: for the Chorus, who do not accept 'purification,' the blood *is* there; for Orestes [and later, for Athena] it is not. Such passages as this, and there are others, should surely also settle the question, existing at least in the minds of some scholars, whether or not the blood with which Orestes is alleged to be dripping ever refers to the pig's blood of the purification-rituals.[29]

Clearly it must always refer to the blood from his matricide: now it is there, now it is gone – depending not only on Orestes' 'state' but also on how the viewers in question 'see' him.)

Suddenly the Chorus breaks in with the excited dochmiacs, interspersed with iambic trimeters, of the second parodos, as the trail grows stronger ('Look! Look! Search everywhere! Don't let the matricide escape unpunished!' 254–6).[30] Outraged, they see Orestes grasping Athena's altar seeking *to be tried* for his deed of blood (ὑπόδικος θέλει γενέσθαι χρεών.)!

> This may not be! The mother's blood once shed upon the ground cannot be recalled. Once shed, it's lost for good! (261–3)

And so the hunting images now give way to the 'vampire' images descriptive of the Furies' primal function:

> Still living, you must requite me with the red blood from your limbs, for me to gulp ... Thinning you alive, I'll hale you to Hades down below ... (264–5, 267)

Nowhere is the antipathy between the Erinyes' Justice and the coming 'new covenant' (already anticipated in the Chorus' shocked '... he wishes to stand trial!' 260) more clearly expressed.[31]

Despite the apparently single-minded vindictiveness of this brief parodos, a somewhat broader view of the Erinyes' functions makes its appearance at the end of of the ode. Here they threaten 'the rewards of Justice' for dishonour done to gods and strangers as well as to kinsmen: all such deeds will Hades, 'men's chastener beneath the Earth,' mark down with his recording mind. This is one of several hints in the early songs of this play of a gradually broadening (beyond the immediate concern with Orestes) of the Furies' outlook on Justice in this play.

3 First stasimon (vv 307–96)

This ode, like the parodos, is preceded by an iambic passage from the Chorus-Leader (299–306) which heralds at least one of the ode's dominant themes. Neither Apollo's nor Athena's power, the Leader assures Orestes, will save him from becoming the food of the enraged Chorus of Erinyes, who will turn him into a bloodless shadow of his corporeal self. 'Now you shall hear our binding song!' (ὕμνον ... δέσμιον, 306).

The first stasimon does, to be sure, mark the climax of the 'vendetta' songs, the vampire-like pursuit of Orestes by the Furies. But interwoven with the vendetta is the Furies' insistence on their Justice, and on their special right, coeval with time and recognized even by the Olympians, to pursue the blood-guilty. It is this theme which the opening anapaests of this Chorus first introduce ('... to declare how this band of ours discharges its special functions [λάχη, 310] among men; for we claim to be righteous in our judgments [εὐθυδίκαιοι], 310–12). In a few moments the Chorus is to turn to the more pressing business at hand, but we shall see that by the end of this long ode it is the more general theme which predominates.[32]

With the change to trochaic metre in the first pair of strophic stanzas (321–7; 333–40), the tone becomes more aggressive, as the Erinyes invoke ancient, pre-Olympian authorities, 'Mother Night, who bore us as Punishment [ποινάν] on the living and the dead' (321–3), and Fate (Μοῖρα), who gave them their special function (λάχος, again) of pursuing murderers of kin. It is in this first strophe that we find the only specific reference to Orestes in this ode, as the Chorus declare their outrage with Apollo for depriving them of 'this cowering hare, fit subject to atone for a mother's blood' (323).

After each of these strophic stanzas, the Chorus switch to a more insistent rhythm, as they sing and dance their binding-song, the frenzied, mind-staggering hymn of the Erinyes, around their victim (328–33, 341–6).[33]

In the second strophic pair, a change of metre, this time to more sombre, 'elevated' dactyls, again accompanies a change of theme. In the strophe (347–53), the Chorus sing of their separateness, in function as in estate, from the Olympians. To them from their birth (γιγνομέναισι) belong the special rights (λάχη) of vengeance, but the gods are exempt from their prosecution, and the Erinyes may not share in the feasts or in the human worship of the other gods. (This lonely isolation is later to be exploited by Athena.) The text of the antistrophe (360–6) is too corrupt for us to be at all sure of its total meaning; it would appear, at any rate, to corroborate, by a reference to Zeus' own attitude and, possibly, intentions in the matter, the exclusion of the Erinyes from all contact, official and social, with the Olympians.[34] Once again, a violent refrain (354 ff, 367 ff?) in the same insistent rhythm as the earlier refrain (328 ff, 341 ff) follows the second strophe and, most probably, the second antistrophe;[35] as before, the hymn of hate, accompanied, no doubt, by the mimetic menace of violent dancing, threatens those households where kin-bloodshed has broken out.

The third strophe and antistrophe (367 ff, 377 ff) continue to celebrate the Furies' assaults. Once again, we find a distinction between the strophic stanzas and the trochaic refrain which interrupts and follows them. In the former, dactylic, passages, first men's high reputations are pictured as wasting away before 'the black-robed assault, the malignant dancing' of the Furies; then the very mind of the victim (now 'particularized,' in the antistrophe, by a shift to the singular) is assailed, as the mist of pollution enfolds him, and Rumour (answering the 'high reputations' of the strophe) proclaims his whole house to be under its pall. The refrain, on the other hand, dwells with insistent trochaic beat on the physical aspect of the Furies' assault, the leaping and tripping of the Chorus' lethal dance.

μένει γάρ: 'for it [the law of retribution] abides ...'[36] In the final strophic pair (381–96) the Chorus return to their initial theme in this ode: their immutable and apportioned rights (λάχη, 386) to exact such retribution, as well as their inexorable efficiency (εὐμήχανοι / δὲ καὶ τέλειοι κακῶν ... δυσπαρήγοροι βροτοῖς, 381–4) in fulfilling them. Also highlighted in this closing set is the ambiguous and paradoxical status of the Furies and their prerogatives. In the strophe, these functions are described as 'dishonoured and despised' (ἄτιμ' ἀτίετα), 'kept separate from the gods in sunless gloom' (385–7).[37] In the antistrophe, we are reminded that the Furies' office (here described as θεσμός, no doubt to rival the new θεσμός which Athena is soon to proclaim)[38] is 'fate-ordained and granted by the gods' (391–3), and the Furies insist that they themselves meet with *no* dishonour (οὐδ' / ἀτιμίας κύρω, 393–4), though keeping their rank in the sunless shadows 'neath the earth. Both attitudes toward the Furies, respect and loathing for these Ishmaels of the Greek pantheon, the only survivors of the chthonic powers, are well represented in the attitudes of Athena and Apollo respectively. Both attitudes are to be exploited in the final reconciliation which Athena will achieve at the end of the play.

4 Third episode (vv 397–488)

The long-awaited arrival of Athena on the scene marks the beginning of a new phase in the play's action. However, Athena postpones notice of her unusual guests (the suppliant Orestes, surrounded by the Furies, at her altar) while she tells of her return from Troy, where she has been taking possession, for her citizens, of land awarded her by its Achaean conquerors (397–404). It is not unusual for gods in tragedy to tell whence they have come: both the great distances covered and the magnificent ease of their travel arrangements enhance their divine stature in contrast with their earth-bound subjects.[39] In the present instance the additional element of Athenian chauvinism contains perhaps another contemporary allusion;[40] at any rate, we shall see in a moment that Orestes makes 'political' capital of Athena's Trojan connection.

In her first reaction to the sight of the Furies at her altar, Athena is careful to avoid Apollo's reaction of horror and disgust ('this strange company,' she calls them and adds, 'I am surprised but not alarmed!' 406–7). Not until both suppliant and pursuers have both been asked 'Who are you?' does she turn her attention to her more egregious visitors. These, she allows, are like to no goddesses or mortals ever seen, but even so she checks herself from any discourteous comment on the grounds that it is unjust to speak evil of those who have not done any wrong (408–14). Athena's initial treatment of the Furies anticipates the careful courtesy with which she is to treat them thereafter, even when she learns their identity and their designs against her suppliant. In the ensuing dialogue, Athena is to make her first breach in the Furies' conception of justice, and the Furies are to make their first (and surprising) concession to Athena. The poet is concerned that these essential developments of his theme should arise as much as possible from the evolving dramatic situation and from the interaction between the characters and the Chorus (which, in this play, has almost the status of a dramatic character). The initial courtesy of Athena is an essential part of this procedure.

Two small points at the beginning of Chorus-Leader's answers to Athena's questions may, perhaps, be worth noticing. One is the choice, for the first time in this play, of the word *Arai* (417), rather than Erinyes, as the Chorus' identifying name. The other is the choice of the word βροτοκτονοῦντας ('homicides,' 421) to describe the object of the Furies' pursuit. Concerning the first point, it is true that *Arai* is elsewhere applied to the Furies. Some scholars take it as a precise equivalent; nevertheless, the term suggests curse-fulfilments in general, not merely ones arising from kin-slaying.[41] So, too, the word βροτοκτονοῦντας broadens (at least for the moment) the scope of the Furies' vengeance and so tends to dissipate (again for the moment) the exclusiveness of their concern with *kin*-murderers. In neither case does this imply a reduction, at this point in the drama, of the Furies' concentration on the matricide, Orestes. In both cases, however, the broader terms used in this first exchange with Athena prepare us for later developments in the play, concerning the functions of the Erinyes and of the Areopagus (soon to be described), once the trial of Orestes is over.

However, by far the most important point in this initial dialogue between Athena and the Furies is the 'new consideration' which Athena introduces concerning the just pursuit of homicides (or, in this case, matricides). For the Furies, it is sufficient that Orestes has admitted the slaying of his mother (425); Athena raises the question whether he may not have acted 'fearing the wrath of another necessity' (426), ie one as compelling as the threat of *their* vengeance for matricide. This is, in effect, one of the most significant verses in the play. In the first place it reminds the Furies (who have, a moment before, declared themselves to be avengers of murderers in general [βροτοκτονοῦντας, 421]) that Orestes was himself acting under the compulsion of his father's murder, ie of 'the Erinyes from his father's blood' (see *Cho* 283–4). (Thus, in this dialogue, the poet, by calling attention to the, as it were, contradictory functions of the Erinyes, is showing us the inadequacy of the old law of retribution.) Secondly, the implications of Athena's question, that there may be extenuating circumstances even for matricide, point the way to the removal of this inadequacy (ie by judicial inquiry into such circumstances). The revolutionary nature of this suggestion is indicated in the exchange which follows. To the Furies' rejection of any such excuse (or 'sufficient goad') for matricide, Athena replies that there may be two sides to that argument. And when the Furies then fall back on the old (and once sufficient) claim that the defendant has refused to take the oath (ie that he has not done the deed), Athena warns them twice (430, 432) not to mistake the appearance of justice (based on such legal technicalities) for justice itself.[42] Still more arresting, and more productive for the future action of the play, is the fact that the Furies, despite their initial surprise at this new way of looking at the matter (427, 431), declare themselves ready to learn from Athena ('... for you are not lacking in wisdom,' 431) and, reverencing Athena's worth and worthy parentage, turn over the judgment of Orestes' case to her.[43]

Not until Athena has dealt (with great diplomatic success) with the pursuers of her suppliant does she turn to question Orestes more closely. If indeed he sits, confident of justice, as a *purified* suppliant (in the manner of Ixion)[44] at her altar, then she would know his country, race, experience, and defence against the Furies' charge.

Athena's reference to Ixion, mythical prototype of the purified suppliant, gives Orestes the cue to stress again his own purified state and so his claim to be able to sit and to *speak* at her altar without fear of polluting it. Once again, the familiar term οὐ ... προστρόπαιος ('not as a polluted suppliant,' 445) and the accounts of purifying rituals performed 'at other houses' are all repeated.[45] This said, however, Orestes, in his self-identification, makes a significant change in his claims on Athena's protection. In his previous speech, as we have noted, he speaks, as it were, like a 'contemporary' Argive, promising the alliance, ἄνευ δορός, of Argos with Athena's people. Now he speaks again as an Argive but more specifically as the son of Agamemnon, who *with Athena* (457) rendered the Trojan people cityless. Orestes has listened to Athena's own account of her recent journeying from Troy, bringing evidence of Athenian honours from that battleground. The skilful pleader follows his diplomatic self-identification by an honest confession of his matricide ('I slew my mother; I'll not deny it,' 463) – sandwiched between human and divine justifications: Clytemnestra's ignoble dispatch of his father, Athena's Trojan ally, and the threats of Apollo (here described as jointly responsible, κοινῇ ... ἐπαίτιος, 465) if he failed to do the deed. Once again, Orestes turns over all adjudication of the matter to Athena, by whose judgment he will abide (468–9).

Athena now gives her decision concerning the judging of this matter of more than usual gravity (τὸ πρᾶγμα μεῖζον, 470). She states clearly why it is not lawful (θέμις, 471) for her to decide a murder case involving grievous wrath. On the one hand, Orestes has come as a properly purified suppliant whom she therefore accepts (or reverences?)[46] as a suppliant blameless in the eyes of the city. (Thus, if rejected, the suppliant might himself prove harmful to the city.) On the other hand, the Erinyes also have their prerogative (lit, 'lot' or 'portion,' μοῖραν, 476) in the matter, which, if it is set aside, will result in a poisonous blight from them upon the land. Therefore Athena announces that she will select judges of manslaughter, sworn to respect[47] the covenant which she will establish for all future time. Both Orestes and the Furies, both of whom have agreed to Athena's jurisdiction over their case, are called to witness these historic arrangements. Athena departs, promising to return after she has chosen 'the best of her citizens' for her new Court.

5 Second stasimon (490-566)

The Erinyes now embark on their great central ode, which, if it came immediately after the two blood-lapping parodoi (143-77, 254-75), might well strike the hearer as so inconsistent with their dramatic personality as to be credible only as a sort of Aeschylean parabasis.[48] However, the first stasimon (307-96), for all the vampire fury of its trochaic passages, has provided at least a hint of the loftier and more universal aspect of the Furies: there they have described themselves as εὐθυδίκαιοι ('righteous-judging,' 312) and their prerogative as a 'covenant [θεσμός, 391] ordained by fate and granted by the gods.' The present ode, with its emphasis on τὸ δεινόν, the healthy fear of retribution, as a moral force in society, expresses the divine 'law and order' aspect of the Furies, just as the two parodoi have concentrated mainly (and appropriately in their dramatic context) on their animal aspect (as Clytmnestra's creatures) of pursuit and vengeance. Thus we do not come quite unprepared for the Furies' still grim but more 'socially conscious' warnings in the present ode.

The ode begins with a series of awful prophecies based on the (to the Furies) dread premise that the cause of the matricide will prevail in the coming trial. First of all, they warn, that will mean the overthrow of the new covenant, the new court being established by Athena;[49] then all men will be enjoined to easy violence and many and certain slayings of parents by their children may be expected in the fullness of time (490-8). In the first antistrophe (499 ff) the minatory tone of these prophecies breaks forth into an explicit threat:

> For then [if the matricide wins his case], there'll be no anger from us, the mortal-watching maenads, for these deeds of violence. We'll let total ruin reign! (499-502)

The threat leads, in turn, to a sudden image of citizens hearing of ever fresh reports of such kin-slaughter and offering fruitless remedies (503-7). The Chorus concludes their prophecies with another reminder of the grim 'sanctions' they'll impose:

> Then let no one smitten with disaster cry out to us: 'O Justice, O sacred thrones of the Erinyes!' For soon might some father or mother, newly smitten, make piteous lament, as the house of Justice totters to the ground! (508-16)

In the second antistrophe (517 ff) the positive aspect of the Furies' theme becomes for the first time explicit:

> There is a place where Dread [τὸ δεινόν] as guardian of men's minds should abide [lit, 'remain seated']. To be chastened, to learn restraint by suffering is right and proper. What man or city fearing nothing 'neath the sun would ever honour justice? (517–25)

The reasonable, didactic tone, replete with genial admonitions ('Praise neither the anarchic nor the despot-ridden life!' 526–8) and benevolent aphorisms ('Prosperity comes from a healthy state of mind!' 535–7), continues for over three stanzas into the fourth strophe. Here we find the Furies dwelling (in thoroughly Aeschylean fashion) on Justice in general and on the positive rewards of the pious life, and including, for the first time, such traditional virtues as hospitality (along with respect for parents) among the values which they champion.

The calm ends as quickly as it came. Mid-way in the fourth stanza we come upon 'the rash transgressor' (553) desperately lowering his sails almost before we are aware of the sea-storm smashing his yard-arm. As in the first half of the ode, warnings change swiftly to vivid dramatic imagery, though this time it is the guilty one, rather than the victim, who calls out helplessly to those who hear him not.

> And the god laughs as he looks down on the passionate miscreant who, all unsuspecting, finds himself helpless, unable to round the cape to safety, engulfed in a sea of woes. Smashing his once fortunate ship against the reef of justice, unwept and unseen for evermore, he perishes! (560–5)

At the beginning of our analysis of the second stasimon, we have accepted Dover's view of the Chorus' opening prophecy, to wit, that if the new court of justice which Athena has just proposed fails to convict the matricide it will, at its very inception, preside over its own destruction. Need we go further and agree with the same critic that *throughout this ode* the Chorus is continuing to sing of this new court, the Areopagus, when it insists on the value of τὸ δεινόν in society and on the choice of a life which is neither anarchical nor enslaved?[50] On the whole, I think not; despite several tempting and indeed suggestive aspects of the argument, there is too much in the text and context of the ode which tells against its total acceptance. For one thing, the new court, as yet unnamed, has not at this point been described in terms which would justify the Furies' enthusiastic account of it as 'the disciplinary element' necessary for the preservation of the State. For another, though the Furies apparently accept the new court, in accordance with their previous agreement to accept Athena's disposition of Orestes' case (433–5), it seems improbable that this acceptance, which implies, as it were, their own demotion, would take this enthusiastic form – unless, of course, we are prepared to think that the poet was, at this point, prepared to sacrifice dramatic considerations entirely to contemporary political interest.[51] However, to my mind the most convincing objection to Dover's argument is the fact that the Chorus' warning concerning the outbreak of multiple kin-murders is directly connected (in sense and in syntax) with the sentence 'For the wrath of mortal-watching maenads [βροτοσκόπων μαινάδων, ie the Erinyes, 499–500] will no longer pursue these deeds.' Just as the destruction of the social fabric is seen (494–516) as the direct result of the disappearance of the Furies' pursuing wrath, so too the enthronement of τὸ δεινόν in the contrasted picture of the just state which follows (517 ff) must refer also to the presence of this same power. Moreover, the expression φρενῶν ἐπίσκοπον (518), in connection with τὸ δεινόν, reminding us of βροτοσκόπων μαινάδων (499–500), reinforces this identification.

Nevertheless, once this has been said, it should readily be admitted that the Chorus' account of the functions and effect of τὸ δεινόν in society transcends to some degree the more limited functions of the Furies, at least as they have been described hitherto in the play. This, as well as the 'political' advice (as Dover has called it), to praise neither the ἀνάρχετον nor the δεσποτούμενον βίον, seems to anticipate Athena's description of her new court, the Areopagus, and the political advice which is to accompany it. However, as we shall see, it is Athena's eventual intention that her court and its influence should function in concert with the Furies when they have become reconciled to their new position at the end of the action. In broadening the scope and interests of the Furies as he does in the second half of this ode, the poet is surely preparing us for this development by putting in the mouths of the Chorus an account of their own function which will accord well with that of the Areopagus when that, in due course, is formulated by Athena. And with the slight attenuation of the dramatic personality of the Chorus involved in this development, we may note a slight increase in what would appear to be specifically 'Aeschyliean' ideas, expressed in characteristically Aeschylean terms.[52]

6 Fourth episode (vv 566-777): the 'trial scene'

The scene now changes from Athena's temple on the Acropolis to the nearby hill, the Areopagus.[53] Though little or no change would be made in the physical setting (apart from the possible removal of the statue of the goddess), Athena's return would itself have a significant spectacular and aural effect, as she leads in her chosen band of Areopagites calling on the Etruscan trumpet to sound and the herald to marshal the people to their places. The proclamation for which the goddess demands silence is, however, postponed to the climactic moment at the end of this scene (681 ff: 'Now at length you may hear my covenant ...'); for the moment, Athena simply announces the *purpose* of the new court, to decide the justice of the case of those who stand before it.

First, Apollo is asked to state his business there.[54] The move is significant of the shift of emphasis from Orestes' to *Apollo's* role in the defence, a shift which is soon to be repeated in the actual trial. Apollo explains his presence as a material witness, first as the defender and purifier of his suppliant, and secondly as the very instigator of Orestes' deed of matricide (576–80). Thus answered, Athena officially opens the trial (εἰσάγω δὲ τὴν δίκην, 582) and calls on the Furies, as the prosecutors, to state their case.

The Chorus-Leader now interrogates Orestes on three points: the fact of the matricide, its method, and its instigation or motive.[55] The first two of these are a formality and readily answered by Orestes ('I slew her' and 'with a sword through the neck,' 588, 592, respectively). Orestes' answer to the third question ('by this god's oracle,' 594) immediately switches the responsibility to Apollo; Orestes' personal motives (enumerated at *Cho* 246–54, 300–5) are suppressed, save for Orestes' expression of willing acceptance (596) of the τύχη ('the happening,' a strange word in the circumstances) to which Apollo's orders led him. When pressed by the Chorus-Leader, Orestes further supports his confidence in his justification and acquittal by reference to the 'twofold pollution' of Clytemnestra, as slayer of her husband and his father (597–602); why, he asks, did the Furies not pursue *her* while she was living (604)? Orestes' arguments, then, imply the superiority of the male (the avenging of the husband-father). Inevitably the Furies counter with the claim that Clytemnestra was not guilty of kin-murder (605) but now, instead of continuing his own line of defence (ie the primacy of the marriage bond, urged by Apollo earlier, at 213 ff), Orestes for the first time seeks, albeit tentatively, to refute the Furies' specific charge of blood-guilt:

> Am I of the same blood as my mother? (606)

The deadlocked issue has at last taken a new turn and Orestes, quailing before the Furies' indignant reaction to this question, asks Apollo not, be it noted, to be an advocate but to be a judge concerning the justice or injustice of his deed (609–13).

Apollo, to our surprise, soon reverts (625 ff) to Orestes' original line of defence (cf 600–2), that it is the murder of the husband by the wife which is the greater of the two crimes. Before doing so, however, Apollo prefaces his argument with an overwhelming claim for all his oracles *which are commanded by Zeus himself*, and a reminder to the jurors:

> ... to understand how much strength *this* claim to justice has and so to follow the father's plan [$βουλῇ$], for an oath [presumably the juror's oath] is not stronger than Zeus. (619–21)

The Chorus is incredulous: could Zeus' oracle so disregard a mother's rights in the interest of vengeance for the father? In answer, Apollo extends something of Zeus' authority to Agamemnon's royalty:

> for the murder of a noble husband, endowed with Zeus' gift of royal power – murder, too, by the King's own wife – is in no wise the same [ie 'far worse than matricide']. (625–7)

Apollo concludes this part of his argument (addressed now to the jury rather than to the Chorus) with a detailed description of the various heinous aspects of Clytemnestra's deed (627–39).

The passage provides, in several ways, an interesting doublet to a passage in the 'pre-trial' scene between Apollo and the Furies. There, at vv 212 ff, the Furies parried the charge that they neglected Clytemnestra's crime by the defence that it was not a kin-murder. There, as here, Apollo prefaces his emphasis on Clytemnestra's greater guilt by a reference to Zeus' authority, for Zeus, together with Hera and Aphrodite, defends the marriage bond. And there too, as we have seen, there is a similar vindication of the priority of divine sanction (that of Zeus, Hera, and Aphrodite, backed by Fate and Justice, in this earlier passage) over even such binding commitments as an oath ('for the marriage bond ... is stronger than any oath,' 217–18).[56]

The Furies try a new tack. Zeus gives prior honour to the father, according to Apollo's argument, but how does this claim square with Zeus' own binding of his father Kronos? Apollo speedily aborts this argument with the reminder of the difference between bonds, which can be loosed, and 'blood once drunk by the thirsty dust' for which there is no recall (640–51).[57]

Orestes' reference to 'bloodshed' immediately prompts the Chorus-Leader, in the inevitable circularity of this contest, to return to *Orestes'* deed. How can Apollo plead for the acquittal of one who has shed *his mother's blood* upon the ground? How can such a one dwell in his father's palace or share the public altars or lustral bowls? (Thus the Furies clearly reject Orestes' claims to 'purification.') Only now does Apollo return to develop the argument which Orestes had introduced, and then handed over to him, at vv 606, 609–10. The mother, he declares, is not truly the parent of the child but only 'nurse of the newly sown embryo.'

> The begetter is the one who mounts, but *she* ['the mother'], as a stranger for a stranger, acts as preserver for the offspring ... (660–1)

A strange doctrine, though not as strange for the Athenian audience as for modern readers,[58] which Apollo immediately supports by pointing respectfully to Athena, a goddess born of Zeus without a mother. Apollo completes his defence with a frank *captatio benevolentiae*: he sends Orestes as a guest to Athens that he may be an ally, and a surety of future allies, to the land.

(This patent suggestion of bribery [which has been anticipated, before the trial proper, by Orestes' own promises at vv 289 ff and by his ingratiation, with Athena, of another kind at 455 ff] would not perhaps have startled an Athenian audience who were not unaccustomed to such devices in courts of justice. This 'contemporary' aspect of the trial scene and other elements in it which scholars have found unedifying or unconvincing has been well discussed by Lebeck and others. I cannot, however, agree with her that Aeschylus intends the trial scene in the *Eumenides* as a parody of Athenian legal practice [nor do the comments which she quotes from Reinhardt entirely support this view] and that further the purpose of this parody is to show the inadequacy of human justice. It may be true of this play, as she states, that 'Man, in the end, can only trust Zeus. Orestes' acquittal does not depend [I would say 'does not *entirely* depend'] upon the trial scene but on divine will,' but I do not think that the poet leads us to this conclusion by making a mockery of the trial of Orestes. If that were the case, the whole presentation of the founding of the Areopagus, on which so much dramatic energy is successfully expended, would lose its point.)[59]

Defence and prosecution have now both completed their respective arguments. Athena secures their agreement[60] that the case should now be handed over the jury for decision, and then embarks on her formal foundation of the new court of the Areopagus.

> People of Attica, now judging the first trial of bloodshed, hear now my ordinance ... (681–2)

It is perhaps remarkable that, in this lengthy proclamation (681–710), only in this initial sentence is the primary function of the court, the adjudication of bloodshed, mentioned, and mentioned, too, in such a way as to describe the function which the court is even now performing. A 'practical' explanation of this summary, almost elliptical, description of the court's judicial prerogative can, no doubt, be easily supplied: in her speech at the end of the preceding episode (470–88), Athena has already declared that she will go and choose just such a court of citizens to try this case of bloodshed which, for the reasons she there gives, she feels she cannot decide by herself. When she returns (at v 566) with the chosen band of citizens, lets the trumpet sound for silence for the court to hear her covenant, *and then begins Orestes' trial*, she has, in effect, already established the new tribuanl, specifically as a court for the trial of homicide.

Why, then, does the poet have Athena postpone her proclamation, her θεσμός, already prepared for in her call for silence at vv 570–3, till after the actual trial (though not the judgment) has been completed?[61] Partly, perhaps, to give this θεσμός greater prominence in isolation, but mainly, I would suggest, to make it easier for Athena to generalize, now that the court has already been seen in operation as a homicide tribunal, on the more wide-ranging powers and political significance she also envisages for the Areopagus. This, at any rate, is precisely what the goddess now proceeds to do.

First Athena ensures the perpetuity of this tribunal (ἔσται ... αἰεί δικαστῶν τοῦτο βουλευτήριον, 683–4). Then she supplies an explanation of the place-name, 'hill of Ares' (where the Amazons, battling with Theseus, sacrificed to Ares, 685–90), which may serve to suppress the memory of the earlier mythical trial of Ares himself by the Areopagus.[62] Next reverent Awe (σέβας) and its kinsman Fear (φόβος) on the part of the citizens are invoked as the familiar custodians of justice in this court, provided only that the citizens themselves do not corrupt the laws with base infusions (690–5).[63] Here the reminder of the salutary aspect of civic fear leads directly (as it did in the case of the Erinyes' account of *their* function in society, 517–31) to political considerations. Athena warns both against the danger of casting fear from the state ... 'for what man is ever just who nothing fears?' (696– 9).[64] In Athena's speech, however, 'the political consideration' is gradually given a firmer institutional context. First, the citizens are promised 'a bulwark of the land, a safeguard of the city, such as no man has ever had,' if they persevere in their reverence for this awesome body (τοιόνδε ... σέβας, 700). But finally, Athena establishes her court as just such a body, 'awesome, quick to anger, a wakeful guardian of the land, watching over its sleeping citizens' (705–6).

In this speech, then, we note a clear transition from the judicial to the political (or at least to the more universally protective) function which the new court of the Areopagus is to perform in the State. Indeed, so subtle is this transition that, at the crucial moment, it is hard to determine whether, in Athena's conditional promise of 'a bulwark of the land,' she requires her people to honour simply 'such a spirit of awe' (τοιόνδε ... σέβας) as we find in τὸ δεινόν (698) or, more specifically, the objectification of that necessary element in the new court itself.

(Long before the time of Aeschylus, the Areopagus had, of course, achieved just such a broadening of its powers from those of a homicide court to those which could, indeed, be loosely described as amounting to 'a guardianship of the state.' Although it was an institution in which the citizens at least of 'the older democracy' at Athens took great pride, this broader authority had, within a few years prior to the production of the *Oresteia*, been much curtailed. It is clear that the playwright had this contemporary issue much in mind when he composed Athena's speech at *Eum* 681–710. It is also clear from our brief analysis of this speech [as well as from certain features still to be noted in the dénouement of the play] that Aeschylus, through the words of Athena, appears to be championing the prestige and civic responsibilities of the Areopagus in terms which go far beyond the judicial functions for which, even in the play itself, Athena has established it. Further than this we are not, at least for the moment, prepared to go. The degree to which Aeschylus may have been taking sides in the continuing debate about the Areopagus, the detailed meanings, for example, which we should, or should not, attach to such apparently explicit pieces of political advice as we find in vv 693–6, have long been matters of debate among scholars. Some consideration of these arguments will be offered after we have completed our dramatic analysis of the play itself.)[65]

While the votes of the new jury are being cast, the Chorus-Leader and Apollo fill in the time with a barrage of thrusts and counter-thrusts. Dramatic interest, however is sharply revived at the end of this sequence, when Athena suddenly (and perhaps surprisingly, in view of her earlier statement at vv 471 ff), asserts her function of giving 'final judgment' (λοισθίαν ... δίκην, 734) in this matter. She will cast her vote for Orestes. The reason she gives is simply that, being born of no woman, she favours the male in all matters (except, in her case, in actual marriage) – this, and the fact that it is the male who is 'the guardian of the house' (δωμάτων ἐπίσκοπον, 740). Athena clearly intends her judgment as a 'casting vote,' declared in advance, for she concludes her declaration with the statement:

> Orestes wins, even if by equal votes the case be judged [νικᾷ δ' Ὀρέστης, κἂν ἰσόψηφος κριθῇ]. (741)

(Controversy, represented by a considerable body of literature on each side, has developed over the question whether the vote of Athena is counted with the votes of the jurors to produce the tied vote [and so the acquittal of Orestes] announced by Athena at vv 752–3, or whether Athena's vote is to be regarded as truly a 'casting vote' resolving the equal votes of the Areopagite jury; Gagarin is the most recent spokesman for the former view; Thomson, and more recently Hester, are among the most eloquent defenders of the latter.[66] Since both scholars rehearse the arguments which have been advanced on both sides [though neither of them, perhaps, with complete objectivity!], I shall content myself here with indicating what I feel to be the strongest arguments for the 'casting vote' view [which I believe to be the correct one] and for dismissing the alleged difficulties in the way of accepting it.

Athena has given advance notice of her vote in favour of Orestes and then, as we have seen, indicates the effect of this vote if there is a split decision, with equal votes on both sides: Orestes will win. The common-sense interpretation of this statement, apart from other considerations [dramatic and historical] which may be urged, must surely be that it is Athena's vote which would break such a tie and so secure Orestes' acquittal and this view is further supported by Athena's use of the particle καί ['*even* if the votes be equal'] which suggests that this condition might render acquittal uncertain, were it not for her already known vote for Orestes. To the argument that it was a historical practice [known to the audience] that tied votes regularly assured acquittal [and so that a tie-breaking vote from Athena is not needed to secure this result], it may be answered that the poet is here supplying a mythological explanation, a sort of aetiological myth, for this practice: hereafter, jurors are to imagine 'Athena's vote' as breaking this tie. There is, indeed, some ancient evidence that this was, in fact, the case: see Euri *IT* 1469–72; schol Aesch *Eum* 735 [where, however, there is some slight textual uncertainty] and Aristides *Or* 2.24. These passages do not, however, provide incontrovertible evidence for the *historical* explanation of the practice [which is not, in any case, the real issue here], since one of the sources is a dramatic text and the other, later ones *may* be expressing inferences based on the Aeschylean and Euripidean passages.

Athena's conditional statement at v 741 is repeated in unconditional form at vv 752–3, when the votes have been counted: the votes are, in fact, equal, and Orestes is acquitted. A little later [795–6], in her attempts to mollify the indignant Furies, Athena is to remind them that, in view of this 'equal vote,' they were not really defeated. Her credibility as a pacifier of the Furies would surely have been jeopardized in advance if she had first of all cancelled, by her vote, an actual vote by the human jury *condemning* Orestes, and then declared in addition that this single vote converted an actual condemnation into an *acquittal*. And this, as it were, 'double' use of her vote would be all the more extraordinary in view of the fact that Athena originally set up the human court of justice because of the particular nature of her own dilemma between the conflicting claims of Orestes and the Furies upon her [471–84]. Surely she would not wish to set aside the judgment of that court as, in effect, Gagarin's interpretation would have us believe. Rather, the only situation in which her vote will have any effect is when it is necessary to break a deadlock between what the human jury find to be the equally balanced but conflicting claims of each side.

Finally, we should consider arguments which are based on inferences from the text concerning the stage action during the voting scene. These are twofold. First it is argued that during the ten couplets [711–30] spoken by the Chorus-Leader and Apollo respectively, ten jurors vote, and during the closing triplet by the Chorus-Leader [731–3], the eleventh juror votes and Athena steps forward to vote. Therefore the jury is of an uneven number and Athena's vote must be included in the eventual tie. This argument I believe to be negligible; we know nothing of any dramatic silences which may have taken place [eg, between the Chorus' triplet at 731–3 and Athena's speech at 734]; we do not know how much, or how little, stage action went on during the Chorus' triplet at 731–3,[67] or indeed whether any activity *preceded* the ten couplets at 711–30. In fact we can form no detailed picture of the stage action during these exchanges other than the fact that the jurors' voting was going on and is completed by the time Athena begins speaking at v 734. The second argument based on alleged stage action is somewhat stronger. Athena states at v 735: 'I, for my part, will hand over [display? show? προσθήσομαι] this vote for Orestes.' We are, perhaps, entitled to ask what Athena does with her vote, or whether she does anything with it. Gagarin argues that she places it forthwith in the urn which will receive the other white ballots of the jurors voting for acquittal and that therefore it is included in the 'equal numbers total' announced at v 753. This strikes me as unlikely: Athena is not a member of the Court which she has set up; at best she is its presiding officer and as such would hardly vote with them, let alone lead off the voting. According to our former argument, she simply declares what her casting vote, should it be necessary, will be – as she makes clear when she states (at 741) what the *effect* of her vote will be in the event of a tie. Some scholars indeed suggest that Athena's 'vote' may be symbolical and that no physical vote on her part need be shown, and this seems a reasonable possibility in the case of a divine statement of decision.

I have argued at some length for the view that Athena's vote is truly a 'casting vote' because the alternative interpretation [that the human jury of the Areopagus votes against acquittal] is germane to Gagarin's further argument that it is the Areopagus and the Erinyes who are the true upholders of *dikê*, regarded [as Gagarin regards it even for *this* play] as the principle of retribution, whereas the gods (Apollo and Athena, under Zeus himself) subvert *dikê*.[68] What this argument fails to recognize is that while the human jury remains on the horns of the dilemma, unable to decide for one side or the other, the divine vote favours the new form of justice, which, as we have seen, admits considerations of motive and circumstance, including those of divine commands, and which depends ultimately on conformity with the will of Zeus.)[69]

A series of tense utterances from Orestes and the Chorus-Leader, then from Apollo himself, serves to heighten the tension as the votes are being counted. Finally, Athena announces the verdict: Orestes is acquitted, 'for the number of votes is equal' (752–3)

Orestes greets Athena's announcement with a great speech (754–77) of gratitude to Athena, to Apollo, and to Zeus τρίτος Σωτήρ. The terms in which the hero addresses Athena, 'You who gave me a home when I lost my father's ...' (755–6), establishes the oneness of Athens and her tutelary god and so the detailed pledge of Argive support to Athens which follows is Orestes' thank-offering to god and people for his delivery from his mother's Furies.

To many readers, the manner of Orestes' acquittal and, in particular, Athena's explanation of her casting vote come as something of a letdown, in a trilogy in which so much has been said and sung about the justice of Zeus and in which so much dramatic energy has been spent in distinguishing Orestes' bloody deeds from those which have preceded them. Nevertheless, these few verses from Athena defending her preference for the male side (736–40) need not be taken as obliterating (as they certainly do not contradict) the more extensive reasons (provided in this play and in the whole trilogy) for regarding Orestes' escape from retribution as more justifiable than Clytemnestra's or even Agamemnon's would have been. While both Agamemnon and Clytemnestra acted as the ministers of Zeus' justice, both were provided with secular motives for their particularly heinous deeds: Agamemnon, in the famous passage rehearsing his 'dilemma,' mentions not the justice of Zeus but his fear of being a 'fleet-deserter' (λιπόναυς, Ag 212); Clytemnestra's motive of erotic passion and erotic jealousy complement her motive of outraged mother-love and both are made explicit in her 'defence' before the Chorus after the murder of Agamemnon. Orestes' personal motives, on the other hand, to avenge his father and to regain his royal patrimony, are strictly in accord with Apollo's (Zeus-inspired) commands and Apollo has reminded us that the royal sceptre of which his mother deprived the King came from Zeus himself (*Eum* 626). These motives, both personal and divinely inspired, are still Orestes' justification for his deed (in a sense they are also subsumed under Athena's explanation of her casting vote 'for the male,' δωμάτων ἐπίσκοπον ['guardian of the house'], as she calls him [740]).[70] These and other preparations (which we have noted) for the vindication of Orestes supply the (admittedly decreasing) human factor in the presentation of Orestes' situation, the necessary degree of sympathy which has been elicited for the only member of his blood-stained family deemed worthy of escape from vengeance. They need not be forgotten simply because that vindication now appears in the impersonal terms (appropriate to this stage of the trilogy) in which Athena expresses it.

Does the trial and acquittal of Orestes represent a solution to the problem of the blood-feud by the introduction of a new form of justice which, for society at large, will dispense with such self-perpetuating sequences of vengeance? Has the establishment of the Areopagus, the first homicide court, put an end to the ancient prerogative of the Erinyes, the automatic exaction of blood for blood? It has become fashionable, of late, to reject this traditional, 'common-sense' view of the action of the *Eumenides*. This repudiation is stated most emphatically by Lloyd-Jones:

> The cliché we have heard repeated all our lives that the *Eumenides* depicts the transition from the vendetta to the rule of law is utterly misleading.

and (to anticipate for a moment the dénouement of the play):

> When the Erinyes become Eumenides, there is not the least question of their giving up their function.[71]

Similarly, Gagarin regards the Furies and the Areopagus alike as the upholders (in spite of the Olympians!) of the unchanged principle of *dikê*, 'the force of law, order, retribution and punishment.'[72] The basis of this view is (for both scholars)[73] the striking similarity between the function of the Erinyes, described by themselves in the second stasimon, and the function of the Areopagus, described by Athena in her 'foundation speech,' namely, that of providing the necessary element of fear and awe ('the formidable,' as Lloyd-Jones translates τὸ δεινόν in this context) essential in a civilized society. Moreover, that the Furies will retain this function is to be established by the honours which Athena showers upon them at the end of the play as the upholders, along with her court, of justice (*dikê*).

It is, of course, clear from the text that, in general terms, the 'disciplinary functions' ascribed to the Erinyes and to the Areopagus, respectively, are similar. If this were all that was needed to establish that *dikê* is to be viewed in the same light before and after the new Court is founded, there would be no problem. But why, if the Areopagus and the 'pre-Areopagite Erinyes' operate with the same concept of *dikê*, do we need the Areopagus at all? Or, to put the matter in its dramatic context, what important difference does the foundation of this Court make in the dramatic action of the play? The answer is clear. If retributive justice, pure and simple, had been allowed to operate, the Furies, according to their ancient prerogative, would successfully have claimed Orestes as their victim. This they were prevented from doing, temporarily by Apollo, permanently by Athena's establishment of her human court of homicide and the subsequent acquittal of Orestes.[74] As we have noted, the point at which a new concept of justice is most sharply anticipated comes in that crucial exchange at vv 426 ff, where Athena introduces to the surprised Furies the new considerations, motive and circumstances, as elements affecting the justification or the culpability of their quarry. The Furies accept 'the new *thesmoi*' (as they themselves call Athena's proposal to found a new Court, which is to adhere to her 'new considerations') but warn that it had better support their ancient prerogatives. That the Furies realize *after the verdict* that these ancient prerogatives *have* been abrogated is clearly demonstrated by their savage outcry in the ode (778 ff) immediately following Orestes' speech of gratitude. If this were not the case, and if Lloyd-Jones and Gagarin were right that 'the old laws' have really not been changed, then the long appeasement of the Erinyes, which we are now to consider, would not have been needed. As we shall see, the Erinyes, honoured as they are in the closing passages of the play, will henceforth operate in an environment (now the environment of the *polis*) unalterably changed by the institution of a human court of homicide.[75]

7 The 'conversion' of the Erinyes (vv 778–1020); the escorting of the Erinyes to their new home (vv 1021–47)

The final movement of the *Eumenides* comprises an exciting sequence of passages, alternately lyric and dramatic, culminating in the pacification and winning over of the Erinyes, the climax of this play and of the trilogy.[76] This dénouement, though a reversal of the hostility of the Furies at the beginning of this 'movement,' yet fulfils certain dramatic expectations provided earlier in the play. The Chorus, it will be remembered, has given notice in the second stasimon (490–565) that if Orestes is acquitted, the new θεσμοί of Athena will be doomed, for the Erinyes themselves will withdraw the fear of retribution from the body politic, and anarchy, especially in the form of kin bloodshed, will inevitably ensue. Yet, by a nice irony, the Chorus' own descriptions of the necessary element of fear which they provide anticipate, as we have noted, Athena's own description (at vv 690–706) of the function of her new court of the Areopagus.[77] Now, after the acquittal of Orestes, it will be Athena's task first to allay the dread curses which the indignant Chorus threaten to let loose on Athens, and then to convert the Furies' destructive power into a positive function in the new scheme of things. As she succeeds, the apparent 'displacement' of the Erinyes by the Areopagus becomes less of a displacement than a redirection, since the new court is to embody those very functions which the Furies, once reconciled, are best fitted to sustain. But the Erinyes are also to acquire new powers of a more beneficent and life-giving kind than could ever have been anticipated from their manifestation as fiends of vengeance in the opening passages of this play.

In formal structure as well as in thematic development, this sequence provides a fitting finale for the trilogy. In its first part, we see and hear the lyric fury of the Chorus' song and dance breaking, wave after wave, against the iambic discourse of Athena's gentle reasoning (778–891). Here *Peithô*, Persuasion, which has appeared in sinister form in the first play of the trilogy (Helen as *Peithô* luring Paris to bring destruction on the Trojans,[78] Clytemnestra as *Peithô* persuading Agamemnon to tread the purple, *Ag* 931 ff), is finally vindicated (and duly thanked by her minister, Athena)[79] as the gentle victor over violence. At this point, when Athena's last arguments prevail, the Chorus, through its Leader, joins Athena in iambic discussion of the terms of the new pact, brief symbolic definitions of what will be expected from each side (881–915). Once these are established, another modified kommos ensues, the now joyful songs of the Chorus alternating with anapaestic chants from Athena (916–1020). Finally, the escorting of the Erinyes/Eumenides to their new home is also accomplisheduby a fresh alternation of iambic and lyric passages (1021–47).

The sequence I have outlined begins, then, with a furious (dochmiac) song and dance (778 ff) by the Chorus, interspersed by Athena's iambic deprecations of the Furies' curses. Athena's first appeal is met with a precise repetition of the opening strophe. Another indignant outburst, somewhat different in tone, follows Athena's second appeal, and this is again repeated, verbatim, after her third. Only after a fourth appeal from the goddess is there any real response, the sudden change in mood being marked by a switch to iambic dialogue. The drama of the passage lies in this modulation and ultimate reversal of the Chorus' fury before the subtler onslaught of Athena's various appeals.

The Chorus' opening song (778–93) is its most lethal one, for it contains, after a furious indictment of the younger gods, the Furies' actual curses in the name of *Dikê*, against the crops and children of Attica (... λιχὴν ἄφυλλος ἄτεκνος). Athena's first (ignored) appeal undergoes a subtle change in her second attempt. Mention of Zeus' will (797–9)[80] is replaced by a casual reference to Zeus' thunderbolts (827–9); offers of caverns and altars at Athens (805–7) by the warmer invitation to share Athena's home and honours (ὡς σεμνότιμος καὶ ξυνοικήτωρ ἐμοί· 833). And the Furies' blighting curse is deprecated by an offer of 'first fruits' (ἀκροθίνια, 834) on behalf of the children and of marriage rites. In the Chorus' second strophe, there is at least an oblique answer to Athena's plea ('oh that I should live in this land, a thing of scorn and hatred!' 838–9); there is as yet no sign of yielding, but the Erinyes at least indicate that they have heard Athena's suggestion. Moreover, self-pity, not curses, now predominates in the Chorus' song.

In her third speech (848–69), Athena offers the Erinyes a seat near the house of Erechtheus, the most 'national' of Athens' shrines. Correspondingly, her deprecations also take on a political and contemporary flavour as fears of civil war ('Apply not goads to bloodshed in my land!' 858–9) replace fears of natural blight and sterility. In her last plea (after the Chorus' repeated chant of bitter hatred) Athena's language becomes still more persuasive ('soft inducements from my honeyed tongue ...' 886) ... *and more political*.[81] No one of these elder gods (she declares) can ever say that she was an exile (ἀπόξενος, 884) from Athens; each, if she wishes, may become a property holder (γάμορος, 890) justly honoured for all time.

The Furies' capitulation (892–900) is as complete as it is sudden. Is it Athena's promise of civic security that wins them over? One is tempted to think so: they continue to employ Athena's legalistic terminology as they ask for security (ἐγγύη, 898) for the promise that no house may prosper without their aid. The Erinyes have become good burghers in the end.

Chief among the honours which Athena bestows on the Eumenides (as we may now call them) is that no house may flourish without their aid (895). In answer to the Chorus' question as to what blessings they should invoke upon the land, Athena ends the reconciliation scene with a splendid evocation (903–15) of the prosperity which

Athens is to enjoy – in crops and heroes, and in the increase, prosperity, and virtue of its citizens. (Here Athena's language prepares us for the coming series of repudiations of the 'corrupt nature imagery' of the first play of the trilogy: 'like a good gardener' [ἀνδρὸς φιτυποίμενος δίκην, 911] she cherishes a race of just citizens free of blight.) The speech serves as a dramatic prologue to the blessings which the Eumenides themselves are to call down in their final chorus on the land which they had blasted with curses in the preceding ode.

This reversal of mood and function on the Chorus' part is answered by a similar though less emphatic change of tone on Athena's part as well.[82] Again the epirrhematic form is used to express the new positions,[83] as Athena intervenes, amid the Chorus' lyrical showers of blessings, with anapaestic chants reminding all of the more sombre aspects of the Eumenides' role. A few examples will suffice to illustrate this curious blend.

In its first strophe, the Chorus undoes its former curses with prayers that the bright sun may cause teeming abundance to break forth from the earth (923–6). Athena follows this immediately with a reminder of a very different aspect of the Erinyes/Eumenides:

> ... Mighty and hard to please
> are the divinities I make to settle here ...
> And he that encounters their anger
> does not know from where come the blows that assail his life;
> for crimes born from those of long ago
> hale him before them, and in silent destruction,
> loud though he boast,
> through their wrath and enmity grind him to nothing.
> (928–37, in part)[84]

Later, the Chorus, in their benevolent mood, seem almost to repudiate this reminder of their ancient punitive role as they pray:

> ... may the dust not drink the black blood of the citizens
> and through passion for revenge
> speed on the ruin to the city
> wrought by murder in return for murder!
> (980–3)

Once again Athena follows with her warning of the price of this benevolence:

Have they [the citizens] a mind to find out
the path of benediction?
Then from these fearsome faces
[ἐκ τῶν φοβερῶν τῶνδε προσώπων]
I see great good for these the citizens.
For if, kind in return for kindness,
you do them ever great honour, both land and city
on the straight path of justice
you shall keep, in every way preëminent.
(988–95)

Other critics have already commented on various reversals in the use of imagery (particularly in the Chorus' blessings) at the end of the *Oresteia*:[85] joyous 'blossom images' where once (as at *Agamemnon* 659) such imagery was used with sinister corrupting irony; images of growth, vitality, and light, where once 'blood shed upon the ground' produced ever more bloodshed, with the chthonic powers sending further destruction rather than nourishment. But it is now Athena's role to remind us that the Eumenides still retain, in its most effective form, that great quality of *to deinon* by which, in the second stasimon, they claimed to maintain justice among men. In this, it would seem, they are to share the role which Athena has assigned to the Areopagus as 'the ever-watchful guardian of the land.'

In certain other ways, however, the newly defined function of the Erinyes transcends that of any merely human court. Among her persuasions Athena has already promised that no house shall prosper if it does not honour the Erinyes (895–7). Later, she compounds this assurance with still more generous descriptions of their prerogatives ('It is their lot to manage all affairs of men' [πάντα ... τὰ κατ' ἀνθρώπους], 930–1) and reminds her new Court (πόλεως φρούριον, 949) that the Furies have the power to bestow joys upon some men, upon others a life of tears (952–5). In stressing these all-embracing life-functions, Athena seems to be reverting to their (Aeschylean?) association, here almost identification, with the Moirai, the Fates; as if in response to this declaration of Athena's, the Chorus, in turn, invoke the Moirai, their 'sisters,' in terms very similar to those which Athena has just applied to themselves (959–67).[86] Could it be that Athena (and the poet) is in some degree compensating the Erinyes for their diminished role in avenging familial bloodshed by adverting to these more wide-ranging prerogatives? Or are these new life-giving and life-begetting powers ones which rightly belong to the original, chthonic Eumenides with whom (as Reinhardt has argued)[87] the Erinyes are here for the first time identified?

However that may be, Athena's valedictory chant (1003 ff) as she sends the Erinyes down to their new home (1006-7), in the caves beneath the Acropolis,[88] stresses again the function which they will perform in their benevolent chthonic capacity, that of restraining the baneful (τὸ μὲν ἀτηρὸν, 1007) and sending up the profitable (τὸ δὲ κερδαλέον, 1008). As the Chorus repeat their blessings (χαίρετε, χαίρετε δ' αὖθις, ἔπη [Weil] διπλοίξω, 1014) Athena bids her own attendant escort them below, 'to the very eye of Theseus' whole land,'[89] and to further honour them with investiture in crimson robes. Thus the trilogy ends with the recurrence of a striking visual symbol: the blood-stained robe of the slain Agamemnon (displayed at the climactic moments of both preceding tragedies) is now triumphantly replaced by crimson insignia proclaiming the new civic status of the Erinyes.[90] A second Chorus acting as escorts sing the Recessional as they conduct the Erinyes/Eumenides off the scene.[91]

NOTES

1 Apollo's 'takeover' at Delphi was not described as a peaceful one elsewhere in the tradition. According to the account at Euripides *IT* 1249-53, Apollo (brought to Delphi by his mother Leto after his birth at Delos) first slays the serpent guarding the chthonic seat of prophecy, then dispossesses Themis (daughter of Gaia, cf *Eum* 2-3) of her oracular seat; Zeus' help is later required to allay reprisals from Mother Earth herself and to reestablish Apollo on the seat of prophecy. (In the Homeric Hymn to Apollo, we are told only that Apollo slew the serpent, mother of the monster Typhaon, guarding the site.) The free gift (as a 'birthday present,' γενέθλιον δόσιν, *Eum* 7) of the oracular shrine to Apollo by Phoebe (another Titanic daughter, succeeding Themis at Delphi) is doubtless Aeschylus' invention ... for the dramatic purposes to be suggested. Cf Kitto *Form and Meaning in Drama* p 54 and Lloyd-Jones, in his note ad loc, in his translation of the *Eumenides*, who also comment on Aeschylus' emphasis on Apollo's peaceful takeover at Delphi. See further Rosenmeyer *The Art of Aeschylus* pp 111 ff, on significant features of the style and content of the Priestess' catalogue of the gods connected with Delphi.

2 '... dripping with blood:' is this blood from the murder of Clytemnestra

or, as some think (eg, Lloyd-Jones in his note ad loc), the pig's blood from the purification ritual referred to later (282–3)? The question will be considered after the various passages concerning Orestes' purification have been reviewed. However, we may note one initial objection to the 'pig's blood' view: the reference in the same sentence to the freshly drawn sword surely suggests that the blood in question comes from Orestes' own deed of violence.

3 This is the more generally accepted view; cf Pickard-Cambridge *The Theatre of Dionysus* pp 44, 107 f. However, we do not really know how this scene was managed. Taplin's view (*The Stagecraft of Aeschylus* pp 369–74), that the Chorus is not visible until the parodos at 140 ff, seems unlikely, since Apollo clearly describes them as being present: ὁρᾷς ... 'you *see* these crazed creatures, overcome, fallen asleep ...' he says (67 f) to Orestes, who clearly *is* present, since he answers at vv 85 ff (Taplin, in defence of his view, is forced to take ὁρᾷς, improbably, as meaning 'understand' here). Taplin's first argument (among several) for the non-appearance of the Chorus before v 140, namely that 'the Chorus ... normally enters *to* the first song, not *before* it,' is nullified (as far as reasonable exceptions go) by his own mention of Euripides' *Supplices*. The argument for the Chorus' entry at the parodos is then reduced to 'unless there is very good reason otherwise' (p 371). Many readers will find excellent reasons for the presence of the Chorus in that they are an essential part of the situation to which the actors in the Prologue (most notably Apollo and Clytemnestra's Ghost) now address themselves.

4 κτανεῖν ... μητρῷον δέμας 84: the peculiar phraseology is perhaps an anticipation of Apollo's 'biological' defence (658 ff) of Orestes' matricide: that the mother is not truly the parent of the child at all.

5 Paley (*The Tragedies of Aeschylus*) explains this obscure verse (104) by the alleged Greek doctrine that the mind's eye sees more clearly in sleep. He also refers to *Cho* 280 (= 285 OCT) but that corrupt and obscure verse (obelized in Page's OCT) offers little help. I accept Prien's deletion of v 105: 'in daytime men's fate is unforeseen' makes little sense in the context and it may be that *both* verses (*Eum* 104–5), which have some connection in sense, belong to the same interpolation, as Lloyd-Jones thinks. See now Podlecki 'The *Phrên* Asleep: *Eumenides* 103–5.'

6 We shall return to the question as to whether the Erinyes properly pursue only *kin*-bloodshed in connection with the Chorus' statement to this effect at v 605 – in answer to a question by Orestes, who has reason to believe otherwise.

7 The gradual and subtle transformation of the Erinyes throughout the

action (and particularly throughout the choral lyrics, which may be regarded as part of the action) of this play has, of course, been noted by other critics. Perhaps the best treatment of it, including discussion of the image sequences involved, is to be found in Lebeck's *The Oresteia*, part 4, passim, esp section 16. Cf also, Winnington-Ingram 'A Religious Function of Greek Tragedy: A Study of the *Oedipus Coloneus* and the *Oresteia*' pp 16 ff, and *Studies in Aeschylus* chapter 8; Méautis 'Notes sur *les Eumenides* d'Eschyle' pp 33 ff. (Both Winnington-Ingram and Méautis compare the initially terrifying and later beneficent aspects of the Erinyes in this play with the allegedly similar effects in Sophocles' *OC*; the differences are, however, more striking than the similarities.)

On the imagery involved in these contrasting treatments of the Erinyes (as well as on contrasts with the imagery in the preceding plays of the trilogy) see, in addition to Lebeck and the studies of Goheen and Peradotto to which she refers (p 131, n 1), Vidal-Naquet *Chasse et Sacrifice dans l'Orestie* esp pp 136–7, 145–8, who comments on the significance of the interweaving of 'hunt imagery' with the sacrifice theme. Cf also Zeitlin 'The Motif of the Corrupted Sacrifice,' to which we have already referred (chapter 1 appendix 1, n 15).

8 In connection with the total treatment of the Erinyes (including their ultimate 'conversion' by Athena) in this play, we should consider Reinhardt's discussion (*Aischylos* pp 154 ff) of the original *distinction*, and the alleged connection, between the Erinyes and the Eumenides in early Greek thought. Reinhardt describes the function of the Erinyes from Homer onwards as 'the power of curse, the denotation of the magic of forgotten blood-shed.' Emphasizing both their 'instantaneous' and their 'specialist' qualities in their hound-like pursuit of the blood-guilty victim, he adds significantly, 'An Erinys can as little bless as a Curse can be recalled or removed' (p 154). The Eumenides, on the other hand, he describes as 'earth-goddesses, worshipped in connection with the Areopagus, on whom all life and fertility depended ... until the Olympians and the State culture deposed them in ethical and political significance.' Reinhardt stresses that it was their separation, in time of origin and in the physical location of their cult (under the rock or Ares or under the *Kolonos Hippios*) which caused them to be regarded with a certain awe or fear ... 'wherefore one gladly calls them (euphemistically) the Well-wishers, Gracious Ones, Eumenides' (p 155).

Reinhardt, I think rightly, rejects Wilamowitz' view (see his reference ad loc) that the Erinyes and the Eumenides were *originally* one, that, when they lost their blood-avenging function as Erinyes, they retained only a vague, gypsy-like capacity, and that it was Aeschylus who restored their original oneness with the Eumenides. Reinhardt argues that in Aeschylus the Erinyes are in no way *restored* as Eumenides but rather are introduced as Eumenides for the first time. This originality on the poet's part he defends mainly from the marked antithesis of Aeschylus' play: curses (the exclusive function of the Erinyes) are the goddesses' only power at the beginning; blessings, their exclusive function at the end. Though one might (as we shall see) question Reinhardt's emphasis on the *exclusively* kindly attributes of the Erinyes/Eumenides at the end of this play, I am inclined to accept (as far as one can in these conjectural matters) his argument as a whole.

9 ποτιτρόπαιος (176): again the technical term for one polluted with bloodshed. Whether or not Orestes has been purified at this point, the Furies would not, and at this point claim they never will, recognize such purification, for they believe that his pollution will cling to him even in the Underworld, after death. In this ode (169–70) and later (204) they upbraid Apollo for sullying his own shrine with the presence of the polluted Orestes.

10 The Chorus make two other significant references to the Fates later in the play at vv 723–4 and at v 961, respectively. In both passages, as Sidgwick points out, the Chorus speak of the Fates as beings quite separate from themselves. Hence it would appear that the present passage (171–2) is an obscurely phrased reference (anticipating vv 723–4) to Apollo's comparable outrage of the Moirai or possibly (as an anonymous reader has suggested to me) a reference to Apollo's destruction of those provisions of the Fates which the Erinyes would expect to follow. It does not (as some commentators, including the Scholiast, have thought) imply a momentary identification of the Furies themselves with the Fates. But cf also vv 895, 903–15, 930–1, 948–55 and below, n 86.

11 Cf Herodotus (III.125, VI.9, IX.112), who attributes such deeds and punishments to the Persians (as Lloyd-Jones has also noted, in his note to *Eum* 186). Cf also Plutarch *Life of Artaxerxes* XVI–XVII.

12 Again we should note the use of the technical term προστρόπαιος for the suppliant seeking purification from bloodshed. A few moments earlier, as we have seen (205), Apollo has answered the Furies' charge that he has received one polluted with bloodshed at his shrine by claiming that he has ordered Orestes to seek purification (προστραπέσθαι) there. Now he reminds us of the special claims that such a suppliant has upon *him*. The precise moment or occasion of Orestes' purification is not here made clear, but as we shall see at the beginning of the scene at Athens, Orestes is there no longer προστρόπαιος, no longer a blood-polluted suppliant.

13 Cf Smyth *Aeschylean Tragedy* pp 214 ff, who discusses this distinction and then goes on to explain that the Apolline cult sought to soften the idea of blood-pollution by introducing purification in justifiable cases. However, in saying of the Furies in the *Eumenides* that Aeschylus 'unconsciously reproduced their primitive function ... The Furies of Clytemnestra are in fact only Clytemnestra herself, her ghostly spirit multiplied to form a group' (ibid p 217), Smyth does not tackle the problem of the apparent inconsistency between the functions of the Erinyes in the *Choephori* and the *Eumenides*, respectively.

The terms 'shame culture' and 'guilt culture' used above are borrowed from Dodds' use (*The Greeks and the Irrational* chapter 2), with careful qualifications of these expressions, to describe the different attitudes of the Homeric and the archaic periods, respectively. For the application of this distinction to the present problem, I am indebted to Visser *The Erinyes* chapter 2, esp pp 120 ff, though the way in which I apply the distinction, and my own conclusions on how the Erinyes function in the *Eumenides*, differ from her more complex treatment.

14 See Hesiod *Theogony* 178–85. Cf also Homer *Il* 19.418, where the Erinyes stop the voice of Achilles' horse Xanthus, as it prophesies Achilles' death. Cf further Heraclitus B 94 (D–K) (to which Munro refers in his note to the above passage from the *Iliad*), where it is said that the Erinyes, 'guardians of Justice,' keep watch over the Sun, lest it transgress its limits.

15 Cf Verrall's note to *Eum* 212 ad fin: 'The limitation of murder to the shedding of kindred blood (according to various conceptions of kindred) was a view which had authority, and the Erinyes of Aeschylus adopt it, *when it suits them*, but generally disregard it.' But cf also Verrall's curious comment (in his note ad loc) on the reference at *Cho* 283 to 'the Erinyes from the father's blood': 'All the conceptions of this passage are far more ancient than the cult of the Erinyes as goddesses; and indeed ἐρινύων (avenging spirits) is not here a proper name.'

16 The other three occurrences of Ἐρίνυς or Ἐρινύες in the *Choephori* also do not support the restrictive function of vengeance for kin-murder which they claim for themselves at *Eum* 212, since they occur in connection with vengeance either on both Clytemnestra and Aegisthus (402) or on Aegisthus alone or for the stain of bloodshed in general (651). The meaning (and text) is a shade uncertain in the third of these passages (648–51); if we take τέκνον to refer to Orestes, we again see the Erinus as bringing the son to avenge the murder of his father, as in *Cho* 283.

17 See Owen *The Harmony of Aeschylus* p 114 for this and the following quotation. Cf the similar view of Kitto *Form and Meaning* pp 61-2. (Kitto rather overemphasizes the view that the Furies, even in this play, are essentially 'Cries for Vengeance' [*Arai*] for *any* sort of violence, when he translates αὐτουργίαι at *Eum* 336 as 'acts of wanton violence' rather than as 'acts of kin violence.' Cf below, p 153, and n 41).
18 Owen, to be sure, appears to recognize this point (though not, perhaps, in the terms I would use) when (*The Harmony of Aeschylus* p 115) he quotes George Thomson with approval to the effect that the identification of the Furies with the customs of tribal society is one of the ways of expressing 'the old dispensation' in opposition to the new ways of the *polis*.
19 See Davies *The Eumenides of Aeschylus* appendix, pp 207-9. Davies notes that Weil had already suggested a lacuna after v 212 but rejects Weil's further suggestion that its purport was simply '*itaque nostrum non est eam persequi*,' which would be merely an expression of what the Furies had already clearly implied in their answer (212) to Apollo's question in the preceding verse. (I have adjusted Davies' and Weil's line numbering to that of the OCT.)
20 Thomson *The Oresteia of Aeschylus* vol II (Commentary), p 198 (note to vv 217-18). Cf also Paley, ad loc (= vv 208-9, in his edition).
21 Kells 'Aeschylus, *Eumenides* 213-214 and Athenian Marriage.' See also Kells' arguments for rejecting the versions of Paley and Thomson (already discussed) as well as that of Wecklein, who explains that the marriage-bed is 'die eheliche Verbindung, über welche Dike wacht ...'
22 For the relevant ancient sources, see Thomson's note ad loc.
23 On the 'change of scene' and on other unusual features involved (eg, the specific time lapse) in the transition at vv 235 ff, see Taplin *The Stagecraft of Aeschylus* pp 377-8. The only visual scenic change needed would seem to be the addition of Athena's statue and even this, as Taplin notes, might have been there from the start and simply revealed at this juncture.
24 I cannot agree with Sidgwick's view (see his notes on vv 41 and 237) that the word προστρόπαιος is used in different senses at v 41 and at vv 234, 237, respectively. The repeated emphasis on this word in different contexts surely tells against this explanation.
25 See Dyer 'The Evidence for Purification Rituals at Delphi and Athens.' Dyer points out (pp 40-3) that most of the relevant evidence concerns rituals which took place outside Delphi, though Delphi gave oracles which might occasionally involve such rituals and might properly be looked to for the authority for a purification system. He concludes

(pp 55–6) that some of the audience might think of the purification of Orestes as taking place at Athens or Troezen, others at Delphi. 'Aeschylus himself is vague.' (Nevertheless, it is hard to imagine the audience thinking of any other place than Delphi when Orestes mentions ἑστίᾳ θεοῦ Φοίβου as the place where he experienced the pig's-blood ritual [282–3], since no other hearth of Phoebus has been mentioned.)

26 This is my own view of this vexed question. Cf also Mazon *Eschyle* II, 126, who also regards Apollo's 'travelling instructions' to Orestes (vv 75–7) as intended to complete his purification and compares the practice at Athens of a year's exile (ἀπενιαυτισμός) for involuntary homicides. (I cannot, in view of vv 238–9, agree with Smyth, *Aeschylean Tragedy* p 219, that Orestes 'does not expressly claim that his many wanderings were a part of a formal purgation.') See also Taplin *Stagecraft* pp 381–3, and further bibliography on the problem there given; Taplin notes the difficulties already outlined, as well as others still to be considered, and reaches a conclusion similar to that suggested above.

27 This seems the simplest and (I think) most generally accepted sense of ἄνευ δορός, ie to refer to an alliance which Athens will not have to fight to obtain, as she did in the case of other 'allies.' But see also the view of Quincey 'Orestes and the Argive Alliance' pp 190 ff, to be considered in the appendix to this chapter.

28 These and other contemporary political references will be considered later in the appendix to this chapter.

29 See above, n 2, on the discussion of v 41 ff.

30 Many commentators think that this passage (254–6) is divided among different members or different parts of the Chorus: see, for example, Verrall's notes at vv 244 and 255 and, more recently, Taplin *Stagecraft* pp 379–80. Taplin also supports the view that the Chorus here enters σποράδην, ie that there was a 'stream of entries' (cf ibid p 140, in Taplin's account of the first parodos, for which he suggests that the present passage supplies 'a striking visual mirror scene,' p 380). Certainly, as Taplin argues, this form of entry would serve to dramatize the persistent hunting images in the present passage.

31 We may note, in anticipation, the contrast between this spectacle of the Chorus of Eumenides as 'vampire avengers,' shocked at the idea of their victim 'coming to trial,' and the impression left at the end of the play of 'reformed' Furies invoked by Athena as (still awesome) supporters of the state and of its new guardians, the court of the Areopagus. (See vv 903–1020, passim; cf 681–710.) It is this contrast which makes one wonder at those who see no real change in the Eumenides of this play; see, for example, Lloyd-Jones 'Zeus in Aeschylus' pp 64–7.

32 Lebeck (*The Oresteia* pp 150 ff) has expressed this point more strongly in her discussion of the apparent disparity between the Chorus' ostensible purpose here (see vv 306 and 331–2) to sing a 'binding-song' over Orestes and the fact that 'the major portion of the lyric concerns the Furies' age-old prerogative ...' (Lebeck is, perhaps, guilty of a slight exaggeration in suggesting that only the first refrain, 328–33 = 341–6, can be regarded as an explicit 'spell to bind Orestes.') The two themes are, of course, related, but I confess to finding far-fetched the elaborate ritualistic argument (involving the 'lot' of the Erinyes being substituted, as in sympathetic magic, for the 'lot' of the victim, Orestes) by which Lebeck explains the connection. Nevertheless, Lebeck's observations on the Chorus' alternating and sometimes ambiguous uses of λάχος/λάχη (referring now to the victim's lot, now to the Furies' own allotted function, now to both together) and on the descriptions of the similar twilight gloom inhabited by the Furies and their polluted prey do help us to see how, by words and imagery, the poet interweaves the two themes of this ode.

33 The metre of these two *ephymnia*, or refrains, is still basically trochaic like that of the strophic stanzas which they follow, but the unusual combinations of resolutions and syncopation give them a very different effect ($\smile\smile — \cdot / \smile\smile — \cdot /$: 'a drum-beat rhythm,' as Verrall has described it) from that of the strophic stanzas.

34 That Zeus is the subject of the verb at the end of this stanza ('Zeus judged this blood-stained hateful tribe unworthy of his company,' 365–7) is almost certain. The main problem is the agreement to exempt the Olympians from the punishments due to the blood-guilty. If we keep the reading of the mss (σπευδόμεναι), it is the Erinyes, and we are left with a *nominativus pendens*; if (following Wilamowitz) we change the participle to agree with Zeus, then we may find an allusion to Zeus' exclusion of the Olympian gods (specifically, perhaps, his own son, Ares) from the pursuit of the Erinyes for blood-guilt. See the notes of Sidgwick (who follows the former version) and of Lloyd-Jones (who follows the latter) ad loc. Other editors (Verrall, Murray, Mazon) adopt Doederlein's separation of σπευδόμεναι δ' to read σπεύδομεν αἶδ' thus making the stanza consist of at least two separate sentences, with the Furies the subject of the first and Zeus the subject of the last sentence. (Verrall and Murray manage in different ways, as ingenious as they are improbable, to insert yet another sentence between these two).

35 I follow the reasonable assumption adopted by Schneider, Kirchhoff, Wilamowitz, and Murray that the second and third *ephymnia*, or refrains (at 354 ff and 372 ff, respectively), are to be repeated after the antis-

trophes in each case as, in the mss, the first refrain (328 ff, 341 ff) is repeated.

36 More precisely, perhaps, the πολύστονος φάτις, the 'mournful cry' proclaiming this law at the end of the preceding antistrophe, may be taken as the subject (despite the intervening refrain). In any case, the strong expression μένει γάρ, of the manuscripts seems, despite the difficulty of supplying a subject from the general context, preferable to Heath's weak emendation μόναι, as an additional modifier of the feminine plural subject. Sidgwick well compares μίμνει, Ag 1563, though there, to be sure, the 'real subject' is at least introduced in the accusative and infinitive in the following verse.

37 ἀνηλίῳ λάμπᾳ [?](386): lit 'in sunless light.' Wieseler, followed by Page, emends to λάπᾳ, an obscure and probably late word for 'slime,' 'mud.' Once again, too-busy textual criticism succeeds in diminishing poetic expression, this time a typically Aeschylean oxymoron.

38 Cf vv 484, 681.

39 Compare Athena's gentle boast, 'wingless, merely rustling the folds of my aegis,' with Ocean's, at PV 286–7, 'guiding my wind-swift bird by mind alone, without a bit.'

40 The promontory of Sigeum in the Troad was of perennial interest to the Athenians. Important for the grain route from the Hellespont, it had long been a matter of dispute between Mytilene and Athens. Pisistratus had finally conquered it and there was a temple of Athena there. (See Sidgwick's note ad loc and his references to the scholiast and to Herodotus 5.95 for the relevant mythological and historical allusions, respectively.) So obtrusive is this passage (though Orestes is to make some 'dramatic' capital of it) that it is tempting to think that the Sigeum question was of some particular significance at this time. Mazon (in his note ad loc, in the Budé edition) cites Zielinski as supposing that the Pisistratids had kept Sigeum as a sort of personal fiefdom, though there is not, as far as I know, any evidence for this.

41 On the first point, cf Lloyd-Jones' note to Eum 417 and his references to Homer Il 9.454 ff and, especially, to Aesch Sept 70. Cf also Reinhardt's view (discussed above, n 8) that this was indeed the original and exclusive function of the Erinyes, primitive spirits whom Aeschylus, in this play, blends with the previously separate and distinct goddesses, the Eumenides. On the second point, cf Kitto's views (cited above, n 17) on the Erinyes as Ἀραί in the trilogy as a whole.

42 At preliminary investigations in Athenian courts, the defendant was asked to swear to his innocence, as the prosecuting or injured party was asked to swear to the offence (cf Sidgwick's note ad loc). The passages

cited in Thomson's edition (Hom *Hymn* IV.312, Herod v.83, Dem xxxix.3, Thuc v.59.5) indicate the traditional nature of this procedure. See also Gagarin *Aeschylean Drama* pp 75-7 and his references, in n 51, to legal studies on this point. (Gagarin's own discussions of various legal aspects of Orestes' trial should be carefully consulted. However, I cannot quite agree with his views concerning the present passage [*Eum* 425-35], that the Furies drop their demand about the oath because this concerns 'a point of law, not the facts' and that 'They are confident that they will win, since they have the law on their side, as evidenced by Orestes' refusal to swear the necessary oath' (p 77). Surely Athena makes it clear to the Furies in this passage that the mere fact of Orestes' having committed the matricide (and so of his being unable to swear otherwise) will *not* be sufficient to secure Orestes' conviction.

43 On this important point cf also Kitto *Form and Meaning* pp 62-3, who rightly regards vv 421-35 as 'a critical passage in the play' for much the same reasons as those suggested above.

44 Ixion, according to Pindar (*Pyth* 2.31-32) the first to be guilty of shedding kindred blood, was purified by Zeus himself (Diod iv.69). (It is curious that Pindar does not mention the purification, especially since the passage concerns Zeus' punishment of Ixion's two offences, kin-slaughter and his attempted *hybris* toward Hera.)

45 Cf vv 237-9, 276-89. See above pp 147-8 and nn 24, 25, 26.

46 It is uncertain whether we should read αἱροῦμαι, the reading of the mss at 475, or accept Hermann's emendation αἰδοῦμαι. Lobel, on the other hand, followed by Page, transposes v 475 to follow v 482, changing ἄμομφον ὄντα σ' of the mss to ἀμόμφους ὄντας to agree with δικαστάς in the following verse and thus supplies (by the transposition of v 475) a verb to govern δικαστάς.

47 Literally, 'respecting the covenant of their oaths' (so Lloyd-Jones), reading αἰδουμένους (Prien) at v 483 for αἱρουμένους, the reading of the mss.

48 Cf Kranz *Stasimon* p 172, who has, in fact, called the central portion of this ode 'a tragic parabasis.'

See also the interesting discussion of this stasimon by Rosenmeyer *The Art of Aeschylus* pp 174 ff; cf pp 164-8. In the earlier of these two passages, Rosenmeyer expresses the view that the Aeschylean chorus (despite and apart from various individual involvements in the action of the play) from time to time adopts what he calls 'the choral voice': 'a product of its fundamental role, which is that of commentator or responder, and not an initiator of action' (p 164). Rosenmeyer treats the second stasimon of the *Eumenides*, particularly vv 528 ff and 540 ff, as one of several examples of this use of 'the choral voice.' 'What happens here,' he tells us, 'is that the Furies relinquish their partisan status ... in favor of a characteristically 'neutral' choral stand ...' which he later characterizes as that of a 'deputy of the community' (p 168). In the later passage (pp 174 ff), Rosenmeyer observes that the second stasimon 'is entirely without the venom of the Furies' earlier singing.' (Rosenmeyer also ventures some guarded comparisons of the use of the Aeschylean chorus which he is here describing with the Aristophanic parabasis; see pp 166–7.) While I find much that is congenial in these views, my own discussion of this particular ode will seek to show that it is more relevant to its particular moment in the play (and in the presentation of the Furies as the play develops) than Rosenmeyer's comments on it suggest. See also Winnington-Ingram *Studies in Aeschylus* p 135, who regards this ode as 'something of a turning-point' in the presentation of the Erinyes in the play. Cf also his comment, ibid n 36, on the conflicting views of Lebeck and Taplin on this matter.

49 Here I follow Dover's arguments for taking θεσμίων as objective genitive and for not tampering with the reading νέων θεσμίων. (Others whom Dover cites have sought to make the opening statement mean 'Now comes disaster from [or 'on the part of'] the new covenant' or to give it some other meaning suggesting that the 'disaster' is really the subversion of 'the old laws,' ie the *lex talionis* supported by the Furies.) See Dover 'The Political Aspect of Aeschylus, *Eumenides* p 231. (I shall, however, venture to disagree below with certain other features of Dover's interpretation of this ode.)

50 See Dover (above, n 49) pp 231–2, on vv 517–65 of this ode. Dover seems surprised at 'the drop in the temperature' of the Furies' mood in this passage. He explains it by accepting the stasimon 'as concerned from the outset with the Areopagus ... τὸ δεινόν will then be taken by the audience as referring to political authority and the transition to μῆτ' ἀνάρχετον κ.τ.λ. is smooth and natural.'

51 See, for example, Livingstone 'The Problem of the *Eumenides*,' who appears to take this view of this and other passages in the play.

52 The idea expressed at *Eum* 533–4 (δυσσεβίας μὲν ὕβρις τέκος ὡς ἐτύμως: 'so surely is violence the offspring of impiety') is expressed, in expanded form, at *Ag* 758–60, 763 ff: in both we find the close association of δυσσεβία (or τὸ δυσσεβὲς ἔργον) with ὕβρις. Also *Eum* 539 ff ('Dishonour not the altar of Justice ... Trample it not ... with godless foot!') carries a strong echo, in language as in sentiment, of *Ag* 381–4 and *Cho* 641–5. Cf Dodds 'Morals and Politics in the *Oresteia* p 23, n 2, who also suggests further parallels of this kind and comments that in

the *Eumenides* passages 'the Furies appear to speak less for themselves than as the poet's persona.' Cf also Winnington-Ingram *Studies in Aeschylus* p 165 and n 38, who also comments (along with other critics there noted) on the similarities between the passages in the *Eumenides* and the *Agamemnon* suggested above.

53 See Taplin *Stagecraft* pp 390 ff and his references to the long controversy on this matter. See also his sage remarks pp 103–7 (in connection with the change of scene in *Persae*) on the whole question of 'scene setting in Aeschylus,' especially the comment: 'A scene which is set in the imagination of the audience, and not by means of scenery, may simply go out of focus, and when it is refocussed, that is, when it is brought back into sharp definition, it is somewhere else.' Cf also Dale's excellent discussion of this matter (to which Taplin refers), in her *Collected Papers* pp 119 ff.

54 Wieseler's attribution of these verses (574–5) is surely right. It is the function of the presiding divinity, Athena, not of the Furies, to ask Apollo to state his role in the matter and it is to Athena that Apollo's answer (576–81) would seem to be addressed. Cf again Taplin *Stagecraft* p 396.

55 The wrestling image (used by the Chorus-Leader at v 589) of the 'three falls' recalls the recurrent motif of triplicity which we have observed throughout the trilogy (cf above, chapter 2, n 47), rather than any set legal procedure, since this is actually the first time that the Furies have been prepared to look beyond the question of *de facto* guilt or innocence. (Cf above, p 154 and n 43 on *Eum* 425 ff.)

56 Gagarin *Aeschylean Drama* pp 75–6, uses Apollo's twice-expressed scorn of the value of oaths, and especially his insistence at v 621 on the primacy of Zeus' will over the jurors' oaths, to support his view that Apollo scorns the whole legal process, a curious position, surely, for the god of Delphi, the font, at least, of sacred law among the Greeks. We shall return to this question at the end of our discussion of the 'trial scene.'

57 Cf *Ag* 1017–21.

58 Of the several ancient sources which Thomson, in his note ad loc, cites in connection with this passage, Aristotle's citation of Anaxagoras and other physiologists to the effect that the seed is from the male whereas the female provides the place (τόπος) comes, perhaps, closest to Apollo's argument. (See Aristotle, *de gen anim* iv.763 b 30 = Anaxagoras A 107 D–K.) Thomson himself regards the doctrine as Pythagorean. However, the passage (Stob *Fl* 1.64) which he quotes in support of this view, while it clearly stresses the greater importance of the

male in providing the ψυχή of the offspring, does credit the female with providing not merely the 'place' (as in the Anaxagorean passage) or the 'nourishment' (as at *Eum* 59) but the 'material' (ὕλη) of the offspring; moreover, the date of this Pythagorean teaching cited by Stobaeus must remain uncertain. Plato, *Timaeus* 50D, also quoted by Thomson, seems too to contain some echo of the view attributed to Anaxagoras; there the mother is called 'the receiver' (τὸ δεχόμενον), the father 'the source,' of the offspring; however, in the same passage, the offspring's 'nature' (φύσις) then seems to be derived from both. There is also an echo of 'Apollo's doctrine' in the *Eumenides* in Orestes' defence before Tyndareus in Eur *Or* 552, when he speaks of Clytemnestra as 'a field [ἄρουρα] receiving the seed from another.'

Gagarin *Aeschylean Drama* pp 102 ff (who also cites the Anaxagorean view quoted above) treats this argument that the father is the only real parent as 'crucial to Apollo's (Orestes') case;' indeed, this and the casting vote of Athena for acquittal (which he describes as based upon Apollo's biological argument) provide, in Gagarin's view, the climax of what he regards as 'one of the central concerns of the trilogy, the clash between male and female forces and values' (p 103). Winnington-Ingram, who also stresses the importance of the male-female struggle in all plays of the trilogy, nevertheless deprecates the 'physiological argument' of Apollo as one to which the audience would be hostile; see his 'Clytemnestra and the Vote of Athena' pp 143-4. Zeitlin, in an interesting article to which we shall return later, seems to me to distract us from the point at issue at this particular moment of the play (viz, 'was Orestes related by blood to Clytemnestra?') when she says of the passage: 'It is the patent absurdity of Apollo's argument that offends our own fully-developed scientific sensibilities, not the principle itself of biology (true or false) as a justification of ideology. The issue of whether anatomy is destiny is still very much with us' ('The Dynamics of Misogyny' pp 171-2).

59 See Lebeck *Oresteia* pp 134-8. (The quotation given above is from p 137; Lebeck's quotation of Reinhardt is in her note 1 to p 134.) Cf Rosenmeyer *The Art of Aeschylus* p 348 and especially pp 359-61, who agrees with Lebeck on the comic aspect of the trial scene in the *Eumenides*, an aspect which he finds to be concentrated mainly on the treatment of Apollo and his arguments. The argument concerning the unique parenthood of the male he describes as 'a conceit' which he thinks the audience 'may have found tolerably amusing.'

60 Vv 676-7 and 679-80 are all attributed to the Chorus in the mss. Obviously the two statements expressing readiness for the jury's deci-

sion must be split up between Apollo and the Chorus. The fact that the second of these utterances adds the advice to the jury to reverence their oaths would surely indicate that these verses should be attributed to the Chorus, rather than to Apollo, who, at v 621, has apparently insisted on the primacy of Zeus' will over the jurors' oaths. (See above, pp 160–1 and n 56.) It is curious that many editors (eg, Wilamowitz, Sidgwick, Murray) follow Karsten's attribution of 679–80 to Apollo in spite of this discrepancy.

61 Several editors, eg, Nauck and Kirchhoff, forestall this question by simply transferring Athena's speech at 681 ff to follow 573. But it would seem preferable to look for possible reasons for the postponement of Athena's proclamation before interfering with the sequence of the mss. Besides, as Sidgwick points out, 'the close of the speech indicates that it comes just before the voting.' Rosenmeyer approves of its position with the comment, 'the central location of our speech, close to the balloting itself, enhances our understanding of the significance of the victory. At the same time, the institutional burden of the address lulls our moral and aesthetic sensibilities' (Rosenmeyer *The Art of Aeschylus* p 345). Taplin, on the other hand (*Stagecraft* pp 398–400), supports Kirchhoff's transposition (and, indeed, fancies various other disruptions and corruptions in the 'trial scene').

62 As editors note, according to other versions the Areopagus was so called because Ares was the first tried there on a murder charge. Cf Pausanias i.28.5 and other references cited by Thomson.

It seems probable, for the various reasons urged by Taplin, *Stagecraft* pp 390–1, that we are to imagine the trial scene as actually taking place on the Areopagus (note the demonstrative expressions at vv 685 and 688).

63 Some of the much-discussed interpretative problems concerning the contemporary political references involved in vv 690–5, and in this speech as a whole, will be considered in the appendix to this chapter.

64 Many commentators have, of course, discussed the obvious similarities between Athena's advice here and the Furies' earlier warning. Not all, however, have noted the precise parallel in the transition from homicidal jurisdiction to social and political authority through the concepts of Fear and Respect.

65 See the appendix to this chapter. In anticipation of this discussion, however, I should like to quote a brief passage from one of the most interesting of recent studies of the political aspects of the *Eumenides* and of the trilogy as a whole: 'the function of tragedy in its social and historical context is not to comment directly on the times, but to raise

to universality and touch with emotion the experience of the dramatist and his fellow-citizens, to interpret in myth and drama their deepest concerns as human beings. Sometimes that includes the use of myths which explain and legitimate something historical, as we have already seen in the *Eumenides'* (MacLeod 'Politics and the *Oresteia*' p 131). With this statement as a general view of tragedy's function in this context, I completely agree, though some slight qualification may be found necessary with regard to certain passages in the *Eumenides* which do seem 'to comment directly on the times.'

66 See Gagarin 'The Vote of Athena'; Thomson, in his note to *Eum* 734–43, especially his summary of the arguments of K.O. Müller (in favour of the 'casting vote view') with which Thomson agrees. Cf also Reinhardt, *Aischylos* p 143, who takes the same view as Müller and Thomson, and Smyth, *Aeschylean Tragedy* p 220, who comments well: 'The parity of the ballots of the impartial human jury is a twofold symbol – first that it is impossible that any human court should of itself decide an issue raised by claims that outrage all human wisdom, and, secondly that each of the divine powers has its proper right.' So also Hester 'The Casting Vote' p 271, adds to his careful assessment of the evidence the comment, '[Athena] breaks a deadlock which was on moral grounds insoluble.'

67 Douglas Young is quoted by Gagarin ('The Vote of Athena' n 6; cf n 1) as making much the same point about vv 731–3 and possible dramatic silence(s) before and/or after the triplet.

68 See Gagarin *Aeschylean Drama* pp 76–9. Gagarin gives as Athena's motive in voting for acquittal the securing of 'the valuable political alliance' which Orestes promises (ibid p 77). Aeschylus may well have his own motives for Orestes' recurrent promises about an Argive alliance (see appendix to this chapter) but they would not, I think, involve impugning the probity of Athena in this way. However, Gagarin also assures us (ibid p 78) that, 'in spite of the verdict in this case,' Athena subsequently promises by implication (cf vv 804–5) 'that *dikê* [which, as we have seen, he takes to mean retributive justice] will prevail in the future.'

Winnington-Ingram who, more than most critics, regards the *Oresteia* as concerned with the battle between the sexes, and who views Clytemnestra as 'a symbol of all wives and mothers who suffer from the inferior status of women in marriage,' sees even the significance of Athena's vote in terms of Clytemnestra's lost cause of women's rights: 'There is a sense in which Athena is the counterpart of Clytemnestra ... Everything ... that Clytemnestra's nature demanded and her sex forbade or hampered, Athena is free to do, by virtue of her godhead ... There is thus a bitter irony, when the goddess who in all things admires the male ... condemns the woman of manly counsel for seeking the domination which her nature demanded.' (See Winnington-Ingram *Studies in Aeschylus* chapter 6, pp 129 and 125–6, respectively.)

69 Cf the comment of de Romilly, who develops a view similar to that expressed above by means of a comparison very relevant to this trilogy: 'La vengeance ne devient justice que parce qu'il était, déjà avant, vengeance divine. La destruction de Troie était déjà un vote divin – un vote comme celui qui acquitte Orèste' ('Vengeance humaine et vengeance divine: Remarques sur l'*Orestie* d'Eschyle' p 75). Grossmann, on the other hand, seems to me to introduce a misleading idea when he suggests that it is pity and forgiveness which motivate the Olympians ('lassen die Olympier ... Gnade vor Recht ergehen') in opposition to the primitive pitilessness of the law of requital (*Promethie und Orestie* p 274).

70 Schottlaender, 'Um die Qualität des Freispruchs in dem *Eumeniden* pp 144 ff, argues that Athena's reasons for favouring the male appear much less subjective when we pay proper attention to the final word ἐπίσκοπος ('protector') in her explanation of her vote. He reminds us that in heroic times the protection of the house was an essential and permanent function of the male, for whom the female could substitute, in this capacity, only during his absence (cf *Ag* 914; cf also 259–60). Thus, Schottlaender suggests, Aeschylus allows Athena to introduce a fresh point of view in the hitherto insoluble deadlock between the claims of the father and of the mother, each of whose blood was shed in vengeance. Schottlaender's view has much to commend it, though it does tend to play down the fact that Athena seems to give more prominence to her own unique birth 'from the father' than to the 'male-as-protector' consideration in explaining her preference for the father's over the mother's claims for vengeance.

71 Lloyd-Jones *The Justice of Zeus* p 94.
72 Gagarin *Aeschylean Tragedy* p 78.
73 Ibid pp 74, 77–8; Lloyd-Jones *The Justice of Zeus* pp 92–4.
74 Orestes is not, of course, acquitted simply by the vote of Athena; the tied vote of the Areopagus is equally essential to the verdict. Gagarin gets around the difficulty (for *his* argument) of the anti-Erinyes verdict in the way that we have already seen: in his view, it is entirely Athena and not the court who is responsible for this decision and Athena in effect promises the Erinyes that this exceptional suspension of the law of (automatic) retribution will not continue to obtain. (See above,

pp 164–6 and nn 66, 68, and references to Gagarin there given.) Lloyd-Jones, on the other hand, seems hardly to admit (at least in his present discussion, *The Justice of Zeus* pp 94–5) that the Furies' rights *have* been curtailed by the court's verdict. He believes Orestes to have been justified in his deeds and adds, 'In the state of Athens, justice comes through the Areopagus.' He then goes on to cite literary and historical evidence for the peaceful coexistence of the Furies and their blood-feuds with the justice of Zeus on the one hand and the law of the fifth-century Athenian *polis* on the other. This may well be true but it is not the situation which Aeschylus is presenting at this moment in his trilogy. It is certainly not the view which the Chorus of Furies take of the matter.

75 In this connection we might well consider the comments of Reinhardt (*Aischylos* p 141), in contrast to the views of Lloyd-Jones and Gagarin (discussed above): 'Man fand in dem *Eumeniden* dargestellt erstens als rechtsgeschichtliche Idee den Fortschritt der Verstaatlichung des Rechtes, den Ersatz der Sippenfehde und der Blutrache durch ein geregeltes Gerichtsfahren. Indem die Gemeinde spricht: die Rache ist mein, wird der Automatismus eines blinden "Zahn um Zahn" durch die Idee eines humanen, öffentlichen Rechtes aufgehoben.' ('One finds expressed in the *Eumenides*, first of all as a concept in legal history, the increase in the appropriation of Justice by the state, the replacement of family feuds and blood-revenge by an institutionalized judicial process. As the community says, "Justice is mine", the automatism of a blind "tooth for a tooth" Justice is replaced by a human public justice.') But as Reinhardt further remarks of the victory of the new Olympian gods over the old gods, of the humane and spiritual over the demonic and terrifying (which in our play is marked as accompanying and determining the development of the judicial process), 'das alte ist im Neuen wieder nicht vernichtet, sondern darein engegangen' ('the old has not been destroyed by the new but is integrated into the new').

76 There will, perhaps, always be disagreement as to whether the dénouement of the *Eumenides* really provides a satisfying thematic conclusion to the trilogy. Rosenmeyer *The Art of Aeschylus* chapter 12, passim, esp pp 344–7, is inclined to cast a negative vote on this point, while admitting the popular dramatic success which the *Oresteia*, 'with its final celebration' (ibid p 346) has enjoyed. Cf also his gentle satire of the view that reconciliation in tragedy means 'that the contending powers ... go off dancing with one another' (ibid p 346–7). The present treatment seeks to show that the resolution in the *Eumenides* comes to rather more than this. An earlier and less sophisticated critic, Livingstone

(above, note 51), has accused the last 350 lines of the *Eumenides* of a far more extreme form of discontinuity as 'a loosely connected episode, stitched on its outside' (p 123) and justified only by the poet's allegedly exclusive political concern at this point in his play. At the other pole from these views is that of Lesky *Greek Tragedy* p 84: 'for what we have here [he concludes of the ending of the *Eumenides*] is not a grafting of ideas on a given theme in order to force it into conformity with life. In its poetic form the play discloses a genuine religious awareness of the Attic homeland's sanctity.'

77 Cf above, p 163 and n 64; pp 156 ff (esp pp 157–8), p 168, and nn ad loc.
78 See *Ag* 385 ff, where the word Πειθώ is used at the beginning of the first passage describing the 'temptation' of Paris. At *Ag* 681 ff, Helen 'the destroyer' (ἑλένας, ἕλανδρος ἑλέπτολις) is named (in the following Chorus) as the embodiment of that temptation, presented more abstractly in the preceding passage. At *Ag* 717 ff the same theme is repeated in figurative terms, by the brilliant 'lion-cub image.' (The actual word πειθώ is not used in the last two of these three passages.)
79 See *Eum* 970 ff. Athena has previously invoked Πειθώ by name, at vv 885–6, in her final, and successful, plea to the Chorus. See also Rosenmeyer's interesting discussion of 'Persuasion' in the trilogy (and in Aeschylus generally) and of its particular significance in the *Eumenides* (*The Art of Aeschylus* pp 350 ff).
80 In her first attempt to mollify the Erinyes, Athena repeats that the vote of the court was equal and therefore that the Furies were not defeated (and so should not vent their wrath on the citizens of Athens) but that Orestes was vindicated (ὡς ταῦτ' Ὀρέστην δρῶντα μὴ βλάβας ἔχειν, 799) by clear testimony of Zeus' own will in the matter (795–9). Here, perhaps, Athena gives a somewhat more satisfactory reason (at least to modern readers!) than at vv 736–40 for her vote in favour of Orestes. The present detailed discussion of *Eum* 778–995 is drawn, for the most part, from pp 340–3 of my article 'Interaction between Chorus and Characters in the *Oresteia*.'
81 Cf Thomson *The Oresteia* II p 65. After enumerating the baneful effects of *Peithô* earlier in the myth and in the trilogy, he remarks, 'Now the same spirit embodied in Athena brings the sufferings of three generations to an end.'
82 Cf Thomson, ibid p 65, who offers a musical analogy: 'It is like a duet in which, after the bass has taken over from the treble, the treble imitates the bass.'
83 Cf not only the earlier part of the present confrontation but also the

comparable 'progression' in the long epirrhematic passage between Clytemnestra (who, like Athena, shifts from iambics to anapaests as the emotional temperature rises) and the Chorus at *Ag* 1407 ff. There, as we have seen, it is Clytemnestra who gradually changes her attitude.

84 This and the following two passages are from Lloyd-Jones' translation of the *Eumenides* pp 68, 70.

85 See Peradotto 'Some Patterns of Nature Imagery in the *Oresteia*.'

86 In Hesiod, the Erinyes are the offspring of Earth, impregnated by the drops of castrated Ouranos' blood (*Theog* 185), while the Moirai are daughters of Night (*Theog* 217) (at least until their Olympian 'reincarnation' as the daughters of Zeus and Themis, *Theog* 904). In Aeschylus, the Erinyes are the daughters of Night (*Eum* 321) and so 'sisters with the same mother' as they say here (961–2) of the Moirai. Thus Aeschylus seems to make the Erinyes 'more primeval' than does Hesiod, placing them on the same level as the Moirai, and also tending to relate their status and functions quite closely. At *Cho* 306 (at the beginning of the 'great kommos'), the Moirai along with Dikê (Justice) are invoked by the Chorus to fulfil just vengeance on the murderous usurpers, blow for blow, in the manner of the Erinyes. At *Eum* 23–4 (cf *Eum* 723–4), the Erinyes compare Apollo's attempt to curtail their prerogatives with his similar treatment of the Moirai concerning the sparing of Admetus' life. At *PV* 16, the Moirai and the Erinyes are described jointly as 'the helmsmen of Necessity' (Ἀνάγκη). (The authorship of the *Prometheus Vinctus* has, to be sure, been doubted by some scholars: see my *Prometheus Bound, A Literary Commentary* appendix 1. Here, however [at *PV* 516] the treatment of the Moirai and the Erinyes seems consistent with Aeschylus' treatment in the passages in the *Eumenides* cited in this note, and might even be used in support of arguments for dating the *Prometheus Vinctus* close to the *Eumenides*, toward the end of the poet's life.) In none of these passages, however, is the identification of the Erinyes with Moirai, or even of all their functions, suggested, and at *Eum* 723–4 both the status bond and the distinction in function (at least as far as the Moirai's concern with the life-span of individual mortals is concerned) between the two sets of 'older divinities' are clearly illustrated. Athena's chant at 949–55, cited above, like the shorter passages which anticipate it (895–7, 930–1), seems to come closer than do the other passages to identifying many functions of the Erinyes and the Moirai, though it should be noted that, unlike the Moirai, the Erinyes are presented as amenable to prayers and good treatment on the part of mortals who would propitiate them (see esp 988–95). This treatment on Athena's part may explain why the Chorus of Erinyes

immediately pray (959-67) to the Moirai for the sort of things, in the destinies of mortals, which Athena has just indicated was in their own power to bestow.

87 Cf above, n 8 to this chapter.
88 Cf *Eum* 805 ff.
89 ὄμμα γὰρ πάσης χθονός ... (1025): it is possible that these words should be taken, as Sidgwick and others have taken them, in apposition with the *subject* of the sentence, in which case ὄμμα will have its other metaphorical sense of 'delight,' 'most cherished object.' It is perhaps more important to note that at the end of this sentence (ie following v 1027) a lacuna of one or more verses is suspected (the construction appears to require this). The allegedly omitted verse(s) may have contained, as Hermann and others have thought, Athena's further mollification of the Erinyes by calling them 'Eumenides,' which, according to Harpocration, did occur in this play. See editions.
90 Headlam, in 'The Last Scene in the *Eumenides*,' was, I think, the first to point out (pp 275-6) the possible contemporary civic significance of the investiture of the Erinyes/Eumenides in crimson robes, for it was in such robes that the μέτοικοι took part in the Panathenaic festival. See Headlam's references ad loc; note also the repeated use of the words μέτοικοι (the technical term for resident aliens at Athens) and μετοικία at *Eum* 1011, 1018. Headlam (p 274) also finds 'Panathenaic overtones' in the description of the procession at vv 1033 ff and comments (pp 275-6): 'What I think is that the whole of this procession was designed by Aeschylus as a reflection of the Panathenaic festival ... and that the treatment of the Eumenides is borrowed from the symbolic treatment of the μέτοικοι at that feast.' (Headlam, however, credits Th. Mommsen [*Heortologie* (1864) 171] with finding a reflection of the Panathenaic παννυχίς in the procession at the end of the *Eumenides*.)
91 See, however, Taplin's defence (*Stagecraft* p 411) of Hermann's suggestion that in place of a second Chorus (which, Taplin objects, has been given no formal introduction apart from Athena's rather casual words at 1005-6) the escort may have been enacted (and sung) by the jurors of the Areopagus. See also Taplin's (somewhat agnostic!) views (ibid pp 411-14) on the actual on-stage complement of the final procession, which some scholars, going to the opposite extreme, envisage as 'super-spectacular' (Taplin's depreciatory expression) Aeschylean extravaganza. Taplin does, however, allow the probable presence of sacrificial victims, '(two would do),' in deference to Athena's reference to them at 1007 ff, and of attendants to lead them; the women, children, and old women of v 1027 are reduced to a textual

uncertainty. With regard to the imagery (and visual effects implied) in the frequent references to the torches in the final procession, see Peradotto 'Some Patterns of Nature Imagery in the *Oresteia*' pp 382–3, to which Taplin also refers.

APPENDIX TO CHAPTER THREE

Some Views on the Political and Social Aspects of the *Eumenides*

i Preliminary comment

So much has been written on the political interpretation of the *Eumenides*, particularly on those passages (already noted) which appear to make direct reference to contemporary political and social issues, that it would be difficult for any critic to claim originality in any fresh treatment of the problems involved. At any rate, no such claim is made for the present appendix. Its purpose is simply to present for readers who may not be familiar with them (or for those who wish to review them) the main questions of contemporary reference raised by the text of the play, along with the relevant evidence provided by other ancient sources, and to suggest what seem to this writer the most probable answers to those questions. Everything (or almost everything) that will be said on one aspect or another of this interpretation has been said by one or another of the commentators (though not all of them by any one commentator!) and so the reader's indulgence is claimed if at least those opinions and inferences of the less exceptionable kind are not interlarded with references to similar conclusions. Indeed bibliographical references will here be restricted to a small selection (of many studies) which have been found particularly useful or provocative, for fuller references to the secondary literature on the subject already exist in several of the studies here mentioned.

Two preliminary observations should, however, be made. The first deals with the kind of political-historical study of the *Eumenides* (or of any Greek tragedy) with which we will not be concerned. A recent work of Gustav Grossmann[1] attempts to place the theme of the *Ores-*

teia and particularly of the *Eumenides* (as well as of the *Prometheus* trilogy) in the total context and sequence of political and ethical ideals developed in Athens from the time of Solon to that of Pericles. It is doubtful whether individual works of art can ever be very precisely illuminated by such wide-ranging accounts of the cultural history of the society which produced them. Grossmann's study is, perhaps, one of the less successful examples of German *Geistesgeschichten* of this kind, partly because its terms of reference (mythical, historical, ethical, rhetorical) are so broad that particular application to the Aeschylean works becomes unclear, partly because the picture of Athenian political and social attitudes is idealized to an almost absurd degree.[2] It is true, as Grossmann argues,[3] that Attic tragedy (or at least much of it) was permeated with the political ideals and concepts of its day, but too often the rosy glow in which he sees Greek history and Greek literature does less than justice both to the harsher elements of Greek tragic myth and to the pragmatic strain in Athenian political policies and judicial practices.[4]

My second general observation is based on some sage advice prefacing a very different kind of study of the social and political aspects of Greek tragedy by Jean-Pierre Vernant. Vernant reminds us that Greek tragedy appeared (by no means accidentally) at a specific moment in history and that, like every literary genre, it appeared 'comme l'expression d'un type particulier d'expérience humaine, lié à des conditions sociales et psychologiques definies.'[5] For this reason the text of each tragedy 'ne peut être pleinement compris que compte tenu d'un contexte.' It is in his account of this 'context' that the kernel of Vernant's advice is to be found. While tragedy makes many references to the worlds of religion, law, politics, and so on, and makes use of various technical legal expressions, it must always assimilate such references and expressions to its own world, thereby submitting them to a transformation which belongs only to that world: 'Chaque type d'institution, chaque catégorie d'oeuvre possède son propre univers spirituel qu'il lui a fallu élaborer pour se constituer en discipline autonome, en activité spécialisée, correspondante à un domaine particulier de l'expérience humaine.' It is this existence of the autonomous world of Greek tragedy (despite its essential links both with the heroic past and with contemporary circumstances) which we must keep in mind when seeking to expound the political references and 'messages' of any given play.

ii Political aspects of the *Eumenides*

As other scholars have observed of the *Eumenides*, there is a radical change in the cultural climate of this play from the mythical, the heroic, and the 'royal' to the contemporary, the institutional, and the communal.[6] The transition is well expressed by Dodds' comment on Athena's opening lines: 'In mythical terms, as her first words show (397–402), we are still within a few years of the Trojan War, but in historical time we have leapt forward to a new age and a new social order. This telescoping of the centuries is characteristic of the *Eumenides*, and, as I believe, essential to its purpose.'[7]

There are, as we shall see, certain major political issues which are highlighted by the most significant contemporary references in the *Eumenides*. However, the new flavour is also imparted to the play by various incidental touches of no great import, political or thematic, which would incline the Athenian audience to feel that the city to which Argive Orestes has been sent as a suppliant is indeed the city which they know and inhabit. In this connection, one thinks of Orestes' (somewhat gratuitous!) guess that Athena, absent when he arrives, might be off helping friends in Libya (the Athenians themselves were, at the time of the play, helping Libyan friends against the Persians);[8] one thinks also of Athena's actual explanation of her absence (*Eum* 397–402), that she was taking possession for the Athenians of spear-won lands in the Troad, an area in which 'historical' Athens had, particularly in the preceding century, and perhaps continued to have, territorial claims.[9] Finally, numerous features of the 'trial scene' itself (including not only the voting procedures and the precedent, here established, for dealing with split-vote decisions, but also, as we have seen, the various extra-legal inducements by which the litigants sought to sway the jury) must all have greatly increased the audience's sense that this legendary trial had much in common with the trials of their own experience.

The areas in which, as most scholars agree, the 'political allusions' of the *Eumenides* seem to take on major significance are three: the allusions to an Argive-Athenian alliance, the terms of Athena's 'founding speech' (681–710) concerning the Areopagus, and the several warnings, in the latter passages of the play, against civic strife and even civil war.[10] The few years preceding the production of the *Oresteia* in 458 had seen the decline at Athens of the conservative, pro-Spartan faction under Cimon and the rise to dominance of the 'radical democrats' under Ephialtes' leadership. The Spartan rejection of Athenian aid at Ithome and the consequent discrediting of Cimon and his policies led to the breaking of the alliance with Sparta and to the forming, under democratic leadership, of a new alliance (in 461-460) with Argos, Sparta's enemy (Thuc 1.102) On the domestic front, the major constitutional reform of Ephialtes concerned the reduction of the political powers of the Areopagus, the conservative Council consisting of ex-archons, which was seen as the main barrier to the full development of the Athenian democracy.

Two features of Aeschylus' treatment of the Orestes legend, both of them in all probability Aeschylean innovations, serve as preliminary indications that the poet intended his final play to draw attention to Athens and to the two major contemporary issues which we have mentioned. In the first place, the trial of Orestes is made (by forced marches, as it were) to take place at Athens and is made the occasion of the founding of the Areopagus (traditionally, the trial of Ares by the twelve gods for the slaying of Halirrothius was the first mythical trial before that court); secondly, Orestes is presented as an Argive and not as, again traditionally, a Mycenaean or (in some versions) a Spartan prince.

Let us consider the 'Argive issue' first. In his early speeches at Athens, Orestes twice stresses his Argive connection (289–91; 455–8). In the first, he wastes no time in promising Argive support, ἄνευ δορός (ie without the Athenians having to fight for it)[11] in return for protection at Athens; in the second (after Athena has referred to Athenian acquisitions in the Trojan War), he reminds the goddess that his father Agamemnon and she were allies in that victorious undertaking. In the same vein, Apollo, in his peroration as Orestes' 'defence attorney,' reminds Athena that he has sent Orestes as suppliant to her hearth so that he and his descendants may be ever after Athens' grateful allies (667–73). Finally, in Orestes' own expressions of gratitude for his acquittal (754–77), the emphasis is again on Argos, whose prince has been restored, and, this time more powerfully and explicitly, on the promised allegiance of Argives of present and future generations to his saviour Athens.

All of these passages, then, stress alliance between Argos and Athens either as part of the mythological order of things (cf 455–8) or as the natural and welcomed result of Orestes' acquittal by Athena and her new Athenian court. Since the whole 'Argive dimension' is, as we have seen, superfluous to (though not destructive of) the legendary and dramatic situation of Orestes, none but the most obdurate formalist could doubt that the poet intends these passages as a sort of sanctification expressed to contemporary Athenians of the recently concluded Argive pact.

The situation is slightly less clear with regard to the other aspects of contemporary liberal policy at Athens and the apparent allusions to it in Athena's speech at vv 681–706. The early history of the Areopagus is, perhaps, impossible to ascertain with any clarity, but we may at least try to piece together what the Greeks of Aeschylus' time and later thought it to be. Here too, however, the discussion will be fraught with uncertainties. Aeschylus' contemporaries themselves may well have been somewhat vague about the early history of this Court and our main evidence for the Greek view of the matter comes from Aristotle's Constitution of Athens (*Athenaiôn Politeia*), composed in the fourth century from sources (as far as early Greek history is concerned) no longer available to us.

Traditionally, the Areopagus appears to have been regarded as originally founded for the judging of homicide cases. This is, at least, the function ascribed to it in the several mythological references to its activities:[12] such myths would appear to indicate what the Greeks thought of the matter (or, just possibly, what they liked to think was the case, for acceptance of such myths allowed them to pride themselves on the divine origins of their court). There is, however, no mention of this homicide jurisdiction in Aristotle's references in the *Constitution of Athens* (*Ath Pol* 3.6, 4.4, 8.4) to the powers of the Areopagus in pre-Solonian and in Solonian days,[13] though much later in this work (*Ath Pol* 7.3, where Aristotle is referring to his own times) it is reported that trials for deliberate murder and homicide were held in the Areopagus. A passage in Plutarch's *Solon* is the only *direct* historical evidence of such powers in the Court's early days. Plutarch (*Solon* 19.3–5), after citing the opinion of most writers that Solon himself instituted the Areopagus, goes on to give evidence, allegedly from Solon's own tables, of a pre-Solonian Areopagus which appears to have had charge of murder and homicide cases (even here there is a slight, but not, I think, substantive, ambiguity as to whether such trials were held by the Areopagus, the Ephetai, and the Kings, or only by the Kings).[14] Demosthenes (23.66) adds further evidence that the jurisdiction of the Areopagus in homicide cases was traditional, but the reference is vague as to the date of origin of these powers.

Whatever the truth about the early 'homicide jurisdiction' of the Areopagus (and Athenian views of it), it is clear from the two passages (*Ath Pol* 3.6 and 8.4: we may omit 4.4) that the Council was thought to have had considerable legal, political, and constitutional powers in the seventh and sixth centuries. Since, in scholars' discussions of Ephialtes' reforms of the Areopagus and of Aeschylus' alleged (and oblique) comments on them, attempts have been made to distinguish between these three areas of influence, it might be useful to quote the relevant parts of Aristotle's statements on the matter.

Ath Pol 3.6 (in Aristotle's account of the constitution before Draco):

> The Council of the Areopagus had the official function of guarding the laws but actually it administered the greatest number and the most important affairs of state, inflicting fines and penalties upon offenders of public order without appeal; for the elections of the archons went by birth and wealth [ἀριστίνδην καὶ πλουτίνδην] and members of the Areopagus were appointed from them, owing to which this alone of the offices has remained even to the present day tenable for life.

(This passage is valuable also for indicating the privileged membership of the Areopagus, by birth and wealth, for as we shall see, this was to remain the case until a year after the production of the *Oresteia*.)

Ath Pol 8.4 (under Solon's constitution, ca 594):

> [Solon] appointed the Council of the Areopagus to the duty of guarding the laws just as it had existed before as overseer of the constitution [ὥσπερ ὑπῆρχεν καὶ πρότερον ἐπίσκοπος οὖσα τῆς πολιτείας] and it was this council that kept watch over the greatest number and the most important affairs of state, *in particular correcting offenders with sovereign powers both to fine and to punish ... and trying persons that conspired to put down the democracy.*

It is clear from the passage which I have italicized in the second of these excerpts that the additional powers conferred on the Areopagus by Solon were supposed to have been in the interests of the people and of the democracy (despite the still privileged membership of that Council, ex-archons who had, by this time, been elected by lot from candidates selected by a preliminary vote [*Ath Pol* 8.1]). It is curious, also, that Aristotle states the *guardianship of the laws* to be the new (Solonian) function of the Council, 'just as it had existed before as over-seer of the constitution,' when in the preceding passage (referring to the pre-Draconian constitution) the function of guarding the laws (but not the constitution) was explicitly attributed to it. This inconsistency, or possibly carelessness, should put us on our guard against seeking to distinguish too sharply the Solonian from the pre-Solonian powers of the Council simply by these terms of nomenclature.

It is from this background information concerning the Solonian and pre-Solonian Areopagus – its privileged membership, its (probable) early jurisdiction over homicide cases, its further powers and political influence deriving from its official guardianship of the laws (apparently augmented by Solon) and of the constitution – that we must understand the subsequent democratic reforms of that Council, somewhat tersely expressed in Aristotle's *Constitution*, and the possible Aeschylean reactions to them implied in Athena's 'founding speech.' First of all, let us consider the crucial passage on Ephialtes' treatment (in 462 BC) of the Areopagus:

> First he made away with many of the Areopagites by bringing legal procedures against them about their acts of administration; then in the archonship of Conon he stripped the Council of all its added powers which made it the safeguard of the Constitution [τὰ ἐπίθετα δι' ὧν ἦν ἡ τῆς πολιτείας φυλακή] and assigned some of them to the Council of Five Hundred and others to the People and to the jury courts. (*Ath Pol* 5.2)

In the following section it is stated that Themistocles, who is here wrongly described as partly responsible, with Ephialtes, for these acts, wished the Council *to be destroyed* [καταλυθῆναι] because he himself was to be put on trial by it for treasonable dealings with Persia (*Ath Pol* 25.3).[15]

Two further passages from the *Constitution* (one referring somewhat indefinitely to events about the time of the *Oresteia*, the other to a major constitutional change about a year after its production) should perhaps be quoted before turning to the Aeschylean text:

> After this [ie after the murder of Ephialtes] when Pericles advanced to the leadership of the people ... it came about that the constitution became still more democratic. For he took away some of the functions of the Areopagus. (*Ath Pol* 27.1)

> ... five years after the death of Ephialtes [ie in 457 BC] they decided to extend to the Teamster Class [the Zeugitae] eligibility to the preliminary roll from which the Nine Archons were to be selected by lot. (*Ath Pol* 26.2)

(This opening of the archonship to the third class of citizens meant, of course, that the Areopagus was also so opened.)

Let us now consider Athena's speech, founding the Areopagus, at *Eum* 681–706. The general tone of the speech, the description of the emotions (awe, σέβας; fear, φόβος, 690–1) which the Areopagus is expected to inspire, and the terms in which its protective role in the State are expressed (701, 706) clearly draw attention not only to the august nature of this Council (Athena calls it a βουλευτήριον 704, rather than a δικαστήριον) but also to the authority and power which Athena intends it to enjoy in the state. The relevance of this emphasis to the political issues of the day cannot, surely, be accidental; nor do I think that anyone listening to these verses could find them compatible with the policies recently expressed by the reforms of Ephialtes. It is true that we do not know (and perhaps never will know precisely) how much was involved in Ephialtes' withdrawal from the Areopagus of its 'additional powers' (ἐπίθετα)[16]. We do know, however, that the eventual intent of this policy was the political emasculation, even destruction (note the term at *Ath Pol* 55.3), of that Council, and the honorific language of Athena in describing it, as well as the tremendous influence which she envisages it as wielding in the protection of the stage, contrasts sharply with the policy and the intent of the 'reformers.' The particular terms (ἔρυμα, 'bulwark'; σωτήριον, 'safeguard,' 701; φρούρημα, 'guardianship,' 706) would appear to draw attention to, and to validate, those very watch-dog functions, over the state and its constitution, which the reformers sought to withdraw from the Areopagus, namely those 'additional powers by which it *was* the safe-guard of the constitution.'[17]

One may, of course, ask why Aeschylus chose to criticize such reformist policies some four years *after* the enactments of Ephialtes. The answer may be that he wished to record his disagreement, but this seems improbable in a play so politically positive and optimistic as the *Eumenides* in its final utterances. The passages quoted above from *Ath Pol* 27.1 and 26.2 indicate that the democrats' policies concerning the Areopagus were by no means completed with Ephialtes' reforms but that it was a process which Pericles and others continued after Ephialtes' death. It may well have been these further reforms (one of which, in particular, we shall consider in a moment) which Aeschylus is particularly resisting through the speech of Athena; nevertheless, in view of what has been said already, it can hardly be claimed (as some scholars have sought to do) that Aeschylus favoured

Eumenides

the reforms of Ephialtes but deprecated further ones.[18] Clearly it was the same general policy, even if it was not implemented all at once.

I have postponed, till after reviewing the general terms (and their possible contemporary implications) of Athena's description of the Areopagus, a particular passage in the speech which has occasioned the greatest division in interpretation along the lines (ie 'pro- or anti- the Ephialtic reforms') already indicated. The passage runs as follows and has, unfortunately, one fairly serious textual uncertainty:

> On this hill, awe [σέβας] and its kinsman fear [φόβος] on the part of the citizens will restrain them by day and by night from injustice [τὸ μὴ ἀδικεῖν] provided that the citizens themselves do not introduce new laws [reading 'πικαινούντων for mss 'πικαινόντων][19] For by polluting clear waters with evil influxes [κακαῖς ἐπιρροαῖσι] you will never find good drinking. (690-6)

The general tenor of the passage ('Don't change the laws!') has a conservative sound to it, at least as far as the Areopagus is concerned. However, while admitting this, Dover argues that the 'evil influxes' which Athena strongly deprecates must refer to the 'additional powers' (ἐπίθετα) which Ephialtes removed from the Areopagus and whose very addition Athena is thus seen in this passage as deprecating in advance.[20] But, as Dodds has subsequently pointed out,[21] it is the *citizens* who are advised against introducing new laws at v 693, and this militates against taking these 'new laws' along with the 'evil influxes,' as Dover does, since the 'additional powers' supposedly acquired by the Areopagus were pre-Solonian and so not granted by the citizens as a whole. This point, taken by itself, *could* perhaps be said to be a quibble, on the grounds that Aeschylus was not concerned with the fine points of constitutional history. Dodds' next point against Dover is more substantive. He points out that κακαῖς ἐπιρροαῖσι can more easily be understood (especially, as we shall see, in the historical context) as 'evil infusions' into the personnel of the Areopagus.[22] I have no hesitation in accepting Dodds' view that the passage warns against the impending measure to open the archonship, and hence the membership in the Areopagus, to the Zeugitae, a measure which was actually passed in 458-457 within a year of the production of the *Oresteia*.[23]

One of the most frequently cited arguments for the 'pro-Ephialtic' interpretation of Aeschylus' treatment of the Areopagus, namely the fact that its only actual function in the *Eumenides*, that of homicide jurisdiction, is the one which Ephialtes left to it, is, perhaps, the easiest to refute. No other function could, of course, be exercised in the dramatic context of Orestes' situation; indeed the fact that Athena goes out of her way to suggest the wider functions which she envisages (in suitably general terms) this Council (βουλευτήριον, 684) as fulfilling tends itself to vindicate rather than otherwise the extra-judicial powers which the historical Areopagus actually possessed, whether originally or by acquisition.

However, the main, and most frequently stated, reason why so many and such eminent scholars feel that Athena's 'founding speech' should, despite the difficulties, be interpreted as acquiescing in the democratic reforms of the Areopagus is the fact that, as we have seen, the *Eumenides* does provide several dramatically gratuitous 'supports' to that other aspect of democratic policy, the Athenian Alliance with Argos. (Another reason, less acknowledged and less logical, may be that critics naturally sympathetic with the democrats' reforms prefer to believe that the greatest tragic poet of the burgeoning democratic *polis* was similarly sympathetic.) But need approval of the democrats' foreign policy necessarily imply approval of all aspects of their domestic policy – unless we view the poet of the *Eumenides* as a card-carrying member of a political party who was totally committed to all its measures?

From this examination of Athena's 'founding speech,' I find it difficult to escape the conclusion, however, unpalatable, that Aeschylus had a certain affection for the 'old Areopagus.' Furthermore, if Dodds' interpretation of 'base infusions' (at *Eum* 694) is sound (as I believe it to be), this drawing back by the poet at an essential stage in the development of complete democracy (Athenian style) surely marks him as, at best, a 'conservative democrat,' though one willing to see good in some of the policies and individuals of the more radical wing. Indeed, since (as we shall see) Aeschylus' final 'message' in the play concerns domestic harmony and the avoidance of stasis, the (dramatically) gratuitous 'Argive pact passages' in the *Eumenides* may have been at least partly designed to indicate this open-mindedness. By the same token, it would surely be a mistake (as I have indicated earlier) to view his defence of the Areopagus as an *attack* on, any more than it is an endorsement of, that part of radical policy which was already a *fait accompli*.[24]

I am inclined, however, to believe that the application of political labels does a disservice to our poet and, more particularly, to an appreciation of the *Oresteia*. Perhaps it is time to remind ourselves of the advice cited from Vernant earlier in this appendix. While tragedy may provide a confrontation between fixed values of the heroic, mythical past and the shifting, constantly redefined values of the dynamic present, its business is to question both, and its world, along with the solutions there presented, is *sui generis*, belonging, in the final analysis, to neither.

The final passages of the *Eumenides* (which we have already discussed in the preceding chapter) offer perhaps the best example in all Greek tragedy of the unique quality, which yet includes the best elements of past and present, of this world. Dodds has seized on 'the famous saying about the superiority of [τὸ]μέσον (*Eum.* 530) ... as an honest and correct description of the author's own position'; Dover, however, has objected (in advance!) that such expressions as this and the deprecation (at *Eum* 26-9) of both anarchy and despotism are 'value-words' such as both oligarchs and democrats could appropriate to their use in approving or disapproving of quite different situations.[25] However, no such cavil can be applied to the evaluation of the two great passages in the final section of the play (858–66, 976–87) which abjure in vivid and uniquely Aeschylean language[26] the civil bloodshed which the poet must clearly have seen as a real and imminent danger. It is significant that the first of these passages is put in the mouth of Athena, tutelary spirit of Athens, in the form of a prayer that the Furies may not implant in her citizens the harsh spirit of kin-blooded warfare (862–3), while the second passage embodies the (now reconciled) Furies' *own* prayer that dust gorged with civic bloodshed may never arouse the citizens to similarly destructive vengeance (980–3). Here, then, we have the paradox that the old order of Furies, themselves the embodiment of the *lex talionis*, pray not merely that this law may no longer apply[27] but that, in a civic context at least, the occasion for it may no longer arise.

In the light of this paradox, it is perhaps easier to understand how Athena can on the one hand advise her citizens that, properly respected, the Erinyes/Eumenides may be a source of great gain for her citizens (990–5), while warning them (928–37) that these spirits are still great and hard to please – and may still strike a man down, all unsuspecting, for the sins of his forefathers, however much he may cry out against this.

Critics have rightly deprecated the idea that the Furies, by their past history, their function in society, and their curiously 'modified' position under the new dispensation, are intended as an allegory for the Areopagites themselves.[28] Nevertheless, the poet may have intended a kind of parallel or comparison between these two forces (presented as equally real in the play) and their destinies. Each represents an older order (the one in the world of myth, the other in the Athenian *polis*), each fulfils the necessary function of τὸ δεινόν and the threat of ποινή in society, each has suffered a limitation or an adaptation of its powers under a new dispensation (ironically, in terms of the present dramatic action, it is the Areopagus which 'limits' the Furies) but each retains its power of τὸ δεινόν which men will ignore at their peril.

Thus, both past and present have been confronted and 'put to question' in this play, but the resolution, the blending of the two in this extraordinary marriage of mythical past and political present, is one which could only have been expressed in terms belonging to the ideal and separate world of tragedy.

iii The 'male-female conflict' in the *Eumenides* and in the trilogy

The theme of male-female conflict in the *Oresteia* is prominent throughout the three plays of the trilogy and, like the ethical and the dynastic conflicts, it reaches its climax and its resolution in the *Eumenides*. We have seen it recur in many forms. In the *Agamemnon* the Queen's constant repudiation of male scorn for emotional womanhood (which she imputes to the Chorus more often than they dare express it) is vindicated on stage in her symbolic victory over Agamemnon in the 'carpet scene' and off stage by her bloody vengeance. In the *Choephori*, the male-female conflict is expanded to a conflict between generations, as the male matricide Orestes takes vengeance on his father-slaying mother, a conflict which is universalized (from the male point of view) by the Chorus' lurid depiction in the first stasimon of male-destroying females from the mythological tradition. In the *Eumenides*, the conflict is given a divine dimension in the confrontation between the Furies and Apollo and is finally resolved by the vote of Athena 'for the male' and by her induction of the Furies into a new social dispensation superseding the age-old antipathy between the sexes.

Egregious though this conflict between the sexes must appear when isolated in this way, I believe it to be a part (though a singularly powerful part) of the total fabric of each play, and the trilogy and its resolution to be inseparable from the single resolution of this and all other elements (ethical, dynastic, and social) of the dramatic whole.

It has not, however, seemed so to all commentators writing on this aspect of the trilogy or of its final play, some of whom, at least, have singled it out for separate treatment coloured, in one or two cases, by the preoccupations of a particular ideological approach.

For George Thomson, whose economic determinism in historical matters tends to be reflected in his literary views, Orestes' dilemma (as an enforced matricide) 'reflects the struggle of divided loyalties characteristic of the period in which, for the sake of the accompanying inheritance, descent was being shifted from the mother's to the father's side, and his acquittal will mark the inauguration of Athenian democracy.'[29] Again, in commenting on the casting vote of Athena, Thomson tells us: 'On the question of paternity she [Athena] endorses the attitude of Apollo, and so lays down the principle of the Attic law of inheritance.'[30]

Earlier, in his Introduction to the trilogy, Thomson has argued for common ownership of property and matrilineal descent in early Greek tribal society in contrast to private ownership of property and patrilineal descent and inheritance in the democratic state. Thus, in Thomson's view, the subjection of women was a consequence of the development of private property.[31]

The hypothesis (in its crudest form, that patriarchy succeeded matriarchy in early Greek society) on which these statements of Thomson's are based has little evidence to support it and is not now generally accepted.[32] However, even if it were sound, readers will look in vain for any real support for the economic inferences (ie those concerning property inheritance) which Thomson so easily draws from Apollo's and Athena's declarations 'for the male' in the *Eumenides*. Nor do Thomson's further statements along similar lines find any stronger support in the text of the *Eumenides*. 'So too,' he adds, 'the principle of male precedence, now formally ratified as the basis of democracy, is accompanied by the declaration that the wealth of the community is now equitably distributed (996).'[33] All that the Chorus has actually bidden the citizens to rejoice in, at *Eum* 996, is 'the happiness of wealth.' Nothing is said about its equal distribution, just as nothing has been implied about 'the basis of democracy' in Athena's assertions (in the case of 'Clytemnestra vs Orestes') of the supremacy of the claims of the male.

In contrast with Thomson's severely impersonal treatment (in terms of economic determinism!) of the dénouement of the *Oresteia* stands Winnington-Ingram's curiously psychological treatment of the subject in connection with the presentation of Clytemnestra in the two preceding plays.[34] It is to this critic's credit that he recognizes (in contrast to Thomson) the vote of Athena as the crisis, the adjudication, as it were, of the theme of sexual conflict which has been developed throughout the trilogy and that (again in contrast to Thomson) he seeks to involve the dramatic characters of the trilogy in his explanation of this theme. Nevertheless, that explanation is vitiated by Winnington-Ingram's curious view of the role of Clytemnestra in the *Agamemnon* and in the trilogy as a whole.

Winnington-Ingram believes that the main motivating force behind Clytemnestra in the first play lay in her jealousy of Agamemnon as a man: for this, he argues, 'Clytemnestra killed her husband ... in order to avenge herself upon his male supremacy.'[35] So, too, Clytemnestra's victory in the carpet scene is taken as the counterpart of her spiritual victory, 'The spiritual context [in which] Agamemnon will be compelled, as his own words reveal (918 ff.), to play the woman's part.' The various sexual antithesis in the *Agamemnon* and the constant emphasis (continued also in the *Choephori*) on Clytemnestra's manlike qualities and 'will to power' are all taken by Winnington-Ingram as pointing in this direction. The Queen's 'personal tragedy' he finds to lie in the fact that 'it was impossible in Clytemnestra's own society, and equally impossible in democratic Athens, for a woman of dominating will and intelligence to exploit her gifts to her own satisfaction and for the advantage of the community.'[36] Clytemnestra's frustrations as a would-be ruler, her jealousy of Cassandra and the various imagined Chryseids who shared her husband's foreign exploits, Orestes' invoking of the double standard to defend the husband's infidelities while condemning the wife's: all, in this critic's view, are illustrations of this tragic situation. Thus Clytemnestra becomes, for Winnington-Ingram, 'a symbol for all wives and mothers who suffer from the inferior status of the woman in marriage.'[37] Thus he takes Athena's vote favouring 'male superiority' as a sign of the poet's recognition of the fact that this was, and is, the way things are – not as a sign of his approval of such a situation, as Thomson is cited as suggesting.[38] Actually, Winnington-Ingram argues, Aeschylus is implying a criticism of the unequal status of women in marriage, through the tragic situation which he has presented: 'Πειθώ [Persuasion] had work still to do, in creating a just social order, which was beyond the imagination of this masculine goddess but not perhaps beyond the poet's.'[39] Two points, at least, need to be made against Winnington-Ingram's view of 'Clytemnestra and the vote of Athena.' There is, first of all, no indication in the *Agamemnon* that Clytemnestra's alleged frustrations are to be regarded as in any way 'tragic.' Her role is, primarily, that of the instrument of Agamemnon's inevitable downfall, inevitable for the various reasons which we have seen in our discussion of that play. To the degree that Clytemnestra is 'characterized' (and Winnington-Ingram 'characterizes' her in greater depth than Aeschylus does), the murder of Agamemnon is rendered the more probable or even (in terms of the human, as opposed to the supernatural, expectations set up in the play) the more inevitable ... and the play is thereby rendered the more interesting. None of this, of course, transforms Clytemnestra into a woman with a 'personal tragedy' either here or in the trilogy as a whole.

Secondly, there is not the slightest indication on the poet's part that the judgment of Athena and, in particular, the *status quo* (of male superiority) which it is taken to represent are to be regarded as anything other than satisfactory. No hint appears either in the closing admonitions of Athena or in the Chorus' prayers for fertility and domestic harmony at Athens that πειθώ (Persuasion) still had work to do in the marriage-counselling department.

M. Gagarin's discussion of 'sexual conflict' in the *Oresteia*,[40] perhaps the most thorough and perceptive of the many treatments of this topic, avoids the fundamental fault of imputing to Aeschylus various ideas which critics, for one reason or another, would like to find in his work. Gagarin traces clearly the pattern which this conflict exhibits throughout the trilogy, and its antecedent action in the myth, showing not only the reciprocity with which each male and female 'offence,' respectively, is answered until the resolution, but also how each deed, itself characterized by the sex of its agent, assails by its particular nature the sex-oriented sphere or values of the offended party. Thus (for example), 'The adultery [of Thyestes] is, of course, an offence against the male-dominated *oikos*, just as the theft of Helen is. The sacrilege of causing Thyestes to eat his children in return is an offence against the family and its religious taboos, a violation of female values, just as the sacrifice of Iphigenia is.'[41] So, too, of the various 'doers' and their deeds: Agamemnon's heinous crime and its 'justification' are those of a military commander; 'Clytemnestra used deceit, which is characteristic of women (as Aegisthus points out, 1636).'[42] This double aspect, subjective and objective, of the sexual conflict is traced by Gagarin in subtle detail throughout the action, speeches, and dialogues of the trilogy. Then, on a larger scale, the first two plays of the trilogy are shown to provide the same well-balanced reciprocity as the various details of speech and action have exhibited. In the first play, Clytemnestra dominates her victim, Agamemnon (both in the symbolic action of the carpet scene and in the off-stage murder itself), as well as the old men of the Chorus and her paramour, 'the cowardly lion,' Aegisthus. In the second play, we witness the complete male dominance of the avenging Orestes, with his male and military values (eg, at *Cho* 303–4, 919, 921), supported by the enslaved and antifeminist (cf 585–61) women of the Chorus and by an Electra playing a very minor role compared with later treatments.

In the *Eumenides* (as Gagarin correctly indicates), the Furies, both by their sex and by their emphasis on the supreme claims of the blood-tie, represent the female element; Orestes and Apollo, with *their* claims on the supremacy of the marriage bond, the male. As we would expect from his emphasis on the precise balance, in the first two plays, between male and female claims, and on the precise reciprocity between their offences against each other, Gagarin finds in the third play the establishment, after much difficulty, of perfect harmony between the sexes – a harmony compatible with, and indeed closely related to, the political and ethical resolutions of this play which we have already noted. More questionably, but again in keeping with the alleged perfect balance of claims in the first two plays, Gagarin argues not that this harmony is achieved by the victory of the male (and the consequent acquiescence of the female) but by the acceptance of their equal claims. The breaking of the deadlock between marriage-tie and blood-tie over the question of Orestes' guilt he finds to consist not in the establishment of the superiority of the former over the latter (for he believes that Apollo fails in this) but rather in the (successful) denial that any blood-tie existed between Orestes and his mother. Thus he takes most seriously Apollo's argument for the male as the only true parent and argues further that it is on this that Athena also bases her vote for Orestes' acquittal. The 'proof' that neither male nor female *wins* in this trilogy, but that they are 'at the last equally balanced,'[43] Gagarin finds in the equally divided votes of the Court (in which, as we have seen, he would include the vote of Athena). Of Athena herself, who votes for the male side but (unlike Apollo) respects the female side, Gagarin observes: 'Thus her bisexuality seems to give her the ability to act as a neutral arbitrator in the sexual conflict and to persuade the Furies that they were not really defeated.'[44] Finally, Gagarin aptly illustrates the sexual harmony achieved at the end of the *Eumenides* by pointing to the feminine blessings of fertility for the Athenians from the pacified Furies matched once again (but this time peacefully) by the masculine contribution of Orestes' promised military alliance.

This is, in many ways, a brilliant account of the sexual conflict in the trilogy and of the harmony which in the end is, indeed, achieved between the two elements concerned. Yet despite the ingenuity of his arguments, what Gagarin says about the *equality* of male and female in that final harmony does not quite accord either with the way in which the trial of Orestes is decided or with the way in which the final harmony is actually brought about. Whatever the nature of the clinching arguments, however one interprets the number of the jury votes, Orestes *does* win, Apollo's argument (at v 625 ff, quite separate from his 'male parent' argument) that Zeus views the murder of King Agamemnon as the greater wrong is vindicated, and Orestes, the legitimate male heir, is reestablished in his royal house. Athena does not base her vote for Orestes on Apollo's argument that the mother is not truly a parent but on her clearly stated prejudice, based, in part at least, on her own *unique* parental situation, for the male (736 ff). Moreover, even if Apollo's argument is as crucial to the acquittal as Gagarin believes, the doctrine that the male is the only true parent of children hardly gives the female equal status in the eventual social harmony established at the end of the trilogy. And finally, the 'equally-voted judgment' to which Athena refers (795), in an (at this point unsuccessful) attempt to mollify the Furies, may (as the poet doubtless intended) help save face for the defeated, but it does not change the fact that, by Athena's own decision and vote, they *are* defeated.

This conclusion must lead us to look again at least in outline at the allegedly equal balance of claims, affronts, and reprisals, between the male and female, on which Gagarin has insisted in his review of the first two plays of the trilogy. However ghastly the sacrifice of Iphigenia, we have never been allowed to sympathize, even in the *Agamemnon* (where, as Gagarin has told us, the female predominates) with Clytemnestra's murder of the King. Resentment of the usurpers does not begin in the second (male-oriented) play: it continues the bitter hostility of the Chorus of old men in the first play, who, critical as they were of Agamemnon's deeds, are nevertheless loyal to the King. Orestes' deed (as Gagarin admits) is presented in a less damaging light than is his mother's and when the third play opens we are prepared for his vindication against the claims of her avenging Furies. Thus the final victory for the male (for that is what it is) is anticipated throughout the trilogy. Only by Athena's persuasion and bribery is the female element (as represented by the Furies) turned to Kindly Ones just as the Furies themselves, for all the powers which Athena bestows on them, have their traditional prerogatives largely assimilated by the new Court of Athenian (male) citizens.

This single but important point (that male dominance is restored in the final harmony), which, I have suggested, is underestimated in Gagarin's account, is corrected (some might say over-corrected) in another recent treatment of 'sexual conflict' in the *Oresteia*. Froma Zeitlin, while not, of course, denying that harmony is achieved at the end of the *Eumenides*, argues that the various impasses created by the female rule of Clytemnestra are overcome only by the 'defeat of the self-willed female principle'[45] and that the pacification of the Furies, while it rescues the female element from sterility (witness the fertile blessings which the Furies finally bestow), does so only by reasserting male dominance in patriarchal marriage; this in turn ensures 'the primacy of the father-son bond in patrilinear succession and the primacy of the male in political power.'[46] For Zeitlin, the role of Athena (a female but a modified and virginal one) in this peaceful resolution only serves to emphasize this same point of male domination. She is authoritative but only as the 'porte-parole of Zeus' ... 'Free from any but symbolic maternal associations, she thus forswears any matriarchal projects.'[47]

Zeitlin's feminist enthusiasm for 'discovering' various symbols of male or female dominance, regeneration, and the like in the images and rituals of the trilogy may at some points strike the reader as excessive.[48] Nevertheless, the particular orientation which she eventually gives to this 'conflict of the sexes' and its outcome in the *Oresteia* is better suited than either Thomson's or Winnington-Ingram's to the actual triumphs both dynastic (the restoration of Orestes to his patrimony) and social (the promise of fertile prosperity for his 'saviour,' Athens) which are celebrated in the dénouement of the trilogy.

NOTES

1 Grossmann *Promethie und Orestie*.
2 See, for example, Grossmann's account (ibid pp 276 ff) of 'das athenische Herrscherideal,' where literary examples, from Aeschylus to Isocrates, of mild, just, benevolent, power-sharing rulers are paralleled by the 'actuality' of just and moderate statesmen from Solon to Pericles.

3 Ibid pp 127 ff.
4 We have already seen one example of this in Grossmann's account of the Olympian 'pity' and 'forgiveness' which save Orestes at his trial (ibid p 274; cf above, chapter 3 n 69). A little earlier in Grossmann's discussion, the freeing of Orestes through the founding of the Areopagus is spoken of as characteristic of the humane and benevolent ideals on which the Athenians prided themselves, particularly in the area of homicide trials.
5 Vernant and Vidal-Naquet *Mythe et Tragédie en Grèce ancienne* chapter 2, 'Tensions et ambiguités dans la tragédie grecque,' p 22, from which the following two quotations are also taken; for the discussion here summarized see pp 21–7. Particularly instructive is Vernant's conception of the confrontation in tragedy between the legendary past and the political, religious, and legal present of the city. Thus though tragedy is rooted in social reality it does not reflect it: 'it puts it in question' (p 25). Both legendary past and present actuality are, as it were, digested and transformed in the matrix of tragedy (my paraphrase). Yet even in the resolutions of so optimistic a poet as Aeschylus in the *Eumenides*, the contradictions between the old and new gods, between the heroic past and the democratic present, do not disappear, for these resolutions are made to depend on the tensions which the poet establishes between them (cf ibid n 3 to p 25).
6 Cf Rosenmeyer *The Art of Aeschylus*: 'The terror of the vendetta is politicized and domesticated for institutionally fruitful ends' (p 344); '... traditional heroism and the desire to live up to one's inner convictions are sacrificed, or at least left unconsummated ... In the place of royal or princely high-handedness, Athena offers popular agreement' (p 345). However, perhaps Rosenmeyer underestimates the compensatory gains which tragedy achieves, and the point that these 'gains' belong as little to the actual present as to the legendary past but to the ideal world of tragedy. (Cf above n 5.)
7 Dodds 'Morals and Politics in the *Oresteia*' p 47.
8 Cf Thuc 1.104.1–2. Dodds 'Morals and Politics' p 47 accepts the 'historical reference,' indicated above, of *Eum* 292–5, rejecting Dover's somewhat pedantic objection that the Athenians actually fought in the Delta, not in Libya itself (Dover 'The Political Aspect of Aeschylus' *Eumenides*' p 237). Besides, whatever their precise location, the Athenians were also (as Orestes imagines Athena to be) 'helping their Libyan friends.' Macleod, on the other hand ('Politics and the *Oresteia*' pp 124–5), deprecates the possible contemporary reference in either this allusion to Libya or (in the following lines) the allusion to 'the Phlegraean fields'

(Chalcidice) as 'at least secondary'; rather (he thinks) the large extent of Athena's sphere of influence is being given honorific attention by mention of its northern and southern extremities.

9 Athens appears to have been involved, off and on, in disputes over Sigeum and in the Troad from the sixth century and even earlier, and trouble of one kind or another seems to have gone on there till after the time of the *Oresteia*. For the earlier disputes, see Herod 5.95 and Sidgwick's note (including his reference to the Scholiast on *Eum* 398). Cf also Dodds 'Morals and Politics' p 47, n 2. Dodds, however, does not press this uncertain historical reference and Dover (*The Political Aspect of Aeschylus' Eumenides* p 237) deprecates it, perhaps rightly.

10 Some or all of the various passages in the *Eumenides* which we will be considering in these three areas have, of course, been discussed in numerous studies of the play, especially in ones devoted to its political implications. Particularly useful are the discussions of Dover and of Dodds, in the articles already referred to (above, nn 7 and 8), of Podlecki, *The Political Background of Aeschylean Tragedy* pp 80–100 (which includes a good bibliographical survey), of Gagarin, *Aeschylean Drama* pp 105–18, esp pp 116 ff and, for certain specific points, of Quincey, 'Orestes and the Argive Alliance.' The more cogent elements of earlier views (some of them now somewhat dated) such as those of K.O. Müller, Wilamowitz, R.W. Livingstone, and F. Jacoby have been successfully preserved in one or another of these studies.

11 See also the view of Quincey 'Orestes and the Argive Alliance,' who argues that this description might mean an alliance in which Athens does not have to promise to fight for Argos in the future.

12 See Hellanicus *FGH* 323aF2, cf F1, both cited in this context by Gagarin *Drakon and Early Athenian Homicide Law* p 126; Gagarin also cites Jacoby *FGH*, vol 3B, Supplements 1.22–5 and 11.19–29 as accepting, from these passages, 'the implication that in its earliest period (before Drakon) the Areopagus tried all cases of homicide.' Gagarin, on the other hand (*Drakon*, p 127), argues that the other three mythological trials (of Ares, Kephalos, and Daedalus) might well have been, like the trial of Orestes in the *Eumenides*, aetiological myths created in the sixth or fifth century. (But even if they were, their existence still indicates that the Greeks of those centuries thought of the Areopagus as being, traditionally and originally, a homicide court, and that is our principal concern here.)

13 The authenticity of chapter 4 of Aristotle's *Constitution of Athens* has been rightly doubted, mainly on the grounds that it contains the only account in ancient Greek literature of a constitution by Draco, partly

also on the grounds of its oligarchical tone 'reminiscent of the intermediate regime of 411/10.' See Rhodes *Commentary on the Aristotleian Athenaion Politeia* pp 84 ff. Rhodes defends chapter 3 (which has also been doubted, due to certain similarities with chapter 4), while admitting 'that 3 and 4 both represent theoretical reconstruction rather than well-documented history' (p 86). Concerning the early history of the Areopagus, Rhodes further suggests (pp 106–7) that an informal council of aristocrats gave advice first to the kings and then to the magistrates and that 'its power was increased as that of the kings was reduced.' He adds the reasonable guess that 'the lost beginning of the *A.P.* stated when and with what functions the Areopagus was created' and that 'the functions assigned to the Areopagus must have included jurisdiction, especially in cases of homicide' (p 107). (See below on Plutarch *Solon* 19.3).

14 Plutarch is quoting (allegedly from Solon's tables) exceptions to the reinstatement of those disenfranchised before Solon's archonship:
Ἀτίμων ὅσοι ἄτιμοι ἦσαν πρὶν ἢ Σόλωνα ἄρξαι, ἐπιτίμους εἶναι πλὴν ὅσοι ἐξ Ἀρείου πάγου ἢ ὅσοι ἐκ τῶν ἐφετῶν ἢ ἐκ πρυτανείου καταδικασθέντες ὑπὸ τῶν βασιλέων ἐπὶ φόνῳ ἢ σφαγαῖσιν ἢ ἐπὶ τυραννίδι ἔφευγον ὅτε ὁ θεσμὸς ἐφάνη ὅδε (Plutarch *Solon* 19.3).Perrin in his translation of the Loeb edition of Plutarch takes the meaning as I do: 'except such as were condemned by the Areiopagus, or by the Ephetai, or in the Prytaneium by the Kings, on charges of murder or of seeking to establish a tyranny ...' So, too, Rhodes (in his approval of Plutarch's rejection of 'the majority view' that the Areopagus was created by Solon) mentions Plutarch's quotation of 'a Solonian amnesty law from which men condemned for homicide or for "tyranny" by the Areopagus or other authorities are exluded' (pp 154–5). (Elsewhere Rhodes (p 24 n 52) speaks of the probable common source of Plutarch and the *Constitution of Athens* on Solon.) Plutarch also indicates (19.4) that he takes the words in this way except that he admits their obscurity and suggests that the reference *may* be to those convicted of charges which would later (at the time of Solon's law) have been in the jurisdiction of the Areopagus. Gagarin, on the other hand, translates: 'except those who, having been proved guilty by the Kings ... , were in exile from the Areopagus or from the Ephetai or from the Prytaneium when this law was announced' (*Drakon* p 129).

15 In Aristotle's *Politics* ii.12, Pericles is assigned the role of acting with Ephialtes in this matter; it could not, of course, have been Themistocles, since the latter had fled Athens not long after his ostracism in 472/1, ten years earlier. However, *Ath Pol* 25.2–3 does indicate that the 'addi-

tional powers' which Ephialtes' decree withdrew from the Areopagus were considerable (as they were now divided between two other bodies) and that, in the author's opinion, they may have included trials for treason and similar 'anti-constitutional' activities, and that the intention of the decree was the destruction of the Council as a political power. For arguments suggesting that this whole passage on Themistocles (25.3–4) is an 'insertion' into the original text, see Rhodes *Commentary* pp 319–20, who adds, 'he [Themistocles] cannot have tried to avert his condemnation by assisting in the attack on the Areopagus and it is more likely that his condemnation helped to provoke the attack.'
Note: The translations of the various passages quoted in this section from Aristotle's *Constitution of Athens* are by Rackham.

16 The easiest and perhaps most generally accepted view is that the expression ἐπίθετα ('additional sc powers') means the various constitutional and law-guarding powers which the Areopagus had acquired in addition to its homicide jurisdiction. However, we have seen that some of these powers seem to have been 'more additional' than others and that, according to Aristotle's reference to the Draconian and even pre-Draconian Areopagus, the Council had considerable powers of this 'non-homicide' type even in these early days. Indeed, as we have noted (above, nn 13–14), Gagarin has argued that the pre-Solonian Areopagus was not a homicide court at all (see Gagarin *Drakon* pp 126–32). However, whatever the precise historical truth may have been, the mythical treatments would lead us to expect that by the time of the fifth century the Athenians would have accepted the Council's homicide function as, traditionally, its original one; nor would the democratic reformers, in seeking to reduce all its 'constitution-guarding' powers, have been likely to distinguish very closely between earlier and later 'additional powers.'

Attempts have been made, however, to define more closely the 'additional powers' of which Ephialtes deprived the Areopagus. Podlecki *Political Background* pp 96 ff has argued that since 'guardianship of the laws' and 'guardianship of the constitution' are distinguished in *Ath Pol* 8.6 (in which Solon is said to have added the former to the already existing latter function of the Areopagus), Ephialtes' reforms *may* have consisted in taking away only the latter function. (We shall see later how Podlecki uses this argument in his political interpretation of Athena's 'Founding Speech'.) Sealey 'Ephialtes' had previously argued that Ephialtes' reforms consisted *entirely* of depriving the Areopagus of its powers of calling magistrates to account. The somewhat crumbly corner-stone of Sealey's argument is that (according to Andoc 1.83.4) the restored democracy of 403-402 BC specifically decreed that the Areopagus should 'take care of the laws' and that *that* would not have occurred, without recorded outcry, if it had been a measure contradicting Ephialtic democratic principles. However, Sealey seems to forget the difference between the democracy of 403-402 BC and that of 462 and, more significantly, the difference between the composition of the Areopagus of 403-402 (which was no longer a bastion of privilege after more than a generation of Zeugite eligibility) and that of 462. Moreover, it is ironic that Sealey should choose (mainly on the basis of fourth-century evidence of Areopagite activity) the function of judging magistrates as the function withdrawn from the Areopagus by Ephialtes: the very decree cited in Andocides 403-402, which Sealey has argued must *not* be in contradiction to Ephialtic reforms, states as its purpose, 'to insure that the magistrates observe the existing laws'!

17 Dover 'The Political Aspect' pp 234-5 has argued that the prestige and authority with which Athena endows her court is in no way inappropriate to a (mere) homicide court in Greek society where political and judicial matters were closely related. This view might be just tenable if the Areopagus had never had constitutional and law-defending powers. In view of the fact that it was in the process of losing those powers, it would seem very odd, if (as Dover thinks) the poet wanted us to think of a homicide court exclusively, that he should have Athena describe the Areopagus in terms of at least suggestive of the very 'additional powers' it seemed in danger of losing. Cf also Dodds 'Morals and Politics' pp 49-50: 'the functions of the Areopagus would seem to be conceived in wider terms than those of a murder court, which does indeed protect the security of the individual but scarcely that of the country as a whole.' More recently, however, Macleod 'Politics and the *Oresteia*' (128-9) has agreed with Dover in regarding Athena's description as applying exclusively to the Areopagus as a judicial body and in relating her references to guardianship of the community exclusively to that function: 'for homicide law is the basis of all law and order.' Thus, for Macleod, Aeschylus' account 'is clearly the mythical charter for the post-Ephialtean Areopagus.' And so the Oxford pendulum swings back and forth.

18 This 'in-between' position on the part of Aeschylus is the one inferred by several scholars from the speech of Athena; cf Lesky *Greek Tragedy* p 85: 'Aeschylus did not register any protest against this [Ephialtes' reform of the Areopagus] in his *Eumenides* ... But the poet views the trend of the new development with misgiving ...'; and Mazon *Eschyle* II pp xvi-xviii, who believes that Aeschylus approved Ephialtes' reforms

but feared the further reduction of their powers (including judicial powers) after the murder of Ephialtes. (Mazon refers to *Ath Pol* 27 in this connection.) Even Dodds, though believing that the language of Athena in the passages which we have cited suggests the powers of the earlier Areopagus rather than those of the reformed court, after Ephialtes, stops short of saying more than that 'the play is no more propaganda for Pericles than it is propaganda for Cimon' (p 50) and describes the Erinyes' praise of τὸ μέσον at v 530) as 'an honest and correct description of the author's own position' (I believe this is true of the poet's overall attitude in the play but not quite an accurate description of his attitude on the Areopagus issue). Perhaps the most detailed attempt on the part of scholars taking the view that Aeschylus here favours Ephialtes' reforms but not further encroachments on the Council's powers is that of Podlecki *Political Background* pp 96 ff. As we have seen (above, n 16), Podlecki believes that Ephialtes' reforms involved taking away from the Areopagus the guardianship of the constitution but not that of the laws (νομοφυλακία) and that it is this later reduction of *these* powers by Pericles and the transferring of them to the board of νομοφύλακες against which Aeschylus is complaining (p 98). Unfortunately the only evidence which Podlecki cites for this particular argument is the mention in Philochorus (see Podlecki's note 52) of this board being set up 'when Ephialtes left only capital cases to the Areopagus.' But surely this suggests that the Nomophylakes were set up as a direct result of Ephialtes' reforms (which in that case must, contrary to Podlecki's hypothesis, have included the withdrawal of nomophylakia from the Areopagus), not as a result of the further reforms by Pericles somewhat vaguely (as regards date *and* content) referred to in *Ath Pol* 27.1.

19 Stephanus' emendation 'πικαινούντων (followed by Sidgwick, and Page) with a stop after νόμους, seems the best emendation of mss' 'πικαινόντων. Alternatively, Wieseler's τι καινούντων, with the same punctuation (cited with approval by Dover), gives much the same sense. 'πιχραινόντων (Wakefield, Dindorf, Smyth) requires the stop to be moved forward to follow κακαῖς ἐπιρροαῖσι, 'discolouring the laws with new influxes': see Dover's good stylistic argument ('The Political Aspect' p 232) for placing the stop after νόμους (and so for retaining θ' of the mss in v 694). πικραινόντων (Valckenaer), 'making bitter the laws by new influxes,' can surely be rejected.

20 Dover 'The Political Aspect' p 234. In support of his view, Dover argues that the word ἐπίθετα may have been not merely Aristotle's description but the actual term which the reformers used for the 'additional powers'

of which they now deprived the Areopagus (even so, κακαῖς ἐπιρ-ροαῖσι would not necessarily suggest these ἐπίθετα to the contemporary audience). Rhodes (*Commentary* pp 314 ff), while agreeing with the first of these two points, remarks on the difficulty in calling these (now deleted) powers ἐπίθετα, as opposed to πάτρια, 'traditional,' 'ancestral,' in view of the accounts of the Areopagus given in pre-Draconian, in Draconian, and in Solonian times by Aristotle in *Ath Pol* 3.6, 4.6, and 8.4 respectively. He suggests (reasonably, in my view) that the Areopagus may have exploited this early acknowledged status as guardian of the laws to justify it in 'new ways of enforcing the law, and that the law-enforcing functions thus assumed ... could easily be represented as accretions by the reformers' (p 316).

21 Dodds 'Morals and Politics' p 48.
22 Ibid pp 48–49; however, the detailed argument for this is given in an earlier article by Dodds, 'Notes on the *Oresteia*.' Cf also Lloyd-Jones' comment on *Eum* 693 ff: 'If "the laws" here simply mean the laws in general, the warning against changing them is presumably connected with the fact that the most important function the Areopagus lost was that of protecting the constitution by vetoing legislation that might transform its character ... and I believe this interpretation is correct.' (This view, though otherwise reasonable, seems to me to give a less specific and significant meaning to 'by evil influxes,' which Lloyd-Jones construes with 'do not currupt the laws,' than does Dodds' view.)
23 See *Ath Pol* 26.2; on the precise date of this measure, cf Dodds 'Notes on the *Oresteia*' p 20 and n 1.
24 I am aware that this is an old-fashioned view of Aeschylus' political stance (namely, that though he approved of the democrats' Argive policy, he still tended to be protective of the Areopagus' diminishing political powers and even of its privileged composition) in comparison with several recent commentators, eg, Dover, Podlecki, as already cited, and Forrest, as cited below. However, this view has received some support within the last twenty years or so; see, for example, Méautis 'Notes sur *les Eumenides* d'Eschyle,' Thomson, in his revised (1966) edition of the *Oresteia* II, note on *Eum* 693–5; Gagarin *Aeschylean Drama* p 116, and Dodds, to the degree cited in the foregoing discussion.

It is worth remembering, too, that Aristophanes consistently depicts Aeschylus as representing the old-fashioned values of the warrier-citizen: see the *agon* of *Frogs*, passim; cf *Clouds* 1364–7, where Aeschylus is admired by the older generation and despised by the younger. The contest between 'Aeschylus' and 'Euripides' in the *Frogs* is not, of course, primarily political in nature, but there are politically conservative overtones in 'Aeschylus' lines at 1010–12, 1085, and 1431–3, in contrast to those of 'democratic' Euripides (952) who taught men skill at speaking and sneers at Aeschylus' old-fashioned pupils (963 ff). At the very least, Aristophanes' picture may be said to exploit and exaggerate popular conceptions of Aeschylus a generation or so after his death.

It is beyond the scope of the present study to consider the possible evidence (in my opinion slim) from his other plays of Aeschylus' political views. For an interpretation of the *Supplices* as a (somewhat belated) championing of the Argive democrats and their courageous acceptance of the exiled suppliant Themistocles, see Forrest 'Themistokles and Argos.' See also Podlecki *The Political Background of Aeschylean Tragedy* (esp chapter 2, 4, 5, and 7), which is in some ways a development of Forrest's views on Aeschylus and Themistocles and subsequent democratic policies and politicians (cf Podlecki ix–x and Forrest at p 236 and notes ad loc; on the 'Aeschylus and the Areopagus' issue, some differences in detail will be noted between Podlecki and Forrest, who agrees more closely with Dover on the matter).

25 Dodds 'Morals and Politics' p 50; Dover 'The Political Aspect' p 233.
26 Note, for example, the vivid conceit at v 861 f: 'Do not, borrowing [lit 'taking out'] the heart of cocks, as it were, implant in my citizens the spirit of kin warfare [Ἄρη ἐμφύλιον].' (Cocks are noted for their readiness to fight with their own kind.) Note, too, the bold expression at 980 ff, in which 'the dust-which-has-drunk-the-blood-of-citizens' is itself thought of as arousing reciprocal destruction.
27 The Furies, in their present benevolent mood, seem more ready to waive the law of requital for bloodshed than Athena herself expects them to be, to judge from her warning at vv 932–7. In the present passage, it may be that the poet, through the Furies, is deprecating vengeful civil strife as a result of the murder of Ephialtes. Cf Dodds 'Morals and Politics' p 52.
28 Cf the political allegory (rather more detailed in its historical references than that suggested above) adduced by Livingstone 'The Problem of the *Eumenides*' pp 125 ff, and Dover's criticism 'The Political Aspect' pp 236–7.
29 Thomson *The Oresteia of Aeschylus* I 51 (= p 46, abridged edition, 1966).
30 Ibid p 63 (1938 edition); p 55 (1966 edition).
31 Ibid p 7 (1938 edition): 'The tribe had been based on common ownership and a system of kinship reckoned through the mother; the Athenian state was based on private ownership and the private family, of which the head was the father. Athenian tradition preserved memories of

a time when women enjoyed equal rights with men and descent had been traced through the female line.' Cf Thomson *Aeschylus and Athens;*[3] p 192: 'Moreover if [as Thomson has argued] the subjection of women in Attica was a consequence of the development of property, it follows that at an earlier time the women must have enjoyed a greater measure of liberty ...'

32 In his notes to *Eum* 212 and 741 (= 738, 1966 edition), Thomson refers to his *Studies in the Ancient Greek Society* pp 149–293 (= chapter 5, 'The Matriarchal Peoples of the Aegean'), for his arguments for early Greek matrilineal organization of society, and to pp 137–9 for 'the cardinal rule of Attic laws of inheritance, which were based on the principle of male succession.' See also Bamberger 'The Myth of Matriarchy' and Simon Pembroke 'Women in Charge: The Function of Alternatives in Early Greek Tradition and the Ancient Idea of Matriarchy' *Journal of the Warburg and Courtland Institute* 30 (1967) 1–35, to which Gagarin (*Aeschylean Drama* p 195) refers in rejecting Thomson's views on this matter. The former of these two articles provides an interesting theory to explain various 'myths of matriarchy'; I have been unable to see the latter article.
33 Thomson *Oresteia* I p 64 (1938 edition); pp 55–6 (1966 edition).
34 Winnington-Ingram 'Clytemnestra and the Vote of Athena.'
35 Ibid p 132 and (for quotations in this and the following sentence) p 133.
36 Ibid p 146.
37 Ibid pp 146–7.
38 Ibid and cf nn 129, 130.
39 Ibid p 147. Doubts about Winnington-Ingram's 'sympathetic' picture of an Aeschylus lamenting the restricted role of women in the Athens of his day need not, of course, push us to believing in the grotesquely misogynistic, male chauvinist Aeschylus which Grossmann depicts (and seems almost, by his enthusiasm, to admire!) at *Promethie und Orestie* pp 226–8. Grossmann points to the undisciplined women of the *Septem*, the man-hating, husband-murdering women of the *Supplices*, and the despotic fiend Clytemnestra, in dubious support of this view (Clytemnestra, he tells us, 'shows what a monster the female can become if the male does not hold her in check'[!]). Grossmann stresses the much greater worth of the man and the master in contemporary Athens. He also (perhaps with justice) regards Apollo's and Athena's view, that Agamemnon's death is far more important than Clytemnestra's, as expressing Aeschylus' own view of the matter as well.
40 Gagarin, *Aeschylean Drama* pp 87–105, esp pp 191 ff.
41 Ibid pp 95–6.

42 Ibid. Gagarin might have added that Aeschylus rejects the version of Agamemnon's sacrifice of Iphigenia that involved the (male) deceit of luring her to Aulis to be affianced to Achilles, as in the epic version (see *EGF* 19 and schol *Il* 17.8), which Euripides followed in the *Iphigenia in Aulis*.
43 Gagarin *Aeschylean Drama* p 103.
44 Ibid p 104.
45 Zeitlin 'The Dynamics of Misogyny: Myth and Mythmaking in the *Oresteia*' pp 156–7. (See also the complete article, which, with its useful bibliography, concerns more wide-ranging issues than can be considered here.)
46 Ibid pp 159–60.
47 Ibid pp 172–3.
48 See, for example, the alleged would-be absorption of mother-slaying 'ophidian' Orestes by the serpentine Furies (ibid pp 158–9); the idea (based on Delcourt's far-fetched interpretation of the 'pig's-blood ritual' as representing the blood of parturition) that the male Orestes is reborn from the male Apollo by means of the ritual at the Delphic ὀμφαλός (ibid pp 165–6). On the other hand, Zeitlin (ibid pp 151–5) makes some interesting applications to the *Oresteia* of Bamberger's theory about matriarchy (mentioned above, n 32).

Bibliography

Editions, translations, commentaries, etc.

Bollack, Jean, and de La Combe, Pierre *L'Agamemnon d'Eschyle, Agamemnon* (Bollack), *Agamemnon* (de la Combe) Lille 1981–2
Davies, John F., ed *The Eumenides of Aeschylus, a critical edition with a metrical English translation* Dublin 1885
Denniston, J.D., and Page, Denys, eds *Aeschylus, Agamemnon* Oxford 1957
Fraenkel, Eduard, ed *Agamemnon* vols I–III, Oxford 1950
Garvie, A.F. *Aeschylus: Choephori* Oxford 1986
Groeneboom, P., ed *Aeschylus, Choephori* Groningen 1949
 ed *Aeschylus, Eumenides* Groningen 1952
Grene, David, and Lattimore, Richmond, eds *The Complete Greek Tragedies* vol I *Aeschylus* Chicago 1953
Headlam, Walter, ed and trans *The Agamemnon of Aeschylus, with verse translation introduction and notes* ed A.C. Pearson, Cambridge 1925
– and Thomson, George, eds *The Oresteia* Cambridge 1938
Hermann, Gottfried, ed *Aeschyli Tragoediae* Leipzig 1852
Hogan, James C. *A Commentary on the Complete Greek Tragedies–Aeschylus* Chicago and London 1984
Italie, G. *Index Aeschyleus* second edition ed S.L. Radt, Leiden 1964
Lattimore, Richmond, and Grene, David, eds *The Complete Greek Tragedies* vol I *Aeschylus* Chicago 1953
Linwood, W *Lexicon to Aeschylus* London 1897
Lloyd-Jones, Hugh, trans *Agamemnon by Aeschylus; The Libation Bearers by Aeschylus; The Eumenides by Aeschylus* translations with commentaries, Englewood Cliffs: Prentice-Hall 1970
Mazon, Paul, ed *Eschyle* II, third edition, Budé edition, Paris 1968

Munro, D.B., ed *Homer, Iliad,* books I–XII, fifth edition, Oxford 1953
Murray, Gilbert, ed *Aeschyli septem quae supersunt tragoediae* second edition, Oxford 1957
Page, Denys, ed *Aeschyli septem quae supersunt tragoediae* Oxford 1972
Paley, F.A. *The Tragedies of Aeschylus* London 1879
Perrin, B., ed and trans *Plutarch's Lives* vol I, Loeb Classical Library, London 1914
Rackham, H., ed and trans *Aristotle, Constitution of Athens,* Loeb Classical Library, London 1935
Rhodes, Peter *A Commentary on the Aristoteleian Athenaion Politeia* Oxford 1981
Rose, H.J. *A Commentary on the Surviving Plays of Aeschylus* Amsterdam 1957–8
Sidgwick, A., ed *Aeschylus, Agamemnon* sixth edition, Oxford 1905
– ed *Aeschylus, Choephori* second edition, Oxford 1924
– ed *Aeschylus, Eumenides* Oxford 1887
Smyth, Herbert Weir, ed and trans *Aeschylus with an English translation* Loeb edition, London 1957
Thomson, George, ed *The Oresteia of Aeschylus* vols I and II, second (abridged) edition, Amsterdam 1966
Thomson, George, and Headlam, Walter, eds *The Oresteia* Cambridge 1938
Tucker, T.G., ed and trans *The Choephori of Aeschylus* with critical notes, commentary, and translation, Cambridge 1901
Verrall, A.W., ed *The Agamemnon of Aeschylus* with introduction, commentary, and translation, London 1908
– ed *The Choephori of Aeschylus* London 1893
– ed *The Eumenides of Aeschylus* with introduction, commentary, and translation, London 1908
Weil, H., ed *Aeschylus. Quae supersunt tragoediae* Giessen 1858–67
Wecklein, N., ed *Aeschylus, Orestie* Leipzig 1888
von Wilamowitz-Moellendorff, Ulrich, ed *Aeschyli Tragoediae* Berlin 1914
Griechische Tragoediae II, *Orestie* Berlin 1900
Young, Douglas, trans *Aeschylus: The Oresteia Translated into English Verse* Norman 1974

Books

Bremer, J.M. *Hamartia* Amsterdam 1969
Conacher, D.J. *Aeschylus' Prometheus Bound: A Literary Commentary* Toronto 1980
Dale, A.M. *Collected Papers* Cambridge 1969

Dodds, E.R. *The Ancient Concept of Progress and Other Essays on Greek Literature and Belief* Oxford 1973
– *The Greeks and the Irrational* Berkeley and Los Angeles 1951
Finley, J.H., Jr *Pindar and Aeschylus* Cambridge, Mass 1955
Frankfort, H.A., trans *Greek Tragedy* by Albin Lesky, second edition, London and New York 1967
Gagarin, Michael *Aeschylean Drama* Berkeley and Los Angeles 1976
– *Drakon and Early Athenian Homicide Law* New Haven and London 1981
Griffith, Mark *The Authenticity of Prometheus Bound* Cambridge 1977
Grossmann, G. *Promethie und Orestie* Heidelberg 1970
Herington, John *Aeschylus* Hermes Books, New Haven and London 1986
Jones, John *On Aristotle and Greek Tragedy* London 1962
Kitto, H.D.F. *Form and Meaning in Drama* London 1956
– *Greek Tragedy* second edition, London 1950
Knox, Bernard *Word and Action, Essays on the Ancient Theatre* Baltimore and London 1979
Kranz, W. *Stasimon* Berlin 1933
Lamphere, L., and Rosaldo, M., eds *Women, Culture and Society* Stanford 1974
Lebeck, Anne *The Oresteia, A Study in Language and Structure* Cambridge, Mass 1971
Lesky, Albin *Die tragische Dichtung der Hellenen* Göttingen 1956
– *Greek Tragedy* trans H.A. Frankfort, second edition, London and New York 1967
Lloyd-Jones, Hugh *The Justice of Zeus* Berkeley and Los Angeles 1971
Mastronarde, D.J. *Contact and Discontinuity, Some Conventions of Speech and Action on the Greek Tragic Stage* Berkeley and Los Angeles 1979
Mylonas, G., and Richmond, Doris, eds *Studies Presented to David Robinson* St Louis 1953
Onians, J.B. *Origins of European Thought* Cambridge 1954
Owen, E.T. *The Harmony of Aeschylus* Toronto 1952
Pickard-Cambridge, A.W. *The Theatre of Dionysus* Oxford 1956
Podlecki, A.J. *The Political Background of Aeschylean Tragedy* Ann Arbor 1966
Prag, A.J.N. *The Oresteia, Iconographic and Narrative Tradition* Warminster 1985
Reinhardt, Karl *Aischylos als Regisseur und Theologe* Bern 1949
Richmond, Doris, and Mylonas, G., eds *Studies Presented to David Robinson* St Louis 1953
de Romilly, J. *Time in Greek Tragedy* Ithaca 1968
Rosaldo, M., and Lamphere, L. *Women, Culture and Society* Stanford 1974
Rosenmeyer, T.G. *The Art of Aeschylus* Berkeley and Los Angeles 1982

Smith, Peter *On the Hymn to Zeus in Aeschylus' Agamemnon, American Classical Studies 5*, Chico, California 1980
Smyth, Herbert Weir *Aeschylean Tragedy* Cambridge, Mass 1924, repr New York 1969
Solmsen, F. *Hesiod and Aeschylus* Ithaca 1949
Taplin, Oliver *The Stagecraft of Aechylus* Oxford 1977
Thomson, George *Studies in Ancient Greek Society* London 1949
Aeschylus and Athens London 1966
Turyn, A. *The Manuscript Tradition of Aeschylus* New York 1943
Velacott, Philip *The Logic of Tragedy: Morals and Integrity in Aeschylus' Oresteia* Durham NC 1984
Vernant, J.-P., and Vidal-Naquet, Pierre *Mythe et Tragédie en Grèce ancienne* Paris 1973
Vidal-Naquet, Pierre *Classe et Sacrifice dans l'Orestie* Paris 1972
and Vernant, J.-P. *Mythe et Tragédie en Grèce ancienne* Paris 1973
Visser, Margaret *The Erinyes, Their Character and Function in Classical Greek Literature and Thought* PHD thesis, University of Toronto 1980
von Wilamowitz-Moellendorf, Ulrich *Aischylos Interpretationen* Berlin 1914
Winnington-Ingram, R.P. *Studies in Aeschylus* Cambridge 1983

Articles, reviews, etc

Bamberger, Joan 'The Myth of the Matriarchy' pp263–80 in *Women, Culture and Society* ed M. Rosaldo and L. Lamphere, Stanford 1974
Bergson, L. 'The Hymn to Zeus in Aeschylus' *Agamemnon*' *Eranos* 65 (1967) 12–24
Booth, N.B. 'Aeschylus' *Choephori* 61–5' *CQ* 7 (1957) 143–5
– 'The Run of Sense in Aeschylus' *Choephori* 22–83' *CP* 54 (1959) 111–13
Borthwick, E.K. 'ἸΣΤΟΤΡΙΒΗΣ: An Addendum' *AJP* 102 (1981) 1–2
Brown, A.L. 'The Erinyes and the *Oresteia*: Real Life, the Supernatural and the Stage' *JHS* 103 (1983) 13–34
Conacher, D.J. 'Comments on an Interpretation of Aeschylus, *Agamemnon* 182–3' *Phoenix* 30 (1976) 328–36
– 'Interaction between Chorus and Characters in the *Oresteia*' *AJP* 95 (1974) 323–43
– Review of H. Lloyd-Jones *Aeschylus, Agamemnon, Phoenix* 25 (1971) 272–9
– Review of Peter Smith *On the Hymn to Zeus in Aeschylus' Agamemnon, Phoenix* 37 (1983) 163–6
Dawe, R.D. 'Inconsistencey of Plot and Character in Aeschylus' *Proceedings of the Cambridge Philological Association* no 189 ns 9 (1963) 21–62

- 'Some Reflections on *Atê* and *Hamartia*' *HSCP* 72 (1967) 89–123
- 'The Place of the Hymn to Zeus in Aeschylus' *Agamemnon*' *Eranos* 64 (1966) 1–21
- Dodds, E.R. 'Morals and Politics in the *Oresteia*' pp 43–63 in *The Ancient Concept of Progress and Other Essays on Greek Literature and Belief* III, repr from *Proceedings of the Cambridge Philological Society* 186 (1960) 19–31 (page references are to *The Ancient Concept of Progress*)
- 'Notes on the *Oresteia*' *CQ* ns 3 (1953) 19–20
- Dover, Kenneth 'Some Neglected Aspects of Agamemnon's Dilemma' *JHS* 93 (1973) 58–69
- 'The Political Aspect of Aeschylus, *Eumenides*' *JHS* 77 (1957) 230–7
- Dyer, R.R. 'The Evidence of Purification Rituals at Delphi and Athens' *JHS* 89 (1969) 38–56
- Easterling, P.E. 'Presentation of Character in Aeschylus' *G and R* 20 (1973) 3–19
- Edwards, Mark W. 'Agamemnon's Decision: Freedom and Folly in Aeschylus' *California Studies in Classical Antiquity* 10 (1977) 17–37
- Fontenrose, J. 'Gods and Men in the *Oresteia*' *TAPA* 102 (1971) 71–109
- Forrest, W.G.F. 'Themistokles and Argos' *CQ* ns 10 (1960) 221–41
- Gagarin, Michael 'The Vote of Athena' *AJP* 95 (1975) 121–7
- Gantz, Timothy 'The Chorus of Aeschylus' *Agamemnon*' *HSCP* 87 (1983) 65–86
- Garvie, A.F. 'The Opening of the *Choephori*' *BICS* 17 (1970) 79–81
- Goheen, R.J. "Three Studies in the *Oresteia*' *AJP* 76 (1955) 113–37
- Hammond, N.G. 'Personal Freedom and Its Limitations in the *Oresteia*' *JHS* 85 (1965) 42–55
- Headlam, Walter 'The Last Scene in the *Eumenides*' *JHS* 26 (1906) 268–77
- Hester, D.A. 'The Casting Vote' *AJP* 102 (1981) 265–74
- Holtsmark, E.B. 'On *Choephori* 585–651' *CW* 59 (1966) 215–16
- Kamerbeek, J.C. 'Prière et Imprécation d'Electre' *Mnem* 14 (1961) 116–21
- Kells, J.H. 'Aeschylus, *Eumenides* 213–14 and Athenian Marriage' *CP* 56 (1961) 169–71
- Knox, Bernard 'Aeschylus and the Third Actor' *AJP* 93 (1972) 104–24, repr in *Word and Action* (Baltimore 1979) 39–55
- 'The Lion in the House' *CP* 47 (1952) 17–25, repr in *Word and Action* (Baltimore 1979) 27–38
- Koniaris, G.L. 'An Obscene Word in Aeschylus' *AJP* 101 (1980) 42–4
- Kranz, W. 'Zwei Lieder des *Agamemnon*' *Hermes* 54 (1919) 301–20
- Lebeck, Anne 'The First Stasimon of Aeschylus' *Choephori*, Myth and Mirror Image' *CP* 62 (1967) 182–5

Lesky, Albin 'Der Kommos der *Choephoren*' SAWW 221 (1943) 1–127
- 'Decision and Responsibility in the Tragedy of Aeschylus' *JHS* 86 (1966) 78–85
Livingstone, R.W. 'The Problem of the *Eumenides*' *JHS* 35 (1925) 120–31
Lloyd-Jones, Hugh '*Agamemnonea*' *HSCP* (1969) 97–104
- 'Artemis and Iphigeneia' *JHS* 103 (1983) 87–102
- 'Interpolations in *Choephori* and *Electra*' *CQ* ns 11 (1961) 171–84
- 'The Guilt of Agamemnon' *CQ* ns 12 (1962) 187–99
- 'The Robes of Iphigenia' *CR* ns 2 (1952) 132–5
- 'Zeus in Aeschylus' *JHS* 76 (1956) 55–67
- 'Three Notes on *Agamemnon*' *Rh Mus* 103 (1960) 76–80
Macleod, C.W. 'Politics and the *Oresteia*' *JHS* 102 (1982) 124–44
Méautis, G. 'Notes sur *les Eumenides* d'Eschyle' *REA* 65 (1963) 33–52
Moritz, Helen E. 'Refrain in Aeschylus' *CP* 74 (1979) 187–213
Neitzel, Heinz '$\pi \acute{\alpha} \theta \epsilon \iota \ \mu \acute{\alpha} \theta o \varsigma$ – Leitwort der aischyleischen Tragodie?' *Gymnasium* 87 (1980) 283–93
O'Brien, M.J. 'Orestes and the Gorgon: Euripides' *Electra*' *AJP* 85 (1964) 13–39
Peradotto, J.J. 'The Omen of the Eagles and the ΗΘΟΣ of Agamemnon', *Phoenix* 23 (1969) 237–63
- 'Some Patterns of Nature Imagery in the *Oresteia*' *AJP* 85 (1964) 378–93
Podlecki, A.J. 'The *Phrên* Asleep: Aeschylus, *Eumenides* 103–5' in *Greek Tragedy and Its Legacy: Essays Presented to D.J. Conacher* ed Martin Cropp, Elaine Fantham, and S.E. Scully (Calgary 1986)
Pope, Maurice 'Merciful Heavens? A Question in Aeschylus' *Agamemnon JHS* 94 (1974) 100–13
Quincey, J.H. 'Orestes and the Argive Alliance' *CQ* ns 14 (1964) 190–206
Rivier, André 'Remarques sur le Nécessaire et la Nécessité chez Eschyle' *REG* 81 (1968) 25–7
Robbins, Emmet 'Pindar's *Oresteia* and the Tragedians' in *Greek Tragedy and Its Legacy: Studies Presented to D.J. Conacher* Calgary 1986
de Romilly, J. 'Vengeance humaine et vengeance divine: Remarques sur l'*Orestie* d'Eschyle' *Das Altertum und jedes neue Gute* Stuttgart (1970) 67–77
Roux, G. 'Commentaires à l'*Orestie REG* 87 (1974) 33–79
Schadewaldt, W. 'Der Kommos in Aischylos' *Choephoren*' *Hermes* 67 (1932) 312–54
Sansone, David 'Notes on the *Oresteia*' *Hermes* 112 (1984) 1–9
Schottlaender, Rudolph 'Um die Qualität des Freispruchs in dem *Eumeniden*' *Das Altertum* 16 (1970) 144–53
Sealey, R. 'Ephialtes' *CP* 59 (1964) 11–22

Solmsen, F. 'The Sacrifice of Agamemnon's Daughter in Hesiod's *Ehoeae*' *AJP* 102 (1981) 353–8
Stinton, T.C.W. 'The First Stasimon of Aeschylus' *Choephori*' *CQ* 29 (1979) 252–62
Trendall, A.D. 'The *Choephori* Painter' in *Studies Presented to David Robinson* ed G. Mylonas and Doris Richmond (St Louis 1953) 114–26
Tsagarakis, O. 'Zum tragischen Geschick Agamemnons bei Aischylos' *Gymnasium* 86 (1979) 16–38
Tyrrell, William Blake 'An Obscene Word in Aeschylus' *AJP* 101 (1980) 44–6
Whallon, W. 'Why Is Artemis Angry?' *AJP* 82 (1961) 78–88
Winnington-Ingram, R.P. 'Aeschylus, *Agamemnon*, 1343–71' *CR* ns 4 (1954) 23–30 (repr in *Studies in Aeschylus* pp 208–16)
- 'A Religious Function of Greek Tragedy: A Study of the *Oedipus Coloneus* and the *Oresteia*' *JHS* 74 (1954) 16–24
- 'Clytemnestra and the Vote of Athena' *JHS* 68 (1948) 130–47 (repr with revised notes in *Studies in Aeschylus* pp 101–31)
Young, D.C.C. 'Gentler Medicines in the *Agamemnon*' *CQ* 14 (1964) 1–23
Zeitlin, Froma 'Postscript to Sacrificial Imagery in the *Oresteia, Ag.* 1235–37' *TAPA* 97 (1966) 645–53
- 'The Dynamics of Misogyny: Myth and Myth-Making in the *Oresteia*' *Arethusa* 11 (1978) 149–84
- 'The Motif of the Corrupted Sacrifice in Aeschylus' *Oresteia*' *TAPA* 96 (1965) 463–508